STRANGERS AT THE GATE
The 'Boat People's' First Ten Years in Canada

Twenty-seven million people in the world are refugees. In this book, Morton Beiser puts readers in touch, emotionally and intellectually, with the reality of refugees in Canada. In the process, he dispels key misconceptions about immigrants in this country and reframes central debates on refugee policy.

The book describes Beiser's ten-year study of 1,300 'Boat People' admitted to Canada between 1979 and 1981. It chronicles the former refugees' struggles to learn English and to establish themselves economically in their new environment, and shows that, contrary to popular opinion, they use fewer health and social services than indigenous Canadians.

Beiser finds that, although most refugees in most resettlement situations succeed remarkably well, no country, Canada included, offers newcomers the welcome they need and deserve. This remarkable study, with its profoundly human dimension, should be read by all policy-makers in the fields of immigration and social and health services.

MORTON BEISER is the David Crombie Professor of Cultural Pluralism and Health, Centre for Addiction and Mental Health and Department of Psychiatry, University of Toronto. He is also director of the Toronto Centre of Excellence for Research on Immigration and Settlement (CERIS).

D1213715

STRANGERS
AT THE GATE

The 'Boat People's'
First Ten Years in Canada

Morton Beiser

UNIVERSITY OF TORONTO PRESS
Toronto Buffalo London

© University of Toronto Press 1999
Toronto Buffalo London
Printed in the U.S.A.

Reprinted 2014

ISBN 0-8020-4282-1 (cloth)
ISBN 0-8020-8117-7 (paper)

Printed on acid-free paper

Canadian Cataloguing in Publication Data

Beiser, Morton
   Strangers at the gate : the 'Boat People's' first ten years in Canada

   Includes bibliographical references and index.
   ISBN 0-8020-4282-1 (bound)   ISBN 0-8020-8117-7 (pbk.)

   1. Refugees – Canada.   2. Asia, Southeastern – Emigration and
   immigration.   3. Refugees – Asia, Southeastern.   I. Title.

   FC106.S66B44 1999   959.704'3'08691   C98-933060-5
   F1035.S66B44 1999

University of Toronto Press acknowledges the financial assistance to its
publishing program of the Canada Council for the Arts and the Ontario Arts
Council.

To Brendan, David, and Vince

Contents

Preface: The Costs and Benefits of Compassion

Twenty-seven million people in the world have nowhere to go (UNHCR, 1995, p. 19). Having fled their homes, they live in refugee camps and temporary holding centres in Africa, Asia, Europe, the Middle East, and Latin America, waiting either for peace to return to their countries, or for another nation to offer them permanent asylum. As the number of exiles swells, refugee-receiving countries are suffering 'compassion fatigue.' The United States, Canada, and Australia are cutting refugee quotas and tightening eligibility criteria. In Israel – a country bound by its law of universal return to offer permanent residence to any Jew requesting it – there are those who would close the doors on some would-be returnees by questioning the grounds for their claiming to be Jewish.

In Germany and Austria, the very countries whose past infamies prompted Israel's law of universal return, the cauldron of failing economies once again spumes out intolerance and xenophobia. Using the rationale that the Bosnian elections held in the summer of 1996 ensured an end to years of horror, Germany began a program of forcible repatriation of Muslims who had fled there as refugees. Since the elections had restored power to the Bosnian Serbs responsible for expelling the refugees in the first place, the Muslims were understandably sceptical about reassurances of their safety.

There have always been refugees. Chances are, there always will be. According to the Old Testament, Jacob and his sons left their homes in Canaan to escape famine. Today, they would be classified as economic refugees, and few, if any, countries would admit them as ancient Egypt did. Generations later, Jacob's descendants had to flee Egypt to escape a pharaoh who had made them into slaves and ordered the deaths of their children. Had their exodus taken place today, they would be classified as political or 'convention' refugees eligible to claim asylum from any of the 111 member state signatories to the United Nations Convention on Refugees.

Neither the disparities between haves and have-nots that produce economic refugees nor the ethnocentrism that creates political refugees shows any sign of disappearing. Each country subscribing to the UN convention is motivated by its own particular blend of pragmatism, political expediency, and humanitarianism. The humanitarianism of privileged countries is deeply rooted in religious and philosophical traditions emphasizing that the quality of a society can be best judged by the way it treats the vulnerable. Biblical injunction, such as the reference in Exodus 12:20 to the 'stranger at the gate,' underlines a moral commitment to offer shelter to refugees.

Although privileged countries cannot ignore the world's uprooted, public debate weighing the virtues of humanitarianism against its costs ultimately determines the amount and quality of asylum an individual nation offers to refugees. Unfortunately, what passes for public debate about refugee policy is, too often, defamatory rhetoric portraying refugees, and indeed all immigrants, as people who either steal jobs from native-born citizens or choose not to work at all, who use up medical care, social services, or other scarce resources, and who become public nuisances through alcoholism, substance abuse, and crime. Few studies have focused on the impact of refugees on host societies or have assessed the balance between the problems refugees cause and the contributions they make. This lack makes informed public debate difficult.

The cost of compassion may be less than many alarmists fear. Although some studies suggest that newcomers suffer more health problems than the host population and contribute disproportionately to the burden of public nuisance, others draw a profile of immigrant and refugee health that compares favourably with that of the receiving society. Furthermore, new settlers are likely to use fewer, not more, services than indigens (Canadian Task Force on Mental Health Issues Affecting Immigrants and Refugees, 1988a; Munroe-Blum et al., 1989).

This book has a number of goals: first, to inform public debate by documenting the successes and failures of a large group of refugees resettling in Canada; second, to contribute to a growing literature on human resiliency; and, finally, to distil policy and practice implications from the research findings.

After living as a Canadian expatriate in the United States, Africa, and

Europe, I returned to Vancouver, British Columbia, in the late 1970s to take up a professorship in the medical school at the University of British Columbia, the university from which I had graduated fifteen years earlier. I discovered in Canada a country more concerned about the plight of asylum seekers and multiculturalism than the one I remembered. Canada was throwing off its old insular smugness in favour of a new-found humanitarianism.

Three Canadian studies provide the data for this book. The first of these was a longitudinal epidemiological investigation, the Refugee Resettlement Project (RRP); the second, a series of intensive case analyses of a subsample of RRP participants; and the third, a government task-force investigation of immigrant and refugee mental health.

Between 1979 and 1981, in response to the 'Boat People' crisis, sixty thousand people from Vietnam, Laos, and Cambodia gained entrance to Canada to make up the largest single influx of refugees in the country's history. In 1981, I initiated a study of 1,348 Southeast Asian refugee men and women, a representative sample of the approximately five thousand refugees resettled in and around Vancouver between 1979 and 1981. After the initial survey in 1981, my research team conducted a follow-up in 1983, with 1,169 of the original participants, and during 1991–2, with 649 of the people from the original group who could be traced and who agreed to be reinterviewed.

The data are both quantitative and qualitative. Large sample surveys offer breadth of coverage together with the statistical power to detect population trends. However, trends offer only a pale reflection of the individuals in the groups, their unique struggles, and their individual strengths (see also Babbie, 1992). To provide a more intimate perspective on the lives of the refugees, I selected a sample of thirty people who seemed to be doing exceptionally well in their new environment, and another thirty who seemed to be floundering. I interviewed each of these men and women throughout the duration of the Refugee Resettlement Project. I also visited several refugee camps in Thailand in 1981; and in 1988 the Hong Kong office of the UN High Commission for Refugees invited me to carry out a brief study of the health effects of deteriorating refugee camp conditions. These experiences provided a firsthand glimpse of the refugees' lives prior to their resettlement in countries offering them permanent asylum.

Descriptions of the methods of science suggest an ordered process of moving from observation to theory, followed by the deductive formulation of testable hypotheses. According to the mythology of science, a researcher's personal history and experience never sully the temple of investigative purity. Science is not so neat. Subjective experience directs the choice of research questions. There is nothing wrong with that: in fact, passion for one's subject matter is probably a good thing. The danger lies in allowing passion to dictate method and observation. Good scientists devise methods to study problems that are as immune as possible to personal bias (see also Babbie, 1992).

When people ask me why I am involved in refugee studies, I often reply that since Canada is one of the major immigrant-receiving nations in the world, studies that could help direct policy are important. That is true. There are, however, more personal reasons as well.

Several years ago, while sorting through my late mother's papers, I found copies of letters she had written to the Department of Immigration and Defence requesting permission to sponsor her fiancé, left behind in Europe, to come to Canada. The exchange of letters made it evident that the government was not interested in making a reunion easy for the Roumanian-born Jewish immigrant and the man she intended to marry. The government had no idea what they were dealing with in my mother, the personification of words like unyielding, determined, and implacable. She had already made it clear to her parents that she was not about to postpone marrying until they could find a husband for her older, and less attractive, sister. Even if marrying before her sister would embarrass the family in the eyes of the entire Regina, Saskatchewan, Jewish community (all eight hundred of them), she would do it.

The exchange began in 1933 with a request from the immigration department for letters from businessmen in the community to verify my mother's claim that she could support a husband. By that time, my mother was running her own grocery store, a business she had started with a loan from her oldest brother. The businessmen were able to reassure the Department that she could indeed support a husband. In a good month, the twenty-eight-year-old spinster was earning as much as one hundred dollars. Letters from the police department followed. According to their records, my mother and her family were law-abiding. Well-intentioned as it undoubtedly was, her rabbi's letter probably did not help. There was probably nothing a rabbi could say that would have plucked the heartstrings of immigration staff reporting to the openly anti-Semitic Right Honourable Charles H. Blair, Minister of Immigration. Certainly not this rabbi, who could barely contain his enthusiasm about the prospect of my mother and father producing a lot of Jewish children in Canada.

The Department's denial of my mother's application was dated Christmas Eve, 1934. Neither of my parents ever talked about how my father eventually got to Canada. Perhaps it was fear that prompted their silence. Although the new country might not have pogroms, it did deport trouble-makers (Avery, 1979). Or perhaps, in those pre-multiculturalism days, there was an unspoken hope that if one never talked about being an immigrant, one might eventually pass for a real Canadian. I don't know how my father managed to get out of the Sudeten in 1935. Since both of my parents are now dead, there is no one to ask. I do know that, just a few years later, it would have been too late to leave.

Canada's forty-year transformation from an overtly racist to a pluralistic society culminated in 1972, with the adoption of an official policy of multiculturalism. The policy gave voice to previously silenced minorities. By the 1980s, Canada's ethnocultural communities were decrying a catalogue of inequities – inequities that were not supposed to exist in a country committed to multiculturalism. In response to lobbying for change by national ethnocultural organizations, the federal government prepared a list of topics it might be prepared to address, and asked organizations such as the Canadian Ethnocultural Council and the Canadian Council for Refugees for some consensus about where to begin. These organizations agreed that the mental health of immigrants and refugees was an important priority.

From 1986 to 1988, I chaired a task force created by the federal government to study this concern. Together with twelve committee colleagues, I reviewed the extant literature, read briefs prepared by more than two hundred immigrant and immigrant-serving groups across Canada, and conducted cross-country hearings. The government published our final report, *After the Door Has Been Opened*, in 1988.

Findings from the longitudinal epidemiological study, the intensive observations of successful and unsuccessful refugees, and the task-force investigations prompt conclusions that thread their way throughout this book. First, most refugees in most resettlement situations succeed remarkably well. The Southeast Asians in Canada are no exception. Second, no country, Canada included, offers newcomers the welcome they need and deserve. Third, although the news about the former refugees is encouraging, it is not uniformly good. There were casualties, many of which might have been prevented. Finally, even successful new settlers encounter avoidable obstacles that make their adjustment more difficult than it should be.

Acknowledgments

Through their stories, advice, support, and scientific expertise, many people have contributed to this book. In particular, I wish to thank my mentor, Alexander H. Leighton; my research colleagues Phyllis J. Johnson, Ilene Hyman, Feng Huo, Sam Noh, and Richard C. Nann; my friend and colleague Dr Soma Ganesan for lending his wisdom to the project, and for acting as my guide to Southeast Asian culture; the project coordinator, Mr Daniel Roshi, and his splendid team of interviewers; project research assistants Nhi Vu, Bich Pham, Esther Kwong, Phongsanith Rajsombat, Pauline Au, and Susan Johnston; and my secretary, Ms Beverley Marson. The book is a chronicle of how a group of remarkable men and women dealt with and, for the most part, overcame almost unimaginable stresses. I owe an overwhelming debt of gratitude to the former Southeast Asian refugees who allowed my interviewers and me to intrude on their time and privacy so that we could collect their stories. My special thanks to Ruth Sigal and Larry Rotenberg, two people whose friendships I have cherished for more than forty years, and whose stories also appear in these pages. A final thank-you to Timothy, who made me quit dawdling.

Studies that involve more than one thousand people and that span more than ten years are expensive. I am grateful to the funding agencies that have supported this project and its author over the years, most particularly Health Canada through its National Health Research and Development Program. Finally, I wish to acknowledge the rare opportunity provided by the Rockefeller Foundation to spend one month as a resident scholar at Bellagio, Italy, with nothing to do other than complete this manuscript.

Note on Confidentiality

Most of the case histories in this book are fictionalized composites based on statistical profiles as well as individual interviews. Ruth's and Larry's stories in chapter 8 are an exception. With the permission of these two remarkable people, I share their stories with the reader. In all other cases, names and other details have been altered in order to ensure the confidentiality of the original material. Although their source has been disguised, all quotations of written material are actual extracts from personal diaries.

STRANGERS AT THE GATE

ONE

Adapting in a New World

Li Wuchin, a fifty-year-old, soft-spoken Chinese whose lined face and dignified bearing suggest a man of substance, was an early resettlement casualty. In the old Saigon, Mr Li (Southeast Asians usually place their family name first) had factories, properties, and servants. The post-1975 communist government stripped them all away. No longer a rich man, he was forced to send his wife and family into the streets to cook and sell tit-bits to passers-by. To ensure his capitalist cleansing, he was sent to a 're-education camp.' After his release, he managed to escape the country with his family. In January 1980, Wuchin, his wife, and three children came to Canada.

Wuchin was happy to leave the Thai refugee camp in which he and his family had been interned. He was grateful to find refuge in Canada. Nevertheless, in June 1980, he picked up an ice-pick and severed the jugular vein on the left side of his neck.

The sixty thousand refugees admitted to Canada between 1979 and 1981 had suffered oppression, were forced out of their homes in Vietnam, Laos, and Cambodia, and endured experiences that seemed to push the capacity for suffering to its limits. They found sanctuary in Canada, though not always welcome.

As a consequence of these experiences, some refugees developed emotional disorders: depressions and anxieties, which they suffered internally, as well as alcoholism and other behavioural derangements that bothered others as much as themselves.

Unlike Li Wuchin, who turned his unhappiness against himself, a handsome, thirty-two-year-old carpenter named Nguyen Bich harmed someone else. In 1978, when the Vietnamese government began expelling Chinese, Bich pretended to be a member of that unwanted minority. When the fisherman whom he had paid to let him on board pushed his boat away from the beach in Vietnam, the vessel held about one hundred people. Three weeks later, only twenty survivors arrived in the Philippines. Like people all over the world, Bich is not above stereotyping others, especially members of a visible and apparently successful minority. He harbours a vaguely formulated suspicion that Chinese such as Li Wuchin became wealthy at the expense of the fishermen, labourers, shopkeepers, and artisans like himself whom they had exploited in the old days.

Human traffickers pay no attention to class distinctions. Everyone – rich or poor, man or woman or child – had to pay ten taels of gold to government officials before they could leave Vietnam. Bich thinks that because the Chinese were wealthy, it was easy for most of them to pay the government's unofficial exit fee. By contrast, he used all his savings to bribe the officials and to buy boat passage for one. He had to leave his wife and two children behind.

Arriving in Canada late in 1979, the Vietnamese carpenter found enough work to allow him to get by, and to send money to his family in Vietnam. But he was lonely and increasingly discouraged by the steadily diminishing prospect of accumulating sufficient savings to bring over his wife and children. In February 1982, Bich began living with a Vietnamese refugee woman he had met through mutual friends. Eighteen months later, the police arrested him for the murder of a woman the newspapers referred to as his common-law wife.

Human beings tell each other many tales. Although the plots and variations are infinite in number, the themes of the stories are few. At their heart, human tales deal with such universals as death, betrayal, suffering, devotion, and triumph. These are the themes of the story of Southeast Asian refugee resettlement in Canada.

Li Wuchin and Nguyen Bich captured headlines in the Vancouver newspapers. Refugee advocates reproach the media for paying disproportionate attention to the Wuchins and Bichs while neglecting refugee successes. Overcoming wretchedness to achieve the mundane (as most refugees do) constitutes a success story, albeit not one spectacular enough to sell newspapers or to lure prime-time viewing. Although no one among the Southeast Asian refugees has become a bank president, a judge, government minister, conductor of a symphony orchestra, or a candidate for a Nobel prize or for the Order of Canada, most have adapted, without drama but with varying levels of achievement, and most are making positive contributions to Canadian life.

Take, for example, Tran Van Ha, a small-framed man with a flat face and broad nostrils. Ha came to Canada with his wife and two young children in 1981. His impressive credentials, including a degree in anthropology as well as in American civilization and literature, together with a natural eloquence and his facility in Vietnamese, Cantonese, and English, made him an ideal candidate for his first job in Canada, a legal interpreter. Subsequently, he took a course leading to certification as a medical interpreter. Now under contract to a community agency, Ha's services are in great demand by hospitals and clinics throughout Vancouver.

When he talks about the old country, Ha never volunteers the information that he was a colonel in the South Vietnamese army. News of that sort would make him less than popular among other Vietnamese expatriates.

Industry, dedication to his family, and scrupulous honesty are some of Ha's strong points. He has overcome a troubled past to accomplish a great deal in Canada. He is not, however, a distillation of virtues: heroic perhaps, but a complex, imperfect human being, nevertheless. In fact, many people dismiss Ha as a snob. They find his excessive deference towards male authority figures and his barely concealed contempt towards women and poorly educated people distasteful. Though he may be a snob, Ha is not insensitive to criticism, nor to the fact that some of the attitudes he brought with him from Vietnam violate the behavioural norms of a country that prides itself for according respect to everyone, regardless of gender, class, or educational background.

Some of Ha's behaviour is rooted in his patriarchal Vietnamese culture. Whatever inclinations towards deference may have been part of his character, they were probably reinforced by experience. In the communist re-education camps, recognizing and respecting differences in power sometimes meant the difference between life and death.

Although the health-care system in Vancouver is benefiting from his services, Ha's job does not measure up to his personal standards for success. It pays enough to support him and his family, and to enable them to put away his wife's wages from her job as a seamstress to ensure their children's university education. It is, however, hard to be a proud person reduced to what he sees as shabby circumstances. Whenever he can, Ha emphasizes his educational credentials, hanging on to these marks of past distinction as if they were medals he can put on to dress up a bit.

Despite the difficulties, Ha is hopeful, indeed eloquent, about his present and his future in Canada. In 1982, he wrote a document entitled 'Memories.' He did it to help others understand the refugee experience. The preface to 'Memories' reads as follows:

My family was sponsored to Canada as 'boat' refugees in late 1979. Three years have passed since our arrival in Vancouver. However, we vividly remember the first Canadian friends who helped us with some pots and pans, with some shoes and boots. They also showed us how to use the bus transfer, [and] what to do when facing a job interview. Our children have received special care from many devoted teachers who led them to the first lessons in English. It is now amazing indeed to see that our children [can] express by themselves their gratitude in the new language, often-times better than in their own tongue.

Like Ha, Le Quyen will never practise the profession for which she trained. However, unlike her fellow refugee, Quyen does not have to channel frustrated personal ambition into hopes for her children. By anyone's standards, she has been extraordinarily successful.

One year before Quyen would have finished her medical degree in Saigon, the communists closed the universities and forced wealthy families like the Les into poverty. The sheltered, upper-class life of her youth did not prepare Quyen to survive as a refugee. Instead, a combination of personal fortitude and luck probably carried the day. With some of her family dead and others still trapped in Vietnam, she was unofficially adopted by a family selected for resettlement. She came to Canada expecting, or at least hoping, that her friends would take the place of her real family. Finding herself exploited rather than helped, she lapsed into despair.

Memories of her early days in Canada sometimes cast a momentary pall over Quyen's otherwise happy life in her beautifully furnished suburban Vancouver home. Even though she and her husband may control the produce outlets in most of the trendy, ersatz farmers' markets springing up all over British Columbia's lower mainland, even though she may have children and family, dresses in smart business suits, and may be invited to sit on prestigious community boards (sometimes, as she realizes only too well, as a 'token ethnic'), she has not been able to forget the poverty and loneliness of a few years ago.

BASING THEIR ACTIONS ON THE PREMISE that compassion is a luxury they can no longer afford, most countries are now closing their doors to refugees. The moral cost of such decisions is incalculable. It is easier to estimate the other side of the ledger – how many dollars a country spends when it offers asylum to people like Wuchin, Bich, Ha, Quyen, and their families. Their stories suggest that the relatively low cost of resettling refugees is more than offset by long-term financial benefit. However, improvements in policy and practice would pay dividends both for new settlers and their hosts.

The studies that form the basis for this book took place during an era when Canada could, with considerable justification, claim to be a world leader in refugee policy and an exemplar of generosity. The Canadian experiment has a great deal to teach about resettlement, not the least its contribution to understanding how and why refugees like Li Wuchin and Nguyen Bich became mental health casualties, while others like Tran Van Ha and Le Quyen became contributing members of society, pursuing the goal of happiness they share with the rest of humankind.

During the early years of the twentieth century, national self-interest fuelled investigations of the mental health of newcomers. People wanted to know if immigrants were more likely to develop mental disorders than members of the host population: if they were, this might mean they would add an element of danger to the life of the community, that they would absorb more than their share of health and social services, and that they might never be able to contribute to the common good. In less than compassionate hands, data supporting the idea that refugees and other immigrants have more problems than the local citizenry have been used to create arguments to keep newcomers out.

After they release their reports, chairs of federal task forces receive invitations to make wise-sounding comments in public places. During my tenure as 'expert,' most questions that came my way were variations on a common theme of 'How are the refugees doing?' To be sure, each person posing the question had something slightly different in mind. Some were worrying about whether the new settlers were making a contribution: they wanted to know if the refugees were working. Others, afraid that the refugees might become a drain on the economy, wanted to know how many were ending up on welfare and whether they were soaking up more than their share of Canada's health-care services. Still others sensed that the influx of so many visibly exotic people threatened the existing order. They wanted to know how quickly the Boat People were becoming part of mainstream Canadian life. The sudden appearance of so many refugees also provoked fears of attendant increases in crime, violence, or other forms of public nuisance.

By chronicling the first ten years of Southeast Asian experience in Canada with a particular focus on the refugees' mental health, this book is an attempt to answer the 'how are they doing?' question.

The refugees' stories also contribute to theory and to resettlement

practice. Ironic as it seems, people like Nguyen Bich and Li Wuchin survive the overwhelming hardships of uprooting and deportation, only to
succumb to emotional disorder after finally achieving asylum. Insights
into what drove the handsome carpenter, Nguyen Bich, to take someone
else's life and what made the former industrialist, Li Wuchin, want to end
his own make an important contribution to mental health theory. An
understanding of what Canada did correctly and what this and other
countries could do to make resettlement faster and easier can make an
important contribution to refugee resettlement policy.

A large proportion of the general population – research places it as
high as 15 to 20 per cent – suffers from emotional disorders of the types
described in the *International Classification of Diseases* (ICD-10) of the
World Health Organization or the American Psychiatric Association's
Diagnostic and Statistical Manual (DSM-IV), the listing of mental illnesses
most frequently used in North America (Robins, Helzer, and Weissman,
1984; Myers et al., 1984; Robins and Regier, 1991). Their commonness
should not blunt our sensibilities to the enormous toll these conditions
exert in individual suffering and in the cost of providing care. For example, at least 30 per cent of all medical-care contacts involve a mental
health problem (Regier et al., 1985; Schurman, Kramer, and Mitchell,
1985; Leaf et al., 1985), and psychiatric conditions like depression interfere more with work and social life than chronic physical conditions like
diabetes, hypertension, and arthritis (Wells et al., 1989).

Like everyone, migrants sometimes suffer emotional distress. There is,
in fact, a popular conception that immigrants and refugees have more
mental disorders than the populations of the countries in which they
resettle. A search of the world literature on migration turns up many
studies supporting this idea. However, an approximately equal number of
studies suggest the reverse: immigrants either have the same rates of disorder as the host country's population, or, in some cases, lower rates
(Canadian Task Force, 1988b).

If research produces contradictory results, it does not necessarily mean
that the people who conduct the studies are confused or incompetent.
Many immigration studies are carefully designed and well executed. The
problem lies with theory, not investigation. The proposition that immigration and resettlement are stressful enough to cause emotional disorder – a premise that drives most studies – is too simplistic.

A revision of theory has to acknowledge that migration *is* a condition of
risk for developing mental disorder, and that migrating as a refugee
places emotional well-being in even greater jeopardy. Risk is double-

edged, harmful both to the individual refugee and to the receiving society. Rather than becoming an asset to their host countries, newcomers who decompensate under the stresses of resettlement are a burden. But risk is not destiny. *Strangers at the Gate* argues that the social and historical contingencies surrounding resettlement as well as the personal strengths individuals bring to the situation determine whether exposure to risk ultimately results in break-down or in personal fulfilment.

Even though only a small minority of refugees become, like Bich, the subject of a sensational murder story, or, like Wuchin, an unfortunate statistic of the health-care system, their suffering and floundering are remembered while the successes of others are too often forgotten. This book is an investigation of the social forces and the individual resources that can make the difference between successful adaptation for the majority, and tragedy for the few.

TWO

Where Did the Refugees Come From?

It has always been difficult to translate the term 'Indochinese.' In the old days, the Chinese, who thought they lived in the 'Centre of the World,' named the land to their west Western Ocean; Japan, East Ocean; and the three tiny nations to the south, Peninsula in the Eastern Ocean. The French, who came here in the nineteenth century, called it Indochina because the countries had been influenced by the two great nations of India and China.

The lyrics of a popular Vietnamese song describe the history of a nation whose people have, for many generations, been struggling to be called Vietnam: 'One thousand years under the Northern invaders, / One hundred years under the Western enemies, / Thirty years of civil war and not a single day of peace.'

The people do not like their lands to be called Indochina any more than they like Peninsula in the Eastern Ocean.

Pham Bich, research assistant to the Refugee Resettlement Project, 1983.

Squeezed onto a stubby peninsula in the South China Sea between China and India, the tiny countries of Vietnam, Laos, and Cambodia have been battled over and fought in for two thousand years.

Vietnam

The political division between North and South is relatively recent; its cultural antecedents are much older. The Vietnamese themselves have long distinguished between the North (Bac Ky), with Hanoi as its cultural centre, the central region, with its traditional royal capital of Hue, and the

South (Nam Ky), with Saigon, now officially called Ho Chi Minh City, as its hub. The North is dominated by groups culturally affiliated with South China, especially the Thai, Hmong, and Mien, while the South still retains Khmer and Indian influences.

In 111 B.C., the Han Chinese ruler Wu Ti invaded and annexed most of what has become today's North Vietnam. During one thousand years of ensuing Chinese occupation (111 B.C. to A.D. 939), the Vietnamese continually resisted their rulers' efforts at Sinicization. An act of resistance in A.D. 40 retains its hold in the Vietnamese imagination. After the Chinese executed a popular warlord, his widow and sister-in-law organized an uprising, drove the Chinese out, and declared themselves queens. Three years later, the Chinese came back. Faced with defeat, the Trung sisters drowned themselves in the Hat Giang River.

Although they adopted written script and many elements of Chinese Confucian political organization, the Vietnamese clung to their own oral language and to important traditions such as animism, totemism, tooth-blackening, arranged marriage, and seasonal festivals. India exerted its influence through Funan and Champa, two states located in the southern part of the peninsula. Over the centuries, Funan evolved into present-day Cambodia, Champa into South Vietnam.

The Trung sisters' defeated rebellion was only one among many attempts to throw off Chinese rule in the north. Finally, in the fifteenth century, the Vietnamese scored a decisive victory over the Ming dynasty. The new Vietnamese emperor, Le Loi, then set in motion a 'March to the South.' During the ensuing 350 years, the Vietnamese defeated the Chams, and annexed the Mekong Delta and Saigon. By the latter part of the eighteenth century, the March to the South was completed, and Vietnam was established in its present form – a narrow country one thousand miles long, divided by history and differences in tradition. The emperor, now ruling from Hanoi, selected mandarins from the local populace to collect taxes and recruit soldiers for the imperial army. Mandarin selection was based on grades obtained in national examinations, a piece of history that may help explain contemporary Vietnamese veneration of scholarship.

As early as the sixteenth century, travellers from Portugal, England, Holland, and France began visiting Vietnam. Eventually, however, all the Europeans, with the exception of the French, gave up their attempts to establish trade and religious missions. Opportunity eventually rewarded France's persistence. In the seventeenth century, two warlord families, the Trinhs in the North, and the Nguyens in the South, began vying for

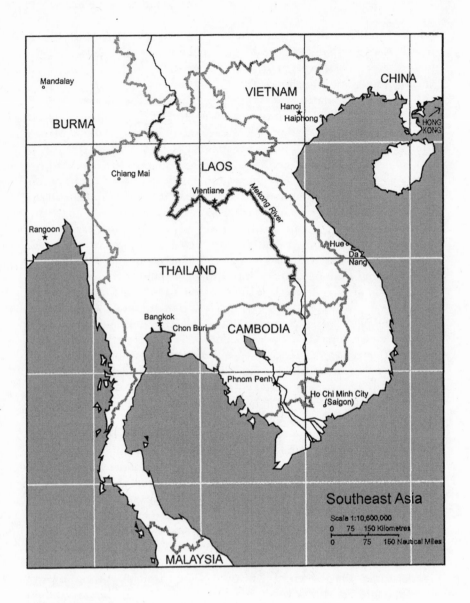

imperial hegemony. French military aid tipped the balance of power in favour of the Nguyens. As a gesture of gratitude, the Nguyen leader, Gia Long, appointed a missionary named Pigneau de Behaine his political and military adviser.

France's enthusiasm for Christian conversion eventually made it an unwelcome guest. Early in the nineteenth century, the Vietnamese began expelling missionaries and persecuting their converts. Rather than discouraging the French, this religious persecution provided just the pretext Napoleon III needed to mount an invasion. After capturing the imperial city of Hue, the French divided Vietnam into a colony, Cochin China, and two protectorates, Annam and Tonkin. In 1893, the French formed the Indochinese Union of Vietnam, Cambodia, and Laos.

The imperialist yoke bit deeply. By the 1930s, 45 per cent of all the large rubber, sugar, and rice plantations of the South were in the hands of six thousand French speculators and a small group of Vietnamese collaborators. By contrast, 62 per cent of the peasantry owned less than one-ninth of an acre of land per household, and another 30 per cent owned less than one-fourth of an acre. The French also controlled the coal, zinc, and tin mines, as well as the country's few industries, such as cement manufacturing. Vietnamese trade was restricted to French markets. The French also established a government monopoly on salt, alcohol, and opium, imposing heavy taxes for which they provided few returns. Despite the taxes, only 15 per cent of all school-aged children received any kind of schooling, while 80 per cent of the population remained illiterate.

French oppression affected Ho Chi Minh's childhood. He apparently never forgot. He was born in 1890, in one of the country's inland provinces, a region poor in resources but noted for its scholars and its reputation for radical thought. By virtue of scholastic achievement, Ho's father had risen above his peasant origins to achieve a post as provincial deputy prefect. He was, however, too candid regarding his feelings about being a mandarin serving a foreign power. The French stripped him of his post, and the family was plunged into a life of poverty.

Like his father, Ho Chi Minh experienced modest success based on scholarship. He even worked for a time as a teacher. However, at the age of twenty-two, he left Vietnam and began working as a mess boy on a French ocean liner. The young expatriate eventually found his way to Paris, where he made a living by retouching photographs and painting made-in-France 'Chinese antiquities.' Ironically, in all probability as a result of exposure to left-wing thought in Paris, Ho eventually welded his abhorrence of French colonialism to an ideology rooted in Leninism and French communism. Imbued with the spirit of revolution, the young Ho moved to post-revolutionary Moscow. In 1925, the leaders of the International sent Ho to Canton to assist the new Chinese revolutionary government. Here, supported by many other young Vietnamese revolutionaries he found living outside their country, Ho founded a government in exile – the Doc Lap Dong Minh Ho, later called Vietminh.

The Second World War presented a scenario of opportunity and of risk. France's defeat by Germany made revolution in Vietnam a real possibility. However, Ho recognized that the Japanese were probably even more dangerous imperialists than the French. Ho created an alliance with the United States and China against Japan. Japan's subsequent defeat brought reward for his prescience. The United States and China supported Ho's return to Hanoi and the establishment of the Vietminh government of North Vietnam.

The French, however, had not given up on Vietnam. Acting on the authority of the Potsdam Conference, they reconquered the southern part of the country. With the help of China, Ho Chi Minh initiated a guerilla war against France. The famous 1954 Battle of Dien Bien Phu was a decisive defeat for France. Following the battle, France and the Vietminh signed an agreement in Geneva that divided the country in two at the seventeenth parallel. The former French protectorate of Tonkin was now reborn as North Vietnam; Cochin China and the former protectorate of Annam, as South Vietnam. Backed by China and Russia, the Hanoi regime took control of the North. The South held elections resulting in the establishment of a unicameral, two-party government headed by President Ngo Dinh Diem.

President Diem's penchant for brutality undermined the enthusiasm of the United States for the man it had initially backed. Worst of all, 'as the Diem regime grew older, the administration began to take on more and more of the properties of a sponge. Money (mainly from the U.S.), plans, and programs poured into it and nothing came out the other end' (Fitzgerald, 1972, p. 93). Internal dissension came from the many Vietnamese who favoured total reunification of the country and the Buddhist majority who resented Diem's favouritism towards Roman Catholics. Diem's overthrow by his army in 1963 set in motion a series of coups and counter-coups. A subsequent Western-backed government headed by General Nguyen Van Thieu and Air Vice Marshall Nguyen Cao Ky met continuing opposition from the Communist-led National Front for the Liberation of the South (NFL). Armed by North Vietnam, the military wing of the NFL – the Vietcong – waged almost continuous guerrilla warfare.

Unable to contain the Vietcong, the government of South Vietnam turned for help to the United States, who first sent advisers, then troops, to aid in the fight. By mid-1965, there were 75,000 U.S. troops in Vietnam. By early 1968, 510,000 U.S. troops were fighting alongside 600,000 regular Vietnamese military.

The prolonged war devastated a country early visitors had described as a tropical paradise. The war claimed more than five million lives, two million North and South Vietnamese soldiers, and three and one-half million civilians. Fifty per cent of the population of South Vietnam lost their homes between 1965 and 1974. Subjected to continuous U.S. bombing, the North suffered even more catastrophic damage.

Since the fall of Saigon in 1975, and its symbolic renaming as Ho Chi Minh City, the Vietnamese Communist party, its membership open to any citizen over eighteen who 'has engaged in labour and is not an exploiter,' has dominated the country's political and social life. However, even though Hanoi has tried to replace organized religion with its own patriotic version of 'Scientific Materialism,' Taoism, Buddhism, Confucianism, and Roman Catholicism have retained a hold, particularly in the urbanized parts of the South. In rural areas, many tribal people cling to animism or to syncretic religions, particularly Cao Dai and Hoa Hao.

Cao Dai, the supreme god of the universe, revealed itself in 1925 to a group of civil servants who were consulting a medium. The sect that developed from this original revelation celebrates the third amnesty of God – the first amnesty being Christ and Moses, the second, Buddha and Lao Tzu, and the third, Cao Dai. The religion's syncretistic symbols unite European ideas of material progress with old patriarchal values and a village-based sense of identity.

Hoa Hao, originating near the border with Cambodia, is a species of reformed Buddhism, expressed through internal faith rather than elaborate ritual. Its founder, Huynh Phu So, preached about the importance of the common man and about the eventual departure of colonialists, who would be replaced by the rule of brotherhood of the Three Religions.

As Saigon was being conquered by North Vietnam in 1975, 132,000 Vietnamese fled the country as refugees. The vast majority of this predominantly urban, middle-class, and well-educated group, many of whom had worked with American military and political personnel, were relocated to the United States. However, about 9,000 resettled in Canada, primarily in Montreal and Quebec City (Montero, 1979).

Shortly after this so-called 'first wave' of refugee exodus, Hanoi sealed the borders of a country plunging into economic crisis. The Sino-Vietnamese war had emptied the country's treasury, and the U.S. military's jungle defoliation offensive had stripped it of one-fifth of its fruit- and lumber-producing forests. Added to these problems, floods and droughts in the late 1970s seriously affected rice production. The crisis prompted the government to send the merchant class (many of whom were ethnic Chinese) from the cities to be 're-educated' as pioneer agricultural workers in 'New Economic Zones.'

Resorting to conquest of its neighbours in order to deal with its internal problems, Vietnam invaded Cambodia in 1978. When China retaliated with military action along its border with North Vietnam, Hanoi began to persecute and expel the country's 745,000 ethnic Chinese residents (Bennaum, Bennaum, and Kelly, 1984), some of whom could trace hundreds of years of ancestry in Vietnam.

The forced expulsion of Chinese, together with the escape of many Vietnamese who felt they could no longer live in their country, set in motion a second wave of refugee exodus, culminating in the so-called Vietnamese Boat People crisis. Although it is a commonly used term, 'Vietnamese Boat People' is misleading on two counts. First, the second wave of Southeast Asian refugees came from the entire peninsula, not just from Vietnam. Second, most escaped their home countries overland, not by boat. Nevertheless, the image of people on boats trying to reach safe harbour in Hong Kong, the Philippines, Malaysia, and Indonesia remains the most potent icon of the Southeast Asian exodus.

Laos

Like Vietnam, ancient Laos was affected by its neighbours: China, India, Burma, Thailand, and Vietnam itself. More recent decades have exposed the country to French, Japanese, Russian, and American influence.

According to most authorities, the Lao originated in southern China. About eight hundred years ago, they fled their homeland to escape Kublai Khan and his Mongol warriors. Entering northern Laos, they established Lan Xang, Kingdom of the Million Elephants. In 1574, the Burmese conquered the capital city of Vientiane, shattering two hundred years of relative peace and plunging the country into anarchy, from which it did not escape for fifty years. In 1637, Souligna-Vongsa ascended the throne, restored order through treaties with Vietnam and Siam, declared the pre-eminence of Buddhism, and made Vientiane a centre of intellectual and cultural brilliance. The sixty years of Souligna-Vongsa's rule are still considered Laos's Golden Age. During the next 150 years, Siam's expansionist ambitions, together with its need to establish a military buffer between itself and Vietnam, led to repeated attempts to annex Laos. By the late nineteenth century, Siam's incursions against Laos brought it face-to-face with France, which had by then made Vietnam into a protectorate. After a number of military clashes, Thailand withdrew and, in 1893, officially recognized the region as a French protectorate.

Japanese domination during the Second World War yielded, in the postwar period, to another period of French ascendancy. By 1949, Laos had become part of the French Union. Internal divisions soon arose. Some Lao leaders, content to work with the French, wanted to remain in the Union. Others, rallying under Prince Souphanouvong, joined the opposing Pathet Lao movement. Before Laos proclaimed its independence in 1953, the Pathet Lao, aided by the Viet Minh, had established a stronghold in the northeast.

Although the 1954 Geneva accords officially proclaimed Laos's neutrality, internal conflict shattered this vision. Reacting to election results that suggested increasing popular support for the Pathet Lao, rightist forces, with military help from the United States and the Philippines, forced Prince Souphanouvong from office and imprisoned him in his capital. From the early 1960s, Laos's fate became increasingly tied to that of Vietnam. In return for the Pathet Lao's support of Viet Minh incursions into South Vietnam along the Ho Chi Minh Trail, Hanoi helped the Lao Communists gain control of Vientiane.

The fall of Saigon in 1975 finally broke the military deadlock. Their morale in collapse, rightist politicians and soldiers began fleeing to Thailand. They were followed by other citizens fearful of what Communist domination might mean and of how the Pathet Lao might retaliate against former supporters of the Western powers. Since 1977, the Lao People's Democratic Republic, with close ties to Hanoi, remains in control of the country.

Cambodia

By comparison with Vietnam and Laos, Cambodia has remained more insular, its origins more obscure, its history more mysterious. Most authorities trace the earliest human settlement to migration from South Vietnam. However, by the first century A.D., it had become Funan, a country firmly under the influence of the great Continent of India. The more

or less peaceful evolution of the Khmer nation reached its peak in the fifteenth century during the Angkhorian era. Three hundred years of internal struggle and of battles with Thailand finally concluded in 1863, when
war-weary Cambodia became a French protectorate.

For the next one hundred years, Cambodia remained largely rural. In
1970, 90 per cent of its five million people still lived in the countryside,
working on family farms. The least economically developed country in
Southeast Asia, Cambodia was almost entirely dependent on two crops,
rice and rubber. In contrast to the almost exclusively ethnic-Cambodian
rural areas, almost half of the urban population consisted of Chinese,
who had begun migrating to Cambodia during the eighteenth century.
Buddhism was the official state religion.

The Geneva Conference of 1953 established Cambodia's independence from France. Under the terms of the Conference, Norodon Sihanouk, crowned as king in 1941, changed his title to become chief of state.
Disregarding earthly titles, many Cambodians worshipped Sihanouk as a
god. His power remained under constant threat, menaced from the outside by Thailand and Vietnam, and internally by dissatisfied right- and
left-wing factions. Pol Pot was one of the leaders of the Khmer Rouge, the
major communist opposition to Sihanouk. The son of a farmer, Pol Pot
had been a student in Paris between 1949 and 1953, where he became
absorbed in left-wing ideology.

In an attempt to placate the Left as well as the Right, Sihanouk permitted the Viet Cong passage through Cambodian territory during the early
stages of the Vietnam war. This tilt to the Left precipitated a right-wing
coup in 1970. Its leader, General Lon Nol, forced Sihanouk into exile in
Peking. Lon Nol was apparently unwilling to stake his continued success
on military muscle alone. It is said that, in order to ensure the defence of
Phnom Penh, he once ordered helicopter pilots to sprinkle magic sand
around the city's perimeter.

In the end, neither muscle nor magic was enough to protect Lon Nol.
After the fall of Saigon, left-wing forces supported by China toppled the
Cambodian general's government. Pol Pot became the country's new
leader.

Some years before Pol Pot's ascent to power, peasants and farmers had
begun streaming into Phnom Penh to seek refuge from the bombing and
guerrilla warfare that had been ravaging the countryside. Between 1970
and 1975, Phnom Penh swelled from a city of five hundred thousand to
two million.

Captured in photographs as a pudgy man with a sweet smile, Pol Pot was described by Western diplomats as unfailingly polite, even deferential. Belying this image, the new premier introduced an idiosyncratic menu of economic reform liberally seasoned with torture and extermination. Declaring musicians and artists 'counter-revolutionaries,' he put to death as many as he could find. He also abolished religion, executed Buddhist monks, banned all forms of private ownership, extended working hours, and declared that all non-labour time was to be devoted to party indoctrination. Fear guaranteed the absoluteness of his rule. A former schoolhouse in Phnom Penh called Tirol Sleng, where people were tortured into making false confessions, has become a national symbol of the era's brutality. Of twenty thousand people imprisoned at Tirol Sleng, only seven came out alive. After closing all the temples and all schools offering instruction beyond the elementary grades, Pol Pot drove urban merchants (many of them ethnic Chinese), priests, intellectuals, and literati into underpopulated areas of the country, where they were to work as peasants in the premier's vision of his new Cambodia, an agricultural commune on a vast scale. During the four years of Pol Pot's terror, between one and two million people died. By 1979, Phnom Penh had been reduced to a city of 270,000.

Vietnam invaded Cambodia in 1979, defeated Pol Pot, and created enough confusion to make escape from Cambodia possible. Supported by the Thai army and by Thai business interests, Pol Pot maintained a comfortable residence near the eastern border of Thailand in 'Office 87,' a compound protected by the Khmer Rouge soldiers and henchmen who supported him during his years of power. From this comfortable base, Pol Pot and his Khmer Rouge followers waged a war of attrition against a coalition government backed by the United Nations, an arrangement that returned Sihanouk to power once again. In 1991, all Cambodian factions, including the Khmer Rouge, signed a peace agreement providing for U.N. peacekeeping and elections. Two of Pol Pot's henchmen, Khmer Rouge president Khieu Samphan and military commander Son Sen, returned to Phnom Penh for the first time since 1979. They left within a day, slightly ahead of a mob determined to lynch them.

Although forced to play his brutality out on a smaller stage in his old age, Pol Pot apparently remained ferocious to the end. On 15 April 1998, he died at the age of seventy-three (*Toronto Star*, 1998).

THREE

Southeast Asian Refugees in Canada: Forced to Rely on the Kindness of Others

Almost two million people fled the Southeast Asian peninsula between 1975 and 1980. Public discourse often relies on mottoes to encapsulate events. Despite the fact that more people left Southeast Asia by land routes than by the sea, the Southeast Asian refugees will probably always be remembered as the 'Boat People.'

Geography dictated some destinations. Cambodians, whose country shares a border with Thailand, made their way to that country by foot. Laotians sometimes used a route through Cambodia to Thailand, as did Vietnamese who had to cross the Mekong River along the way. Of the 900,000 people who did leave Vietnam in leaking, overcrowded boats, 150,000 either died at sea or were killed by pirates (Pottier, 1982). Wind and season played important roles in their choice of harbour. During the winter or early spring, the winds blow south across the North China Sea. People who set out during these seasons were most likely to end up in Malaysia, Indonesia, Singapore, the Philippines, or Thailand. The winds shift and blow northwards in summer and fall. The shift makes Hong Kong the most likely landing at that time of year. The refugees knew that their Southeast Asian neighbours had no intention of becoming permanent hosts. Making the journey to one of the temporary asylum countries was only a first step. Both the exiles and their temporary hosts were depending on countries like Australia, Canada, the United States, Sweden, and Israel to offer the refugees a permanent home.

Although there were many individual reasons for becoming a refugee, the desperation and fear in Min Ran's story were common themes.

Chan Min Ran

'I'm so nervous, I can't talk English with you.' Corpulent, a little flushed, Chan Min Ran sat in her kitchen mopping her forehead, apologizing to me for everything from her reliance on an interpreter to the dilapidated state of her crowded east-end Vancouver apartment. The disorganized piles of garbage on the floor, the stove covered with layers of brown grease, the empty egg cartons taking up every available inch of counter space seemed to reflect the internal jumble of her mind. In Min Ran's opinion, she lost her mind during the years before she left Cambodia. She expected to feel better once she got to Canada. She doesn't. In fact, she feels worse.

Min Ran and her sons came from Cambodia. They are survivors of Pol Pot, the former engineer who ranks with Hitler and Stalin among history's most notorious butchers. The wife of a teacher and the daughter of the owner of a food-processing plant, Min lived a comfortable upper-middle-class life in Phnom Penh until 1975. She was well educated and multilingual. She spoke fluent French, Khmer, and Vietnamese, as well as her mother tongue, Cantonese. English came into her repertoire much later.

One day, without warning, Khmer Rouge soldiers arrived with their rifles at Min Ran's house. They rounded up fourteen members of her family: Min herself, her husband, their six children, her mother and father-in-law, two of Min Ran's cousins, her husband's brother, and his young wife. For the crime of having run a prosperous rice-processing factory, the family was marched at gun point into the forest to do hard labour.

Writing was forbidden. Despite the danger, Min Ran's husband kept a diary on scraps of paper that he hid in his clothes. Although Min managed to save the diary, she could never bring herself to read it. Instead, she gave the precious scraps to me. She felt that, by publishing what her husband had written, I might help my fellow Canadians understand how much she and others from Cambodia had suffered. My translator told me that she could not do justice to the diary's intense poetry. In my opinion, the translation lacks nothing in power:

Highway Number 3 was filled with Chinese people. The procession was several kilometres long, heading aimlessly. The army were like wolves to this scurrying herd of sheep. Using the excuse of a baggage search they snatched valuables. I lost my jewellery and my watch. I need food and clothes. I hope I can leave this nightmare behind soon. Meantime, silence covers my fury.

When exhaustion combined with lack of food dried up Min Ran's breasts, the couple's three-month-old baby died. The baby was not to be the only loss. When their ordeal came to an end four years later, Min and two of her children were the only survivors of a once large family.

During their years in the forest, the adults had to learn how to plant crops, how to carry heavy loads of produce and water on their backs, and how to avoid irritating their guards.

People have to build their own houses from mud and straw. The rainy season came early this year. Storms tormented us, then diseases followed. The elders and the kids were the first to fall ill. People died every day. There were bodies in the river. The old and the weak died from drinking this water. I saw an old woman collecting firewood one morning and, in the afternoon, she was already lying on the ground. Her grandson tried to wake her, to make her play with him. Several days later, orders came for us to move again. I pitied this poor child who had nowhere to go.

When they finally stayed in one place long enough to build a hut, Min Ran's husband went on writing on scraps of brown wrapping paper, which he hid in the roof thatch. Life continued to be harsh.

When we can find them, we eat wild vegetables, bananas, bark, crabs and frogs. Empty stomachs rumble like thunder while sweat falls like rain. Faces are unrecognizable, pushed to work like cows. The Chinese are in danger living as outcasts among southern barbarians. Although no whips are used, the language is worse than weapons, because it hurts the heart. It is wise to act deaf and dumb, to vent your anger on the lands you are forced to work.

Tolling bells announce the return of a herd of cows. A beautiful sight, but my mind does not enjoy it. The warmth of a sunset fails to reach my heart. I am in a painting, but I do not see its beauty because of the curse hanging over our lives.

We work until sunset. Finally, the bells. We line up for rations. The children get half a can of rice, the adults one each.

One day, Min Ran's seven-year-old son was in the hut with his father. The soldiers came and took the older man away. Recalling the incident, the thin, intense twenty-one-year-old, who has called himself Thomas since he arrived in Canada, says he wasn't too concerned. The soldiers were always taking people away, and most of them came back. His father never did.

The Khmer Rouge soldiers came back for Thomas about a year after his father disappeared. Following a new Pol Pot policy, they took the eight-year-old away from his mother to live in a separate encampment for children. One day, the guards caught the lonesome youngster trying to sneak into the adult compound. They made Thomas an example for others who might be tempted to risk acts of disobedience. After hanging him by his heels from the branch of a tree, the guards swung his body in a circle: as Thomas's body passed in front of each of them, the soldiers forced the young boy to hit himself in the face with his fists. Someone told Thomas's mother that, when the soldiers cut her son down, his face was so swollen he could barely see.

One by one, members of Min Ran's family died, some victims of starvation, others of diseases for which there were no medicines.

In 1979, the Vietnamese invaded Cambodia. After that, everything, in Min Ran's words, turned 'messy.' She became part of the swarm trying to escape from Cambodia over the country's eastern border with Vietnam. Afraid of being captured either by Cambodian or Vietnamese soldiers, Min Ran carried her two children on her back, slipping over the border during the night. She had heard that, when the border guards caught would-be fugitives, they punished them by tearing out their eyes or cutting the tendons in their feet.

Although Vietnam's post-1975 Communist government did not rival Pol Pot's in ferocity, it did not spare its ideological and military adversaries. The regime purged the wealthy of their businesses, their lands, and their factories, and it imposed ruinous taxes on small-business owners.

Both North Vietnamese army deserters who had fled south, and South Vietnamese members of the resistance had a great deal to fear. Constantly in danger of arrest and execution, they became part of a large underground population in South Vietnam. Intellectuals, political officers in the pre-1975 regime, former police, South Vietnamese army officers, and formerly high-ranking civil servants also faced the prospect of retaliatory arrests. Rather than execution, these arrests usually meant long sentences to camps in the countryside, where forced labour, isolation, and semi-starvation could be applied in order to inculcate appropriate communist values. If they survived to be released, political detainees confronted new problems. Denied any prospect of finding work, they became social outcasts. Some people escaped the camps by fleeing to the countryside. Even though they took on new identities, they could never completely escape the threat of exposure.

A prominent minority in Vietnam for eight centuries, the Chinese were singled out for persecution, then virtually expelled by the Hanoi government. The Chinese typically left Vietnam in family units after first paying government bureaucrats an unofficial exit price: ten taels (about twenty ounces) of gold per head. While Laotians also typically fled as whole families, many ethnic Vietnamese migrated as singles, leaving parents, siblings, spouses, and children behind.

During the late 1970s, the height of the 'Boat People' crisis, Sino-Vietnamese departures from Vietnam were semi-official. Ethnic Vietnamese flight was always clandestine. When I asked him why he left his wife and children, Nguyen Bich, the Vietnamese carpenter, told me of a hope shared by many refugees: he would find a way to the United States or Australia, earn a lot of money, then bring his family to join him.

Accident dictated other separations. Lien and her husband, Thanh, had planned their escape carefully. After bribing the owner of a fishing boat to let them on board, Lien thought of something she had left behind. Today, living in Canada, the young single mother cannot even remember what it was. Back then, it seemed so important that she insisted that Thanh run back to their house to get it. By the time he returned, the boat had left. Lien's mother wrote to tell her that Thanh was later arrested. They heard that he went crazy in prison; he used to beat his head on the wall and scream Lien's name all the time.

Government policies in countries offering permanent asylum accounted for other separations. For example, although some rural Southeast Asians practise polygyny, Canada and the United States do not accept the concept that a man can have more than one wife. According to Canadian and U.S. guidelines: 'A man may take all his children, or the rejected wife can keep her children and arrive in the country as the head of the household, but a single parent' (Palmer, 1981, p. 6). Men with more than one family had to choose which wife and which children to save.

Internment

Before they reached Canada, the 1,348 refugees who took part in the Refugee Resettlement Project (RRP) spent an average of twelve months in a refugee camp somewhere in Southeast Asia. Some stayed in camps as little as a month or two, others as long as five years. Figure 3.1 shows the

Figure 3.1   Southeast Asian Pre-Migratory Incarceration

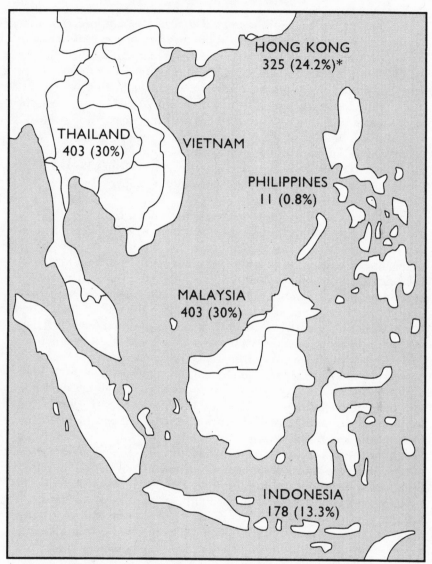

*Number (percentage) of the cohort in the Refugee Resettlement Project

location of the camps, and the proportion of the RRP sample interned at each of the sites.

Tran Van Ha, the linguist who worked as one of the interpreters for the Refugee Resettlement Project, recalls the first days of relative safety after arriving at a refugee camp in Malaysia: 'I slept for three days. That was the first time in years I could sleep and feel pretty sure I would still be there in the morning, that I would not have a rifle pointed at my head or that I would not be taken away during the night. At first, to be safe in the camp seemed so good to us. Then we began to see the bad things.'

Most camps housed a few thousand refugees, usually two to three times the maximum number for which they had been built. Some were in the countryside. Others were in the downtown core of cities like Bangkok and Hong Kong, separated from the surrounding hum of city life by concrete walls and armed guards.

According to a UN-sponsored accord, first asylum countries in Southeast Asia agreed to admit refugees to the camps with the understanding that other countries who were party to the accord – principally the United States, Canada, and Australia – would offer permanent asylum.

Economic hard times, concerns about unlimited population growth, discrimination, and apathy combined to erode the openness that characterized Canada's immigration practices between the end of the Second World War and the early 1980s. During the decades immediately following the war, Canada had been admitting an average of 130,000 new settlers per year. In 1985, a year during which the country was just beginning to recover from a severe recession, immigration figures dropped to a low of 85,000. Oblivious to how economic problems were blunting the generosity of the industrialized world, people kept fleeing their homes in Vietnam, Cambodia, and Laos, and pouring into the refugee camps of first asylum countries. Compared to the numbers arriving, few left. Rather than temporary places of passage, many camps became semi-permanent homes. Some changed from closed to open camps and began to permit the adults to go out for daytime work, the children to attend school.

There was a relentless similarity to Southeast Asian refugee camps. The inmates lived in human warehouses, open at two ends, with corrugated metal walls and roofs. Inside the buildings, people lived in 'bunks,' three-tiered, six-by-eight-foot wooden palettes supported by metal poles. At first glance, the bunks, lined up in rows with twenty to thirty per section, looked like floor-to-ceiling shelves with narrow, dark aisles running between them. To make it easy for children to climb in and out, a family usually got the bottom shelf, while two or more adults shared bunks on the second and third tiers. It was not unusual to find a family of four or five living in the bottom, table-sized apartment, while three young men slept together and ate their meals on the top floor. To achieve a little privacy, couples blocked off their bunk space with scraps of sheets or towels they might have managed to bring along from home or else scavenged in the camps. To cook the food brought in by international relief agencies, the detainees set up small charcoal burners in the aisles between the bunks. There were never enough toilets. When the drains backed up, as they often did, the sewage and dishwater emptied first onto the concrete floors of the barracks, then trickled out in dirty rivulets onto the roadways between buildings.

The longer-established camps with schools, youth centres, medical clinics, offices for governmental, UN, and non-governmental voluntary agency personnel (VOLAGS in international shorthand), and food-stalls, began to acquire an air of semi-permanence. Despite the trappings, these places were prisons. Like refugee camps elsewhere, the ones in Southeast Asia had 'the artifacts of community but not the spirit' (Chan and Loveridge, 1987, p.749).

Among all the miseries of camp life, enforced idleness claimed pride of place. According to Tran Van Ha, camp life was, 'life without meaning, without hope. You can't work, you can't do anything.' Many people were passing the prime of their lives in the camps, with little, if anything, to do. 'Killing time' took on new meaning.

Getting out preoccupied everyone. Most camp inmates had the United States as their goal, a country made familiar by twenty years of American presence as well as through Vietnamese-language broadcasts over the Voice of America. In comparison, Canada and Australia were relatively unknown.

During the time Tran Van Ha was being held in the re-education camp in Vietnam, his older brother Tran Bang escaped with his family. In one of the surprising coincidences of flight, Ha found himself briefly reunited with his brother in a refugee camp in Malaysia. By the time Ha reached the camp, Canadian immigration officers had already selected his well-educated, French-speaking brother Bang for resettlement in the francophone province of Quebec. Brother Bang's happiness about leaving the camp was tempered by what people were saying about life in eastern Canada. He had heard that the climate was so harsh that people worked and went out of their homes only six months a year. During the winters, no one did anything. Orientation films, shown in the camp and from which Bang remembered only 'blank white landscapes, few trees, and no people,' confirmed the rumours. The exception to all this was Vancouver, where the climate was reputed to be at least tolerable. Bang counselled his younger brother not to repeat his mistake: Ha was not to admit he spoke French. During the months Ha waited in the camp with his wife and children, he wondered whether telling someone he spoke French might move them up in the immigration queue. Finally, however, his patience brought what he wanted. Ha is still grateful that he and his family came to Vancouver rather than to Montreal. Although Ha now knows that people in the east do not really hibernate for six months, Bang tells him the weather in Montreal really is despicable.

In 1988, on my way back from a lecture tour to China, I stopped in Hong Kong. I wanted to investigate some disquieting rumours. During the late 1970s and early 1980s, the prosperous British colony was the most humanitarian first asylum country in Southeast Asia. By 1988, however, it had begun changing its stripes. Hong Kong's change of heart was understandable. Although other first asylum countries had sealed their borders to refugees by this time, Boat People were continuing to arrive at the port of Hong Kong at the rate of about two thousand per month. With countries like Canada and the United States defaulting on their promise to take in large numbers of Southeast Asian refugees, Hong Kong was becoming a de facto permanent asylum. Rumour had it that, to stem the tide of refugees, the government was about to introduce legislation defining everyone who arrived from Vietnam an illegal alien subject to deportation, rather than a refugee eligible for asylum (this prediction proved to be true). To pressure some of the refugees now living within its borders to consider voluntary repatriation to Vietnam, Hong Kong was unofficially but determinedly making life in the camps difficult.

When I arrived at Camp Sham Shui Po, walled off from one of Hong Kong's busiest market and industrial areas behind corrugated metal and barbed wire, someone suggested that Trinh Ngoc act as my guide and interpreter. Ngoc was more than happy to do so. Even though I tried to convince him that nothing I said or did could possibly affect his chances of being accepted as a refugee by Canada, he constantly steered our conversation to his suitability. He argued that he would be a good bet for Canada because he spoke such good English (he did not), because he was so resourceful (he was), and because he was so industrious (I imagine he would be, if given the chance). Twenty-six years old when I first met him, Ngoc had lived in refugee camps since he arrived in Hong Kong at age seventeen, the only member of his family to survive the boat trip from Vietnam.

A Southeast Asian refugee camp was a stifling, dangerous place. Partly because of his natural intelligence, partly because many years spent as an internee had taught him 'camp smarts,' Ngoc came as close as was humanly possible to mastering his environment while never giving up the hope of someday escaping it. Thanks to the clothing drives conducted by some good-hearted citizens of Hong Kong, the consumer capital of the world, Ngoc was always well turned out, his designer jeans, cotton shirts, and Reeboks complementing his slim frame and black, shoulder-length hair.

Despite Trinh Ngoc's charm and intelligence, immigration officers continued to overlook him when they chose likely candidates. Ngoc then evolved a new strategy. Knowing that receiving countries considered families a better bet than single men, he planned to marry one of the young Vietnamese women in the camp. Although there was no romantic interest between them, it seemed a fair arrangement to both the prospective bride as well as her groom. By marrying Ngoc, the young woman would take him out of the 'single male' category, the one immigration officers liked least. In return, while sharing her bunk, Ngoc would protect his bride from abuse and possible rape, constant threats to unattached women.

I do not know what happened to Ngoc and his young wife. I do know that many marriages of convenience like theirs fell apart after the refugees arrived in Canada. By that time, there were often children, and a forced, loveless interdependence degenerating into hostility.

In a situation very reminiscent of Ngoc's, Dao Huy and Dao Phuong met and married in a camp in the Philippines. About a year after the couple arrived in Vancouver, they came to our attention through a referral from a community mental health centre. The referral chain began with a call to the police from the Daos' neighbours. They complained about the screaming and crying coming from the household. The confusion attendant on a midnight call coupled with a language barrier made it impossible for the police officers to piece together a coherent story. They recorded a few scraps of Dao Huy's report about his wife, Phuong. 'She wants to kill herself and the baby,' he said. 'She's crazy.' The police took the young mother to the emergency room of a downtown hospital. After giving her a sedative, the hospital sent the woman and her child to a community shelter to spend the night under supervision.

When they discovered that Dao Phuong had disappeared during the night, the shelter personnel called a local mental health centre for help. After she finally answered one of the repeated calls to her home, Phuong told the worker she was fine, then began sobbing and quickly hung up the telephone. Soon after, a staff psychiatrist and a Vietnamese-speaking mental health worker arrived at the Daos' apartment, a second-floor walk-up in Chinatown. The young husband blamed his wife for all their problems. He wanted the mental health workers to make her more reasonable. The woman felt the same way about her spouse, and wanted the same thing from the workers.

The only son of an upper-class family in Vietnam, Dao Huy had run many of his father's businesses before the Communists took everything away and Huy became a refugee. In a camp in the Philippines, Huy met and married Phuong. When their son arrived, they sold whatever they could to the camp guards in order to get the milk supplement the infant required. Phuong says she was very unhappy that she had to sell a ring her mother had given her. After arriving in Canada, the young couple quickly found work, Phuong as a seamstress, Huy as a dishwasher. While they were both working, Huy sent every cent from his pay cheque to his parents in Vietnam. Phuong kept her money to support their little family in Canada. During the recession of the mid-1980s, Huy was laid off. Huy then had to resort to asking his wife for money to send to his parents. Her refusal humiliated him. Unlike Phuong, the young husband was not thinking of saving for a second-hand car or a down payment on a house. He was worried that his parents might be starving, while he, their only son, was failing in his obligations to them.

Phuong soon discovered she was going to have another baby. To her troubled young husband, Phuong's pregnancy seemed the last straw. Huy wanted his wife to get an abortion. She refused. Huy wanted money for his parents. Always ambivalent about the man she had married to get out of the camp, Phuong now found her husband's lack of commitment to her, to their baby, and to the possibilities of life in Canada increasingly intolerable. Life together was degenerating into cycles of fighting and mutual recrimination.

From Refugee Camp to Canada: A Long and Difficult Step

The Canadian mantra 'A country of immigrants' may be getting a little shop-worn, but its truth is never in doubt. In 1867, 15 per cent of the 3.5 million people who came together to form the Confederation of Canada had been born somewhere else. One hundred and thirty years later, the ratio is the same: among Canada's 30 million inhabitants, one in six is still foreign born.

In 1996, Canada granted landed immigrant status to 223,238 people; approximately 85 per cent entered the country as immigrants, the remaining 15 per cent as refugees (Statistics Canada, 1997). The policy that dictates eligibility for each of these categories is straightforward. A person with a talent Canada needs, enough money to have a positive effect on the country's economy, or close family who will guarantee support can usually become an immigrant. A refugee is someone who can claim asylum by establishing that his or her situation conforms to the internationally accepted definition of refugee initially set out in the United Nations Convention Relating to the Status of Refugees (1951), and then modified in the 1967 Protocol.

Competing interests continually shape immigration policy. Expediency, respect, and compassion frequently line up on one side, and nativism on the other. Business and industry have frequently championed immigration in the name of economic expediency, ethnocultural communities argue that respect for the family and for equity should be determinants of policy, and advocates for compassion urge us not to forget the persecuted and the dispossessed.

Nativists urge caution. They point out that immigration has already changed the country's balance of power and influence, and that it threatens to undermine our distinctly Canadian (by which they mean European-based) culture. Over the years, the voice of each group has sometimes been in the ascendancy, and, at other times, muted .

At the Beginning: Immigration under the Sway of Nativist Sentiment

Of the 3.5 million people making up the Canada of 1867, 1 million were French, 1.2 million were from the United Kingdom, and 1.3 million were of German, Dutch, Spanish, Portuguese, Swiss, and Chinese extraction. During the next twenty-five years, Canada gained an additional 1.5 million people through immigration, mostly from the United Kingdom and the United States.

The official government policy of the time, emphasizing the selective admission of people from Great Britain and northern Europe, was probably comforting to nativist sentiments. The policy was very much in keeping with the nativist view that charter members of the new society should decide about jobs to be filled and about the right kinds of immigrants to fill them (Porter, 1966).

Then, as now, Canadians made themselves feel better by identifying some point of superiority over the United States. The Dominion's first prime minister, Sir John A. Macdonald, told his countrymen that Canada's restricted immigration would protect them against the ideological pollution that their southern neighbour's open-door policy invited: 'Look at that mass of foreign ignorance and vice which has flooded that country with socialism, atheism and all other isms' (Macdonald, in the *Empire*, 1890).

Immigration and Economic Expediency

Economic opportunity and economic opportunism changed the face of immigration. Between 1896 and 1914, more than one million immigrants came to Canada. They came not only from Britain and northern Europe, but from everywhere. Chinese immigrants built the West Coast links of the country's two transcontinental railroads, while Italians, Austrians, Hungarians, and Galicians were building the eastern links. Ukrainians, Poles, and Doukhobors opened up the Midwest for farming; Scandinavians, Finns, and Slavs cut timber, and Italians and Slavs went down into the mines. Expediency now overruled nativist sentiment: Canada needed a lot of cheap labour. Many of the captains of industry lobbied for the admission of central and eastern Europeans, whom they considered to be better and more willing workers than people from Britain. They may also have felt that employees who had no language in common would have a difficult time mobilizing any collective actions, and that non-English speakers could hardly use local media to publicize labour abuses. In a word, they would be docile (Avery, 1979).

The government of the day was clear about what it was looking for. Clifford Sifton, the minister responsible for immigration between 1896 and 1905, summed up a predilection for eastern European labour in this often-quoted remark: 'I think a stalwart peasant in a sheepskin coat, born on the soil, whose forebearers have been farmers for ten generations, with a stout wife and a half dozen children is good quality' (quoted in Avery, 1979, p. 19).

From the turn of the century until the beginning of the First World War, economic expediency handily eclipsed nativism. However, although they may have become muted in the din of economic expansion, nativist voices were never completely subdued. As early as 1884, nativists on the West Coast were complaining about Chinese immigrants. In the great Canadian tradition, the government appointed a royal commission.

Although the commission exonerated the Chinese of allegations of bad conduct, it went on to recommend restricting future immigration. In 1885, Parliament imposed a head tax on Chinese immigrants, a noteworthy instance of racist immigration policy. Prior to that Act, only criminals, paupers, and the destitute were tagged as inadmissible. A parliamentary act of 1908 added East Indians to the list. In 1909, the East Indians already living in Canada were stripped of their right to vote even though, as British subjects living in a Commonwealth country, their entitlement was theoretically equal to that of people born on Canadian soil. The South Asian community had to wait until 1947 to have its right to vote restored.

Nativists and immigrant sympathizers coalesced around one issue. Both groups were concerned about the natural tendency of immigrants with common backgrounds to seek each other out and to form ethnic neighbourhoods. According to popular stereotypes, the neighbourhoods were places of 'filth, immorality and crime' (Avery, 1979, p. 41). Sympathetic social reformers such as the Reverend C.W. Gordon may have unwittingly contributed to the negative stereotype. Using the *nom de plume* Ralph Connor, Gordon wrote a popular novel, *The Foreigner* (1909), in which he described immigrant communities as breeding grounds for heavy drinking, violence, and anarchy.

The First World War stimulated a relatively brief reascendance of nativist sentiment. Under the cloud of fear hanging over a country at war, Canada passed the War Measures Act of 1914, providing for censorship of the ethnic press, suppression of socialist organizations, and the detention and deportation of suspected enemy aliens. Between 1914 and 1918, 8,500 people were interned under the Act as prisoners of war, among them 6,000 Austro-Hungarians, 2,000 Germans, 200 Turks, and 99 Bulgarians (Avery, 1979). In 1917, spurred by fears that the Russian Revolution might spill over into Canada, the government began to actively suppress ethnic newspapers, as well as socialist and anarchist organizations. Finns, Ukrainians, Russians, and Italians were particularly suspect (Avery, 1979; Malarek, 1987).

Nativist ideology had to retreat in the face of Canada's postwar prosperity, a development that once again demanded cheap and plentiful labour. In 1922, Sifton, the earlier champion of men in sheepskin coats, claimed that the country now needed another 500,000 'stalwart peasants.' The seemingly insatiable hunger for labour led to what seems, in retrospect, a bizarre development. The Railway Agreement, in effect from 1925 to 1930, granted Canada's two railroad companies the right to recruit potential immigrants, including people from previously 'non-preferred' locations, such as Estonia, Latvia, Lithuania, Russia, Poland, Czechoslovakia, Yugoslavia, Austria, Hungary, Romania, and Germany. With the industrialists now recruiting immigrants, government officials were left with little to do other than to check health records and inspect passports (Avery, 1979). During this era of unprecedented economic expansion, beginning about 1910 and lasting until the early 1930s, the proportion of foreign- to native-born Canadian residents soared from 1 in 6 to almost 1 in 4 (Citizenship and Immigration Canada, 1996; Statistics Canada, 1997).

The Great Depression squelched the economic argument for immigration. Canada's entry into the Second World War not only suppressed immigrant flows, but cast a blanket of suspicion over foreign-born nationals. Repeating the pattern of the previous great war, Canada interned persons whose sympathies might have been on the wrong side. This time, it was the Japanese and the Italians. In 1991, the government issued official apologies to these communities, and paid reparations to the Japanese.

Since the Second World War, Canada has emerged as an economy to be reckoned with, one sufficiently powerful to be included among the Group of Seven. Immigrant flows have accelerated along with the pace of economic development. From the 1950s through the mid-1980s, Canada admitted approximately 150,000 immigrants per year. In the late 1980s and the early 1990s, the Conservative government of the day began promoting increased immigration levels. Their Liberal successors continued the policy. Both governments stressed that immigration was a way to help guarantee the perpetuation of Canada's economic prosperity.

Both political parties introduced a new dimension to the expediency argument. According to the new discourse, Canada needed not only money, talent, and labour, but simply more people. Canada is, after all, an underpopulated and, in many ways, a lonely land. It is probably no accident that, per capita, Canadians own more telephones than any other people in the world. By the 1990s, Canada's birth rate had dropped to an all-time low, and demographers began predicting dire consequences. Without immigration, according to some projections, Canada would actually begin losing population no later than the year 2040. By 2095, it would have fallen from its 1998 level of 30 million to 20 million people (Baxter, 1997).

Immigrants, so the argument continued, would help ensure that Canada's population remained stable, if it did not actually increase. In addition, selective admission could help correct a potentially explosive demographic imbalance. Like all industrialized countries, Canada has an aging population, a product of increased longevity and of historically low birth rates. Immigration could supply a 'youth tonic' (Baxter, 1997) to help ensure that the number of dependent elderly would not eventually exceed the capacity of younger persons to support them.

In the late 1980s, the number of immigrants admitted per year climbed to about 220,000. It has remained more or less at that level ever since (Citizenship and Immigration Canada, 1996).

The Southeast Asian refugees arrived during a period when Canada was re-examining its immigration policy. Successive federal governments had been promoting immigration to help ensure Canada's economic position and to help correct demographic imbalances. At the same time, changing immigration patterns were raising concerns. For example, immigrants were no longer going everywhere to settle. Instead, they seemed to be concentrating in only four of Canada's ten provinces. In addition, there was increasing immigrant diversity. Prior to 1960, only 5 per cent of all immigrants were of Asian origin. By the 1980s, 50 per cent of all immigrants were coming from Asia. Such diversity sparked fears that the era of European-derived cultural hegemony was coming to an end.

Contemporary Patterns of Immigrant Settlement

Ontario, British Columbia, Alberta, and Quebec lead the list of immigrant-receiving provinces. Much to the annoyance of its neighbours, the province of Ontario has become the country's industrial and commercial hub. Banks, major industries, and commercial enterprises are headquartered in Toronto, both geographically and politically close to the nation's capital in Ottawa. In the late 1980s, southern Ontario, along with southern California and Florida, was one of the three fastest-growing regions in North America. Although Ontario is a natural magnet, attracting more than 50 per cent of all newcomers to Canada, the resource-rich province of British Columbia offers a sufficiently appealing alternative to attract 20 per cent of the country's immigrants. Unlike the weather elsewhere in Canada, which conforms to the stereotype of blazing summers alternating with freezing winters, British Columbia's West Coast climate is temperate and mild. As with most resource-based economies, however, this region is subject to boom and bust with corresponding highs and lows in employment opportunities. Boom and bust is even more a feature of life in British Columbia's neighbour to the east, the oil kingdom of Alberta.

The good times are good enough to place it among Canada's leading immigrant-receiving provinces. In recent years, it has attracted about 7 per cent of all new immigrants.

Quebec is Canada's second most populous province. The demographic argument for immigration is particularly powerful in Quebec. The province has the lowest birth rate in Canada. Furthermore, the decades-old threat of separation from Canada has spurred an exodus of anglophones and a flight of anglophone and international investment. To help solve the problems of a declining population and a declining tax base, Quebec has become very interested in attracting immigrants. In 1990, Quebec became the first and, so far, the only province to articulate its own immigration policy, one that assigns priority to francophone immigrants and refugees. Quebec attracts approximately 15 per cent of all new settlers (Statistics Canada, 1997).

In the early years of the century, immigrants went where the jobs were – to cities and towns on railway lines across the country, to lumbering and mining towns in British Columbia, Alberta, Ontario, Quebec, and the Atlantic Provinces, and to farms in the Prairie provinces. Settlement patterns have changed. At the end of the century, immigrants are gravitating to Canada's large cities, and to Toronto and Vancouver, in particular. According to the 1996 census, 57 per cent of the total population of Canadian-born people were living in a metropolitan area. By comparison, 93 per cent of all immigrants who arrived between 1991 and 1996 were living in cities (Statistics Canada, 1997).

Canada's Role in Protecting Victims of Persecution

Canada admits immigrants because they can contribute to the country's economic or cultural life, because they can benefit the demographic situation, or because they are rejoining family. As in many other countries, one federal department is responsible for both immigrants and refugees. A 1997 report by a government-appointed committee recommended uncoupling immigrant and refugee legislation (Immigration Legislation Review, 1997). The idea is a good one: the historical, moral, legal, and ideological grounds for accepting refugees are entirely different from those that drive countries to recruit immigrants. Countries have traditionally welcomed immigrants if they expect to benefit from their presence. Present-day Canadian immigration policies favour admitting the rich, the young, and the talented, and then allowing the chosen to sponsor other members of their families.

Although the tradition of offering sanctuary to the forcibly displaced is deeply rooted in history and in many of the world's religions, refugees did not really become a world problem until the conclusion of the Second World War. A committee set up by the Council of Europe estimated that 11 million refugees had poured into Western Europe at the end of the war; by 1951, 4.5 million were still waiting to be resettled. Some were survivors of the Nazi concentration camps, but they were not the only refugees. With the Cold War in effect, many Germans who had been expelled from the Soviet Union could not go back, and many Poles and Czechs did not want to. The magnitude and the intransigence of the problem created a phenomenon that had never existed before: '... premodern times knew no camps where masses of civilians could be interned for lengthy periods and needed no special category to suspend them outside the framework of civilized community' (Marrus, 1985, p. 5).

In 1950, the UN created the United Nations High Commission for Refugees (UNHCR) as a response to an untenable situation. UNHCR had little funding; it was meant to be an advocate for refugees' legal rights, and to leave the job of providing services to governments and to non-governmental organizations (Marrus, 1985). One year later, in 1951, UNHCR crafted the Convention definition that has remained the basis for refugee determination ever since. According to the UN definition, a 'Convention Refugee' is

> a person who, as a result of events occurring before 1st January, 1951 and owing to well-founded fear of being persecuted for reasons of race, religion, nationality, membership of a particular social group or political opinion, is outside the country of his nationality and is unable or, owing to such fear, is unwilling to avail himself of the protection of that country. (Convention Relating to the Status of Refugees, 1951)

Considering its enormous influence, the inadequacies of this aging framework are disquieting. Most of the twenty-six delegates attending the UN Convention to formulate the protocol were North Americans or Europeans. Only three representatives came from South America, three from the Middle East, and none from Africa or Asia, the four areas which today produce and contain most of the world's 27 million refugees. The assumption that one becomes a refugee only as a result of belonging to certain groups, particularly those singled out for persecution during the Second World War, underlies the Convention (Jackson, 1991). In addition, the Convention is framed in the language of the Cold War, with an eye to escapees from behind the Iron Curtain (Marrus, 1985).

The 1967 Protocol Relating to the Status of Refugees altered the Convention in two ways. First, it removed the time limitation. Second, while the Convention was designed as a response to the plight of refugees and displaced persons in Europe after the Second World War, the Protocol increased its coverage to apply to people anywhere in the world (Jackson, 1991; Bauer, 1997).

De facto modifications in applying the Convention reveal some of the definition's inadequacies. For example, a Canadian refugee board decision makes clear that there are groups singled out for persecution who are not included in the 1951 Convention definition. In 1992, impressed by a Salvadoran's claim that he had been detained and tortured because of his homosexuality, Canadian immigration officials granted him refugee status. There is now precedent for basing a refugee claim on fear of persecution because of one's sexual orientation.

Three other developments, one in Canada and two in the United States, have even more far-reaching implications.

In 1993, an Iranian woman visiting in Canada asked for asylum. She based her claim on an incident during which she had been taken to a local police station in Tehran and beaten for the crime of dancing with male guests during a dinner party at her home. Although her case did not strictly fulfil the criteria set out in the UN Convention, she was allowed to stay in Canada. Shortly afterwards, Canadian refugee determination boards received a new set of guidelines: they stated that persecution under the laws and customs of a country that violates rights guaranteed by Canada's Charter of Rights and Freedoms could justify a claim for refugee status.

On 20 January 1994, a U.S. federal judge ruled that a young couple who had fled China because they were resisting sterilization orders stemming from their home country's coercive population-control policies were eligible for U.S. asylum. The judge, Thomas S. Ellis of the Federal District Court in Alexandria, Virginia, based his opinion on the premise that the right to bear children is one of the basic human rights.

In June 1996, the U.S. Board of Immigration and Appeals granted refugee status to Fauziya Kasinga, a nineteen-year-old woman from Togo. When Ms Kasinga was fifteen, her family arranged a marriage for her with an older man. Fauziya fled the country rather than submit to the ritual premarital circumcision that was required. The Board's decision sets a binding precedent on the 170 immigration judges in the United States.

Local culture provides governments the legitimacy to proscribe male-female dancing, to dictate the number of children a couple can produce, and to condone female circumcision. Canada's decision to boycott South African products while that country practised apartheid was a clear indictment of a perceived violation of human rights. Although decisions about who can and who cannot be considered a fugitive from repressive governments may seem a less obvious form of censure than economic sanctions, such decisions do, in fact, amount to a condemnation of practices that offend North American sensibilities. Recent Canadian and U.S. decisions regarding refugee status have strayed beyond the boundaries of the UN Convention definition of a 'well-founded fear of persecution.' Seen in the most positive light, they are part of the evolution of a universal code of international human rights.

Motives are often complex. High-minded principle may not be the only factor prompting apparently high-minded action. For example, the temptation to score ideological brownie points over an international rival arguably influences decisions such as the United States' granting of refugee status to a Chinese couple who wanted to have more than one child. Critics (Stoffman, 1997; Bauer, 1997) also point out that, given the country's far from blemish-free past, Canada's newly acquired willingness to impose standards of morality on others is startlingly arrogant.

Although Canada can claim that it provided haven to blacks escaping slavery in the United States, and to Doukhobors fleeing religious persecution in eastern Europe, it was far less welcoming during other periods, most notably the 1930s. With its economy battered by the Great Depression, Canada shut its door to all but a highly select few.

Canada's protection would have spared some people a terrible fate. From the rise of Hitler in 1933, prescient Jewish citizens of Germany began trying to find a way to get out. North and South America were the obvious choices for refuge. However, Canada was unwilling to provide a haven. Charles H. Blair, Canada's director of immigration from 1936 to 1945, stated: 'People should be kept out of Canada instead of being let in' (quoted in Abella and Troper, 1982, p. 7). Blair was a product of his insular, inward-looking times. He was also openly anti-Semitic.

As the shadow of Nazism crept over Europe, none of the Western countries was overly anxious to admit Jews searching for a safe haven. Canada was more successful than any other country at keeping them out. From the mid-1930s until the end of the Second World War, the United States admitted 200,000 Jews from Europe; the United Kingdom, about 70,000; Argentina, 50,000; Australia, 15,000; and Canada – fewer than 5,000. As the noted historian Harold Troper (1984) observes: 'Measured against the millions who were murdered and the irreparable damage their deaths caused the spirit of humanity, no nation stands out for its generosity of heart. No nation, however, was as cold to the suffering of others or as deaf to their cry of pain as was Canada' (p. 190). In 1939, a delegation of Canadian Jewish leaders met with Minister Blair to ask how many Jews Canada would be willing to admit as refugees. Blair replied, 'None is too many' (Abella and Troper, 1982).

Fear can make the familiar appear strange. During the Second World War, fellow citizens and neighbours, Japanese and Italians, in particular, were recast as foreigners, just as Austro-Hungarians had been in the First Great War. Perhaps nations learn from their history. Perhaps conscience comes with learning. Or perhaps what seemed like change will turn out to have been only an appearance of generosity, based on temporary prosperity and exposure to world opinion. In the immediate postwar period, Canada admitted 500,000 displaced persons, or DPs, and then did its best to wall itself off from world refugee affairs.

Even with UNHCR in place, the world community remained ambivalent about refugees, and possibly suspicious of the motives of the United States, the country that had championed its creation. For example, although the UN Convention was drawn up in 1951, it required at least six signatures before it could have any binding power. Australia became the sixth signatory in 1954, three years after the protocol had been initially drafted.

Canada did not become a signatory to the UN Convention until 1969. However, it followed an official policy of honouring the Convention principles. Canada admitted 37,000 Hungarian refugees in 1956, and 12,000 Czechoslovakians in 1968. After signing the UN Convention, Canada's refugee protection activities increased: 8,000 Ugandans were admitted between 1972 and 1973; 10,000 Lebanese, between 1976 and 1978; 60,000 Southeast Asians, between 1979 and 1981; 12,000 Poles, in 1980; and, in more recent years, large numbers of Chileans, Salvadorans, Eritreans, Ethiopians, Iranians, Kurds, Bosnians, and Somalis. The humanitarian impulse underlying these actions was translated into official government policy in the Immigration Act of 1976, which recognized the need 'to fulfil Canada's international obligations with respect to refugees and to uphold its humanitarian tradition with respect to the displaced and the persecuted' (section 3 [8]). With the receipt of the United Nations' Nansen Award in 1986, Canada's reputation for humanitarianism reached its peak. Until that event, the Nansen medal had always been reserved for individuals; it had never before been given to an entire nation.

Canada's response to the Southeast Asian refugee crisis marked a transition from indifference to caring. As is so often the case, this historical turning point came about through a confluence of well-documented social trends, together with less well recorded small events and quirks of personality that sometimes make all the difference. The media helped stir·worldwide sympathy for the refugees fleeing their homes in Vietnam, Laos, and Cambodia. Television images of, and newspaper reports about, frightened refugees being turned away from safe harbours elicited an atavistic emotional response from Canadian viewers and readers. Even though many refugees escaped overland rather than by sea, the evocatory power of the 'Boat People' image ensures its continuing currency in public discourse.

Television's capacity to offer comfortable mortification and easy absolution is part of its appeal. A television special about a famine, a natural disaster, or an atrocity such as the Southeast Asian refugee experience provides viewers an opportunity to look on and listen with a mixture of indignation and compassion. After worthy sentiment has created momentary ennoblement, most people go back to business as usual. Some Canadians did more. National organizations such as the Mennonite Central Committee, the Christian Reform Church, the Canadian Jewish Congress, and the Canadian Medical Association petitioned government to help. The people demanding aid for the refugees made up less than an overwhelming majority of Canadians. However, their voices reached some receptive ears.

After seventeen years as the official opposition, Canada's Conservative party won a stunning victory in the 1981 elections. The all-important position of minister of employment and immigration in the newly formed government went to Mr Ron Atkey. In the spring of 1988, I interviewed the greying, impeccably dressed former minister in his twenty-seventh-floor law offices with their sweeping view of Lake Ontario. Over tea served in elegant porcelain cups, Mr Atkey talked with obvious pride about the role he and his government had played in admitting refugees. I asked him what had prompted a country that had not been notably generous in the past to bring in so many Southeast Asians. The former minister recalled the headiness of being a member of a freshly elected cabinet leading a prosperous nation, and seizing on a global issue like the 'Boat People' crisis to show both its U.K. parents and its U.S. big brother that Canada could do better. The new government recognized that the country was not unanimously behind them. However, frequent private polls conducted during the height of the publicity surrounding the crisis in Southeast Asia reassured them that a significant number of voters favoured a generous Canadian response.

Public opinion became more conservative in the wake of a government announcement about what it would actually do for the refugees. According to Howard Adelman, former head of the York University Refugee Study Centre, three polls conducted immediately after Canada announced its intention to admit 50,000 refugees in two years, reported that one-half to two-thirds of Canadians 'clearly opposed' the gesture (Adelman, 1982).

Speaking more personally, Mr Atkey mused that one is not often given the chance, as he put it, 'to make a difference.' It probably did not hurt the cause of those lobbying for a generous response to the Southeast Asian crisis that the minister had spent the weekend prior to announcing Canada's goal for refugee admission reading a pre-publication draft of *None Is Too Many*, Irving Abella and Harold Troper's historical account of Canada's infamous refusal to grant asylum to Jews trying to flee Nazi Germany. Atkey told me: 'I didn't want my children to have to remember me as somebody who said "None is too many."' Most scholars harbour a fond hope that their work will make a difference: few will ever witness their scholarship directly affecting public policy, as Abella and Troper have been privileged to do.

The admission and resettlement of the Southeast Asian refugees called for the coordination of federal, provincial, and private efforts. Having set a goal of 50,000 refugee admissions for the period 1979 to 1981, Canada's Conservative government of the day then looked for a way to share responsibility with the private sector. A provision for private sponsorship of refugees included in the Immigration Act of 1976 became an important part of the strategy. To encourage individuals as well as organizations such as church groups to become private sponsors, the government promised to match every refugee admitted under private auspices with another to be sponsored by government. According to initial projections, approximately 25,000 refugees would come in under private sponsorship, the remaining 25,000 under the government's matching quota. However, citizen response proved greater than anticipated. Enough private sponsors came forward to support the admission of 40,000 refugees.

Citizen vigilance is always a good idea, nowhere more so than in immigration issues. The federal government's next move – to suggest that, in order to attain the original quota of 50,000 refugees, it would now only be required to sponsor an additional 10,000 – aroused the public indignation it deserved. Succumbing to public pressure, the government compromised by raising its ante from 10,000 to 20,000, finally arriving at a two-year quota of 60,000.

The federal government resettled the refugees in all of Canada's ten provinces and two territories. Relocation quotas varied according to the proportion of the total population of the country living in a region (for example, since it accounted for roughly 12 per cent of Canada's population base, British Columbia, the site of the Refugee Resettlement Project, received 12 per cent of all the Southeast Asian refugees). Like all citizens and permanent residents of Canada, refugees were entitled to provincially administered, insured health care. Many received language training in federally funded but provincially run programs, and their children attended schools supported by provincial tax dollars.

Canada: The Ideal Resettlement Country?

All nations cultivate myths, not myths in the sense of untruths, but myths in the sense of stories and idealized images that help people define who they are. The Canadian myth would be something like the following:

Once upon a time there was a country everyone else in the world envied. It stretched between the two mightiest oceans in the world. It was a land of abundance, with farms, fish, forests, and factories. The people in this country had two parents, each of whom spoke a different language: to preserve harmony and mutual respect, all the country's children learned to speak both parents' languages. There were also grandparents and ancestors living in the country. In the past, the children had been guilty of neglect and even mistreatment of these ancestors. However, when they became mature, they resolved to treat their forebears with the respect they deserved.

Some of the children in the country were white, others were black or brown, and others mixtures of the two. Some people wore hats. Some wore turbans. Some drank wine; others avoided it. Some ate with wooden sticks and others with forks and knives. A lot of people believed in God, but they had different names for their deity. Despite these differences, they all respected each other, delighted in their diversity, and made sure that everyone was treated equally. Since they knew that, with the exception of the ancestors, everyone living in the country had come from lands across the sea, they welcomed newcomers. They knew that new settlers would help build a stronger and livelier country.

Underneath its fairy-tale trappings, the myth is a fairly accurate précis of the Canada clause of the failed constitutional accord promulgated by the Canadian government in 1991.

Canada's myth, as well as many of the country's laws and policies, create the picture of a theoretically ideal country of resettlement. The 1960 Bill of Rights articulated the vision of a racism-free society. The 1971 multiculturalism policy, based on the recommendations of an advisory commission on bilingualism and biculturalism, went even further. The 'bi' prefix attached to language and culture was based on the principle that Canada had two founding nations, England and France. By now a significant minority, the descendants of the immigrants who had worn sheepskin coats successfully campaigned both the commission and the government to redefine Canada, not as bicultural, but as multicultural. The metaphor for this new national policy was a cultural mosaic.

Although its emphasis on preserving cultures attracts more attention, Canada's multiculturalism policy assigns equal weight to integration. In keeping with this part of the policy, Canada provides programs to help newcomers learn at least one of the country's two official languages. The Canadian Charter of Rights and Freedoms, Part I of the Constitution Act, 1983, guarantees equality of opportunity as well as equal access to services regardless of gender, social class, or ethnocultural origin. The Canadian Multiculturalism Act (Bill C-93), adopted on 21 July 1988, translates into law the principle that 'diverse groups and communities are free to retain their respective identities while joining one another as equal partners in a united country' (Multiculturalism and Citizenship Canada, 1989, p. 1).

A pluralistic society provides options. People can choose to retain their cultures, give them up in the pursuit of assimilation, or create a new synthesis of their past and their present. Since having options is presumably good for mental health, Canada should be able to provide the rest of the world a lesson in successful resettlement. Unfortunately, like all other signatories to the 1948 UN Declaration of Human Rights, Canada's rhetoric is loftier than its achievement. A national report, *Equality Now*, issued by a Canadian House of Commons special committee in 1984, documents widespread ethnocentrism in the job market. A later report, *After the Door Has Been Opened* (1988), describes the obstructions, frustrations, and inequuities that ethnocultural minorities encounter in their search for health care. At the end of three decades of change, immigrants are no longer predominantly white-skinned Europeans; instead, they come in all hues and from everywhere in the world. Reaction to this profound change has fuelled the appeal of groups such as the ultra-conservative Reform Party, frankly racist organizations like the Heritage Front and the Church of the Creator, neo-Nazis, Holocaust revisionists, and right-wing skinheads.

Closer acquaintance with Southeast Asian refugees converted some of the sympathy with which the Canadian public had greeted their arrival to ambivalence. Opinion polls have repeatedly shown that economic downturns diminish enthusiasm for immigration. The 1982 recession put Canada's generosity into a straitjacket. By 1985, immigration quotas sank to 85,000, half the number they had been at the beginning of the decade. Studies documenting that, overall, immigration supports Canada's economic health offered little comfort to individuals for whom the newcomers were becoming the villains in a drama of competition for jobs and resources. For example, some of British Columbia's fishermen, complaining that aggressive Vietnamese were ruining the rich oyster beds of Vancouver Island, demanded that they be stopped. Pointing out that the Vietnamese were fishing with the same licences and under the same laws as everyone else did little to placate the outrage inspired by the newcomers' daring to infringe on what some people considered exclusively Canadian territory.

Canadians who value this country's commitment to multiculturalism are fond of making a favourable contrast between this policy and the 'melting-pot' ideology of the United States. The philosopher/historian Charles Taylor traces the melting-pot concept to the ideals of Jacobin France, according to which everyone was to be considered equal and free, but everyone, newcomers included, was also expected to conform to established parameters of social behaviour. By contrast, multiculturalism recognizes that newcomers are often not willing to assimilate to the status quo. Some may wish to assimilate. Others will choose to be isolationists, living as much as possible in a community that resembles the one from which they have come. Still others will become bicultural, synthesizing new and old to create something that never existed before. Multiculturalism acknowledges the mutuality of accommodation: both immigrants and the receiving society change as a result of contact.

According to public opinion polls, Canadians continue to support multiculturalism. In a 1989 poll, 63 per cent of the general public affirmed their commitment to this policy (Kopvillem, 1989). However, a crossborder survey provided a surprise. Answering the question 'What do you think is better for [the country]: that new immigrants be encouraged to maintain their distinct culture and ways, or to change their distinct culture and ways to blend with the larger society?' 47 per cent of Americans compared with only 34 per cent of Canadians thought it better for newcomers to preserve their heritage, than to assimilate. The findings suggest that the United States, a country formerly committed to homogenization, is becoming more interested in heritage, while its northern neighbour, which for twenty years has called itself a mosaic, is experiencing a backlash.

The contrast between Canada's multiculturalism and the U.S. melting-pot is probably overdrawn. In certain areas, most, if not all, immigrant-receiving countries are pluralistic. For example, few countries (Israel being an interesting exception) include religion among their criteria for accepting newcomers, or would consider the limitation of religious freedom as a resettlement policy. However, all countries do limit choices in some areas, notably language. To date, at least, the United States is officially monolingual; its new settlers are expected to speak English when they arrive, or to learn it as soon as possible. The same assimilative strictures apply in Canada, the only difference being that the language required is French in Quebec, English everywhere else (see also Zolberg and Woon, 1997). Knowledge of one of the country's two official languages is a requirement for Canadian citizenship.

Most immigrant-receiving countries recognize the importance of cultural pluralism. Although Canadians may be guilty of exaggerating the contrast between the U.S. melting-pot and the Canadian mosaic, the *Economist* magazine offers some encouragement that Canada's beleaguered policies of promoting respect for ethnic heritages and promoting mutual accommodation have worked, and are still working: 'Racism and discrimination can be found in Canada, just as they can everywhere, but probably to a lesser extent than in practically any other country and certainly in any other country that receives so many newcomers' (*Economist*, 29 June 1991, pp. 10–11).

Multiculturalism was supposed to facilitate immigrant integration. The available evidence suggests that it has. For example, naturalization rates have increased since 1971, the year of the policy's adoption. Furthermore, people from the so-called non-traditional source countries are more likely to apply for Canadian citizenship than are immigrants from the United States or from the United Kingdom (Kymlicka, 1998). The incentives to apply for citizenship are not overwhelming. Landed immigrant status confers the right to work in Canada, and to receive social benefits in the same way that Canadian citizens do. The only real incentives for naturalization are a wish to identify with Canada, to carry a Canadian passport, and to participate in the political system – in other words, to become part of the country.

Political participation provides an important measure of the success of multiculturalism. Prior to the adoption of the policy, first-generation immigrants were less likely than other Canadians to be involved in the political process (Richmond and Goldlust, 1977). By the 1980s, however, immigrant groups were about as likely as the Canadian-born to vote, to belong to a political organization, or to take part in a political campaign (Chui, Curtis, and Lambert, 1991).

Immigrants do not form new political parties to promote their interests. Instead, they affiliate with the established parties in Canada (Kymlicka, 1998). The immigrant voice, nevertheless, is becoming increasingly strong. Before 1960, non-British or non-French groups were under-represented in Parliament. However, by the late 1990s, the number of members of Parliament coming from immigrant backgrounds had become roughly proportionate to their representation in the population at large, although visible minority immigrants were still proportionally under-represented (Black and Lakhani, 1997).

Social trends before and after multiculturalism are also revealing. Intermarriage rates have increased dramatically since 1971, as has approval of intermarriage. In 1968, prior to the adoption of multiculturalism, 48 per cent of Canadians said they approved of black-white marriages; by 1995, 81 per cent said they approved (Kymlicka, 1998).

And what evidence does the inevitable comparison with the United States produce? Canada can boast of naturalization rates that are almost twice those in the United States, higher rates of official language acquisition, higher rates of inter-ethnic friendships, and higher rates of political participation by ethnic minority groups. In a 1997 survey, people in twenty countries were asked whether they agreed that 'different ethnic groups get along well here.' Seventy-five per cent of Canadians agreed with the statement, compared with 58 per cent in the United States (Kymlicka, 1998). Although the gap between Canada and the United States is narrower than official rhetoric implies, it is probably fair to say that Canada still tries a little harder.

Value Conflicts

Any discussion about the stress of resettlement inevitably touches on the conflict between the values people bring with them and the values they encounter in North America. Although such conflicts may become manifest in many different forms and in many different situations, a few themes strike to the core of differences among people and the way they organize their societies. These themes include family, authority, male-female role differences, and the emphasis placed on achievement.

Although the family is a fundamental unit in all societies, opinions about what constitutes family are surprisingly diverse. Until recently, Canada was a frontier society, its people constantly on the move to find homesteads, gold, or job promotions to support the good life. Since wanderers need to stay mobile, Canadians have come to think that the portable nuclear family – parents and dependent children – is *the* family. Canadians promote independence from family as a virtue and then keep in touch with grandparents, aunts, uncles, and cousins through the most extensively used telephone network in the world. Southeast Asians have a different definition of family, one that assigns a much more central role to people whom Canadians only think of as relatives one has to invite to weddings, wakes, and bar mitzvahs. Three-generation families are not uncommon for Southeast Asians, nor are large households in which several related nuclear families might live together and share resources.

The structure of Southeast Asian family life presents a dramatic contrast to what North Americans consider normal. This structure only hints at the value differences attached to the family as a societal institution. Middle-class North Americans value their independence from the families into which they were born. People who have trouble becoming emancipated from their parents often end up receiving counselling, therapy, or rehabilitation. For many Southeast Asians, a self that is not part of an interdependent extended family is an absurdity.

In a survey of almost seven thousand adult refugees from Vietnam and Laos living in five different U.S. cities, the University of Michigan–based behavioural scientists Nathan Caplan, John K. Whitmore, and Marcella H. Choy attempted to identify core values. One of the core values of the refugees was family-based achievement, which, according to the three research workers,

> emphasizes the family as a central institution in Asian culture, within and through which achievement and knowledge are accomplished. [This] point[s] to the mutual, collective obligation among family members, plus the subordination of individual needs and desires to those of the larger family unit. Finally, cohesiveness, cooperation, and harmony characterize the quality of the working milieu required for the family if it is to accomplish its goals. (Caplan, Whitmore, and Choy, 1989, p. 45)

Canada was created by people who explored and conquered a new land on their own. By contrast, China and the countries of the Southeast Asian peninsula have evolved from feudal societies that, in turn, developed into great empires maintained by values of fealty and the omniscience of authority (usually male). For people used to Southeast Asian norms, Canadian families are shockingly egalitarian. A microcosm of the larger culture, Southeast Asian families perpetuate the pattern of deference to authority. Children are expected to defer to their parents, the young to the old, the commoner to the leader. Traditional gender roles are patriarchal, and authoritarian as well. Ideally, a Vietnamese woman serves her father in childhood, her husband in marriage, and her sons in her old age (Shepherd, 1987). The wars in Southeast Asia affected traditional gender relationships. With their husbands drafted into the army, women became increasingly used to assuming the responsibilities of a head of household and raising children on their own.

According to Caplan, Whitmore, and Choy, part of the Southeast Asian core value system derives from an amalgam of Confucian and Buddhist traditions:

> The emphasis on respect, genealogical family, and kinship are strongly Confucian in origin; seeking salvation and conformity with nature are more in accord with Buddhist tenets ... These values continue to constitute a source of motivation and guidance dealing with contemporary problems set in a land vastly different from that in which these values originated. (Caplan, Whitmore, and Choy, 1989, p. 45)

Confucianism stresses love for the past and veneration of one's ancestors. Traditional Vietnamese gain knowledge about the conduct of their own lives through study of the writings of Confucius and his commentators. The premise that there is nothing new under the sun is radically different from Western thought, which stresses that everything under the sun is new.

Few cultures have valued hard work and scholarship as much as those of the Chinese and Vietnamese. Although most Canadians espouse hard work, restraint, and self-discipline for the sake of future reward, they were not prepared for the entrepreneurial and scholarly competitiveness of the Southeast Asians who became their neighbours. The children's sometimes dazzling successes in school (Caplan, Whitmore, and Choy, 1989; Rumbaut and Ima, 1988) and their parents' aggressive approach to business were to become sources of ambivalence. The refugees were admired and simultaneously resented by their Canadian hosts.

Arrival

From the moment they arrived, the refugees had to begin learning new ways. They also had to face an important conundrum – how to incorporate into their lives and behaviour enough of what was uniquely Canadian to enable them to get along with their new hosts, while not losing themselves in the process.

As part of his 'Memories,' Tran Van Ha recalled his first hours in Canada:

> I am sitting by the window of a small apartment facing to the Sea. My beloved country is lying somewhere in that direction, but very far away ... Three years ago, I left my country, bewildered, not knowing where would be my next destination. I brought along with me three children and a wife, but there are now four. The last but not least son was born. He was named Van to remind us [of] the new place of his birth: Vancouver.
>
> My mind is wandering back to the old days, which however seem to reappear vividly in front of my eyes.

After escaping from Vietnam, Ha and his small family made their way in a crowded boat to Malaysia, where they spent almost a year in a refugee camp. They were finally selected to be resettled in Vancouver, British Columbia, a city where the mountains cascade down to the sea to form a natural harbour, its shores now planted with rows of skyscrapers that have replaced yesterday's tall cedars. The city's 1.6 million inhabitants take pride in the beauty of the mountains, the lush rain forests, and a relaxed lifestyle, symbolized by the city's nickname, 'Lotus-land.'

> Ever since we knew that our family was sponsored by the Church, our hearts filled with joys and worries. We were happy to convince ourselves that our sponsor certainly must be so kind, so generous to accept us, who were totally unknown and strange to them. However we worried about how we could behave ourselves in order not to displease our sponsor. At times, we had wished that our family's name were on the list of those who were sponsored by the government like many of our friends. The term 'government' seemed to us very vague, very aloof, but connoted the power that could help us more effectively. Some of those who were sponsored by the government commented that the Church preferred to sponsor refugees of less capability in trade, skill or language. These refugees needed more direct and personal care. If this was the case, we were indeed suited. I took the three day waiting

period from the day that the departure list was posted to the day we left the camp for Canada to teach our three kids aged, 10, 8 and 6 the basic greetings in English: 'Good morning, Good afternoon, Good evening.'

Our plane touched down at the Vancouver International airport one afternoon in September three years ago. Our hearts were pounding with excitement. Moments after we got into the waiting lounge, the kids rushed towards me and asked: 'What are we going to say: Good afternoon or Good evening?' I looked at my watch. It was 5:55 p.m. It was too late to say 'afternoon' but still early to use 'evening.' At second thought, I reckoned that there would be another five to ten minutes before meeting our sponsor, so I gave a rather firm answer: 'Good evening of course.'

To my great surprise, when our charming lady sponsor rushed towards the kids with open arms, they all said, almost at the same time: 'Good evening of course!'

Distance from the event makes it possible for Ha to recall his family's first meeting with their sponsors with a sense of amusement. He has not forgotten, however, the anxiety. Although poor and needy, he was proud of his education and of his professional accomplishments. Like any father, he wanted his new friends to understand that he and his family were special people. The importance of 'face' in Asian culture reinforced Ha's very human wish to please and to impress.

Another element was probably even more important. Ha had a long history of being beaten down by authority. After the fall of Saigon, he was sent along with many other young men like himself to 're-education' camps, where the North Vietnamese used hard labour and abuse to clear their 'students'' minds of the taint of French, American, and capitalist influences. Although the refugee camp in Malaysia was a gatepost of promise, Ha's little family's well-being and, ultimately, their freedom depended on the goodwill of camp guards, international observers, and immigration officers. The carefully honed obsequiousness that pervades his 'Memories' helped his family to survive and to realize their goal of getting to Canada.

It was difficult for the refugees to understand private sponsorship. A family could be expected to share what they had in order to save people from the camps. The refugees could not, however, understand generosity offered by absolute strangers. Not knowing what they were expected to do in return for their sponsors' actions, the refugees became vulnerable to exploitation. Sometimes knowingly and sometimes not, more than a few private sponsors took advantage of the helplessness of their beneficiaries.

At the first meeting with these strange Canadian people, Ha was cautious, a little suspicious, worried about how he and his family looked, and concerned that they all act correctly:

At the waiting lounge of the airport ... we were surrounded by three large suitcases, which were full of old clothes given to us while staying in the camp. Most of the clothes were in good condition still, but too colourful and never fitted us both in length and in waist or chest at the same time! When we rushed ashore on the Malaysian coast, we were on bare feet and had nothing. Approaching the departure day, we each tried to get a decent outfit. We were afraid of offending our sponsors by our ragged clothing at the first acquaintance.

The first meeting with their sponsors provided Ha and his wife an opportunity to correct stereotypes, as well as a quick introduction to cultural differences in male-female relationships:

I was puzzling about who was the head of the household of the sponsor's family, because it was our cultural politeness that I should greet this person first, and I had expected a big, tall gentleman, hairy, speaking with a loud, guttural voice as many G.I.'s in Saigon did. I was surprised to see a gentleman, rather small built, with a broad smile but soft and endearing voice approach my wife – who was so timid and walking three steps behind me – offering his hand for the welcome handshake. I did not foresee this situation to alert my wife, so she grasped my hand and pushed it forwards to meet our sponsor's as though asking me to do the handshake for her.

Still the anthropologist, even in compromised circumstances, Tran Van Ha introduced his wife to some ideas about cultural difference:

Later I explained to my wife that ladies are first in this society and I also went further. Ladies always come before gentlemen. When people are delivering speeches, it's 'Ladies and Gentlemen.' In Vietnam, we say 'Gentlemen and Ladies.'
My wife still blushes every time I mention about that incident.

The first glimpse of their new home was a relief:

We were so impressed by the sceneries passing our car windows. It was so beautiful along the road from airport to downtown Vancouver. We remember the first Canadian film shown to us, as orientation to Canada, at the transition camp in Kuala Lumpur. The title of the film was 'Snowstorm in Winnipeg.' I could not help laughing every time when I recall the miserable smile on the face of a friend of mine on knowing that his family was going to make a final stop in Winnipeg in the winter. Before his departure, we prepared a dinner with some extra buy-on-your-own-money foods to show our gesture of comfort for his unlucky destiny!

Ha's sponsors had rented a basement suite for the family:

We were shown to every room in the basement suite. We were so touched by all the preparations for us. 'These beds belong to you, these appliances belong to you, the sofa, the desk, chairs, all are yours.' I could only mumble: 'We own everything now.' One lady, perhaps by instinct, she turned to me and said: 'This house is rented! This house does not belong to you, we have to pay rent every month.' I said, 'Yes. The house is not belong to us.' I could not [respond to] the puzzling expression on the face of our lady sponsor at that moment. When my English was much improved later on, I could explain the different way of reasoning in our native language when answering questions in English. The word 'yes' in our response is only used to indicate that we understand the question, then what follows is the main idea to be conveyed. I understood what she told me but I couldn't explain that I understood.

Although difficulties were not slow in coming, Ha treasures the memory of his family's long-awaited taste of freedom:

That night, our first night in Vancouver, it was cold to us even though the temperature was above ten degrees (centigrade). I told my wife that our sponsors had treated us like a newly-wedded couple. In our home land, parents always try to provide their sons with everything they can for their marriage. We were happy and acted as if we were a freshly-married couple.

FOUR

Migration, Resettlement, and Mental Health: Models and Measures

Li Wuchin, the fifty-year-old former industrialist from Vietnam, tried to kill himself by slashing his throat with an ice-pick. Another employee, who arrived for his shift earlier than usual on that particular morning, found his fellow worker on the floor and called an ambulance. The hospital gave Mr Li blood transfusions, sewed up his wounds, and kept him under observation for a few days. At the time of discharge, the hospital doctors referred him to a local mental health centre for treatment of what they diagnosed as a major depressive disorder.

The British Columbia courts judged the Vietnamese carpenter Nguyen Bich guilty of the second-degree murder of his common-law wife. Bich said that, just before smothering his partner, he heard a voice telling him to kill her. Although Bich's lawyer considered entering a temporary-insanity plea, he eventually decided against it. It was never established whether or not Bich had been drinking on the night of the crime.

Chan Min Ran spends most of her days alone in her messy, claustrophobic apartment. When the memories she tries to shut out become too insistent, she cries. At night, she has nightmares. She suffers from both major depressive disorder and post-traumatic stress disorder.

Concern for new settlers is a blend of compassion and self-interest. Although humanitarian instincts fuel the drive to make resettlement as easy as possible – especially for people like the Southeast Asian refugees whose pre-migration lives were marked by so much suffering – receiving societies also need and want to assess the risk that immigrants and refugees will become societal liabilities rather than assets. Mental illness, which could strain health-care resources or erupt into social pathologies threatening to the public order, constitutes one index of liability. Concern about mental illness among immigrants and refugees has prompted a considerable amount of research, particularly in Canada and the United States (Canadian Task Force on Mental Health Issues Affecting Immigrants and Refugees, 1988b).

Models of Mental Health

Three major paradigms have dominated scientific and popular conceptions of migrant mental health. The first is that migrants bring pre-existing mental disorders with them; the second, that the stresses of resettlement jeopardize previously mentally healthy individuals; and the third, that mental illness in migrants results from an interaction between personal predisposition, on the one hand, and risk as well as protective factors, on the other.

Migrants as Ill before They Come

During the early years of the twentieth century, the paradigm of the mentally and morally weak immigrant dominated popular discourse. A turn-of-the-century article in the influential Toronto newspaper the *Mail and Empire*, describing immigrants as 'freaks of creation,' reflected the accepted wisdom of the times (quoted in Malarek, 1987, p. 7). A few years later, a member of the Quebec legislature summed up his government's opposition to the federal government, whose immigration policies threatened to swamp the province with 'drunkards, paupers, loafers and jail-birds' (Malarek, 1987, p. 8).

Although pre–Second World War science used far less repellent language, both researchers and clinicians were influenced by the same paradigm, one that tended to attribute immigrant mental health problems to personal predisposition and mental fragility. One explanation was that individuals who chose to emigrate from their homes were likely to be the least well integrated, and perhaps the least competent people in their respective societies (see Salvendy, 1983; Goldlust and Richmond, 1974).

Views about refugees used a somewhat kinder version of the same model. For immigrants, mental fragility tended to be viewed as resulting from a flaw of character. Instability in refugees was more likely to be attributed to traumatic experience. However, the difference was only relative, not absolute. The Canadian high commissioner, charged with formulating the country's contribution to resolving the post–Second World War displaced-person problem, received a report cautioning against ac-

cepting Jewish refugees because of 'dirty living habits and general sloven-
liness' (Abella and Troper, 1982, p. 225).

The theory that immigrants and refugees are mentally fragile pro-
pelled a host of studies comparing rates of disorder between migrants
and people from their home communities who did not move, or between
migrants and natives of the receiving society. The results of approximately half the studies were consistent with the prediction that immigrant
mental health would be worse. However, the other half failed to show any
mental health differences between migrants and indigens or between
migrants and stay-at-homes (Canadian Task Force on Mental Health
Issues Affecting Immigrants and Refugees, 1988b).

Methodological problems account for some of the research inconsistencies. Many of the results showing a mental health advantage for indigens over migrants were based on group comparisons of the rates of
hospitalization for mental disorder (Carpenter and Brockington, 1980;
Cheung, Dobkin, and de Rios, 1982; Dean et al., 1981). However, hospital
admission statistics confuse the amount of mental disorder a group suffers with the resources they can call upon to deal with problems. When
mental illness strikes a member of a small, isolated, or fragmented social
group, he or she may experience different treatment than someone suffering the same type of disorder but who belongs to a well-established
community. Hospitalization – usually the last resort in an episode of illness – may take place quickly in the first case. In the second case, traditional healers, supportive family, and health-care professionals who
understand the language and share a patient's ethnocultural background
constitute important resources than can obviate the need for institutional
care.

In the 1950s, community surveys began to replace analyses of hospital
statistics as the favoured way to measure the mental health of populations. Despite the methodological advantage of the community survey,
the procedure has not resolved the problem of discrepant results in studies comparing indigen and immigrant mental health. For example,
although Mexican immigrants to the United States suffer a high burden
of distress (Vega, Kolody, and Warheit, 1985), Indian immigrants to
England have no more psychological disturbances than a comparison
sample of native English (Cochrane, Hashmi, and Stopes-Roe, 1977;
Cochrane and Stopes-Roe, 1981). Some community-based inquiries have
even suggested that immigrants have fewer emotional problems than
native-born persons (Halldin, 1985; Kallarackal and Herbert, 1976; Roskies, 1978).

Stress as Inherent in the Process of Resettlement

Research inconsistencies that prove intractable to explanation call for a revision in theory, or what Kuhn (1970) calls a paradigm shift. Research in the field of immigrant mental health produced results that were incompatible with the view that all migrants were predisposed – either by genes or circumstance – to develop disorder. In addition, the mental fragility paradigm failed to explain why some immigrants and refugees developed mental disorders, while others did not. In the hope of resolving these difficulties, attention shifted to the possibility of differential exposure to stressful experiences during the process of resettlement.

Theoreticians and clinicians developed lists of possible resettlement stressors, including intolerable memories (Meerloo, 1946; Pedersen, 1949; Goldfield and Lee, 1982), culture shock (Handlin, 1951; Eisenstadt, 1954; Oberg, 1960; Kuo, 1976), social isolation (Kuo, 1976; Weinberg, 1961; Handlin, 1951), and structural characteristics of the new society that block opportunity or oppress newcomers (Beiser and Collomb, 1981; Parker and Kleiner, 1966). Although these lists have become part of accepted wisdom about the difficulties of resettlement, very few researchers have actually investigated the effects of putative stressors on the mental health of migrants.

'Acculturative stress' is one of the rare exceptions. According to the acculturative stress concept, resettlement demands rapid accommodation not only to physical change but to new cultural forms. The greater the discrepancy between the familiar and the new, and the more rapid the pace of change required, the greater the risk to individual mental health (Beiser, 1982; Inkeles and Smith, 1974; deVos and Miner, 1959).

Research within the acculturative stress framework has yielded inconsistent results. For example, a well-known study comparing the mental health and blood pressure of South African Zulu who migrated to cities with those who remained in traditional villages demonstrated that, as predicted, urban migrants developed higher levels of distress and elevated blood pressure (Scotch, 1963). Following up on the South African results, I conducted a study among the Serer tribe of Senegal, West Africa, investigating the same question and employing similar methods. In contrast with the Zulu study, my results showed that urban migration posed no threat to health (Beiser, Collomb, Ravel, and Nafziger, 1976). Despite the enormous social and cultural changes brought about by exposure to the cosmopolitanism of urban life in Dakar, the capital of Senegal, Serer migrating from one of the most traditional areas in Africa had no higher levels of distress and no higher blood pressures than villagers who stayed at home.

Such widely discrepant findings suggest a flaw in either the methods of one or both studies, or in the theory prompting the prediction that culture change constitutes a mental health risk for all migrants. Flawed theory is the most likely explanation. Migration is undoubtedly stressful, but context conditions the impact of stress on individual mental health. Context for the Serer and for the Zulu could hardly have been more different. Migrating South African Zulu had to confront the racism and blocked opportunity of official apartheid; Serer who came to the cities were citizens of a black republic. The ethnic enclaves the Serer formed within the cities provided them important emotional support together with a continuing sense of the value of their traditions. Under apartheid, South African police monitored the Zulu's movements. The Serer living in the cities were poor, but free.

The disillusionment model is another example of the 'resettlement stress is inevitable' paradigm. A number of widely quoted studies have suggested that the psychological process of adapting to a new country follows predictable phases (Tyhurst 1951, 1977; Holmes and Masuda, 1973; Grinberg, 1984; Rumbaut, 1985). During an initial phase – sometimes called the euphoria of arrival – the mental health of immigrants is equal to, or even better than, that of the host country's population. The second phase, inevitably overtaking the first, is a phase of disillusionment and nostalgia for the past that was abandoned in order to move to a new country. During this phase, people are at high risk for developing psychiatric disorders. Eventually, adaptation to the new environment takes place; new settlers begin to act more and more like people in the majority population and their mental health approximates that of their hosts.

Figure 4.1 traces the level of depression among the refugees in the Refugee Resettlement Project (RRP) sample according to the length of time they had been in Canada. At the time of the first survey, refugees who had been in Canada ten to twelve months had higher levels of depression than people who had arrived earlier or later. This peaking supports the 'inevitability of resettlement stress' paradigm.

However, figure 4.2 presents a more complex analysis, one suggesting that stress alone does not explain changes in mental health. This figure compares depression scores for four subgroups of refugees at early, mid, and late stages of arrival. The subsamples are defined by ethnicity and marital status, namely married and unmarried Chinese, and married and unmarried non-Chinese.

Figure 4.1   Relationship between Depression and Length of Time in Canada for Southeast Asian Refugees

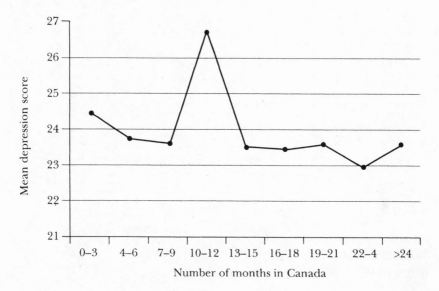

The ethnic composition of Vancouver at the time the refugees first arrived in that city created a natural experiment to investigate a concept known as 'critical mass' theory. According to this theory, immigrants who settle in areas in which there is an established like-ethnic community have a mental health advantage over immigrants deprived of such community (Murphy, 1955, 1973, 1977). At the time the refugees came to Vancouver, the city could already boast a Chinese population of more than 150,000, but no pre-existing Vietnamese, Laotian, or Cambodian communities. According to critical mass theory, the Chinese refugees should have had a mental health advantage over the non-Chinese.

Research suggests that the presence of a spouse protects mental health (Berry and Blondel, 1970; Hirschfeld and Cross, 1982; Brown and Harris, 1978). According to this body of research, refugees who were married and who had their spouses with them should have enjoyed a lower risk of developing depression than people who were single, who had been forced to leave their spouses behind, or who were separated by choice, divorced, or widowed.

Figure 4.2 demonstrates the mental health significance of community and marital status. Married Chinese, that is, people with two protective

Figure 4.2   Relationship between Depression, Ethnicity, Family Type, and
Length of Time in Canada for Southeast Asian Refugees

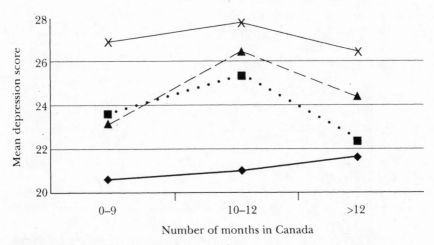

♦ Attached Chinese   ■ Unattached Chinese

▲ Attached non-Chinese   X Unattached non-Chinese

factors, were the least depressed to begin with, and they showed no
change in depression levels over time. The other three groups did show
the expected peaking at ten to twelve months, presumably the period of
greatest mental health risk. However, the unmarried non-Chinese, that is,
the group with no protective factors, had the highest levels of depression
throughout the entire early period of resettlement. The two groups who
had at least one protective factor had levels of depression that were inter-
mediate between the well-protected and the unprotected groups, and
their scores were fairly equal to each other throughout.

Although stress counts, it does not tell the whole tale about mental
health. A comprehensive resettlement model needs to take into account
predisposition, mental health risk, protective factors, and the context,
including resettlement phase.

Towards a Model of Predisposition, Risk, and Context

Although migration and resettlement are potential threats to mental
health, risk is not destiny. The contingencies surrounding the experi-

ence, such as the kinds of stress endured, the availability of social support, and differences in personal make-up, determine whether re-settlement will result in psychiatric disorder, social pathology, or realized opportunity.

Since the RRP obviously could not study the refugees before they came to Canada, the study has little to say about the effect of personal predisposition on the development of psychiatric problems. However, considering the fact that this group of refugees managed to survive extraordinary adversity in their home countries, the rigours of escape, and the crushing atmosphere of the internment camps, it seems likely that they were, on the whole, exceptionally resilient people. Furthermore, research with Southeast Asian refugees suggests that, during the early years of resettlement, the past affects mental health less than what newcomers face during resettlement (Westermeyer, Vang, and Neider, 1983b; Rumbaut, 1988; Hinton et al., 1997).

Strangers at the Gate focuses on people adjusting to a new country and a new culture, the stresses that make adjustment difficult, as well as the psychological and social factors that help make the transition from the familiar to the new a little easier.

Experience becomes stress when it challenges habitual coping patterns. Extreme stress may overwhelm the personality and result in psychiatric disorder. Though rarely applied to refugee resettlement, stress process theory (Pearlin et al., 1981) provides a useful framework for understanding what happens to refugees and how they respond. Building on a stress process model, figure 4.3 depicts the effects of stress and protective factors on refugee adaptation. Pre- and post-migration stresses place mental health and adaptation in jeopardy. Personal and social resources contribute to personal well-being and to the achievement of successful adaptation.

Because the Refugee Resettlement Project emphasized the refugees' present and future more than their past, the study included only one specific pre-migration stress, internment in refugee camps. As mentioned above, previous studies have suggested that what happens to refugees after coming to a resettlement country has more profound mental health implications than their pre-migration experiences. It is difficult to know what to make of these data. Do they constitute a confirmation of well-worn clichés about the indomitability of the human spirit? Probably, at least in part. However, the research has some shortcomings. For example, most investigations cover only the first few years of resettlement; it may well be the case that it is only long after investigators have lost contact with the subjects of their studies that the past emerges to haunt memory and to jeopardize mental health. Perhaps, too, there is something wrong with what is studied. It could well be the case that loss of family, uprooting, terror, and threats to survival – a pre-migration chain of stressors that could be though of as 'cumulative trauma' (Keilson, 1992) – make themselves felt in forms other than depression. For example, an increasing number of studies suggest that post-traumatic stress disorder (PTSD) is one of the legacies of either an overwhelming- ly stressful discrete experience or of cumulative trauma in the pre-migration period (Levav, 1998; Mollica, Poole, and Tor, 1998; Beiser, 1998).

Research concerning the effects of pre-migration stress on mental health is making an important contribution to theory. However, from a practical standpoint, resettlement countries can do nothing to change refugees' past lives. They *can* do something about what happens to people after they resettle: post-migration stresses are potentially remediable. In figure 4.3, the arrow linking post-migration stress to mental health is heavier than the one relating mental health to pre-migration stress, a pictorial device meant to underline the RRP's emphasis of contemporaneous challenge over past vicissitude. The specific stresses studied include unemployment, underemployment, and discrimination, each of them a potent challenge to refugee adaptation. Social and personal resources make important contributions to mental health, affecting it either directly or, by altering the experience of stress, buffering a person against its effects.

At a microsocial level, the family provides emotional as well as more tangible forms of support. Feeling loved and valued by one's family nourishes mental health; deprivation jeopardizes well-being. Family support can also help cushion people against the traumatic mental health effects of adversity. For example, on the whole, married people have better mental health than singles (Turner, 1983). Furthermore, marriage can act as a buffer, preserving mental health when it is challenged by severe stresses such as losing a job (Gore, 1978).

Two macrosocial forces – the ethnic community and the reception accorded by the host society – affect refugee mental health both directly and indirectly. Testimony presented during the national hearings of the Canadian Task Force on Mental Health Issues Affecting Immigrants and Refugees emphasized the importance of the ethnic community in promoting mental health and preventing disorder. Research supports this testimony. For example, one investigator discovered that mental hospitalization rates for immigrant groups in Canada increased as the size of the

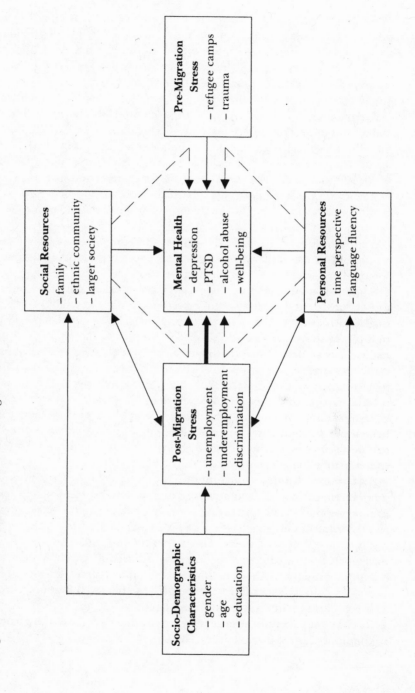

Figure 4.3   Stress, Protective Factors, and Refugee Mental Health

Pre-Migration Stress
– refugee camps
– trauma

Social Resources
– family
– ethnic community
– larger society

Mental Health
– depression
– PTSD
– alcohol abuse
– well-being

Personal Resources
– time perspective
– language fluency

Post-Migration Stress
– unemployment
– underemployment
– discrimination

Socio-Demographic Characteristics
– gender
– age
– education

like-ethnic community decreased (Murphy, 1973). Another Canadian study of hospitalization for schizophrenia showed that, although migrants as a whole were not over-represented, minority ethnic and linguistic groups had admission rates higher than would be expected given their numbers in the general population (Bland and Orn, 1981). An early RRP study, conducted during the first year or two of resettlement, also high-lighted the importance of the like-ethnic community (Beiser, 1988).

To investigate the hypothesis that a 'critical mass' of like ethnics confers a mental health advantage, we included equal numbers of Chinese and non-Chinese in the sample. Measuring ethnicity is not straightforward. For the purposes of this study, we were interested in ethnicity as a factor making it possible to communicate with, and to be accepted as a member of, a significant social group. We used three criteria to define ethnicity: family name, father's ethnicity, and first language, with the last two superseding the first. For example, someone with a Chinese family name, but whose father was Vietnamese and whose mother tongue was Vietnamese, was considered Vietnamese.

Some commentators have suggested that receiving countries offer different 'levels of hospitality' to newcomers (Aylesworth, Ossorio, and Osaki, 1977; Aylesworth and Ossorio, 1983). Although the proposition that the more hospitable the reception the better the chances of maintaining good mental health (Starr and Roberts, 1982) makes intuitive sense, testing the proposition is difficult because hospitality is hard to measure. Reasoning that refugees sponsored by private groups would receive more individualized attention than others left to the care of government bureaucracies, we stratified our sample to include equal numbers of private- and government-sponsored people. We hypothesized that privately sponsored refugees would enjoy better mental health than those sponsored by the government.

As a result of innate constitution and experience, some people have more strength to deal with adversity than others. Although the idea has intuitive appeal, conceptualizing the personal strengths that contribute to emotional well-being has not proven easy. Guided by clinical experiences with refugees who were coping and with those who were not, we developed the concept that the way in which people psychologically handle time influences their mental health, particularly during stressful experiences like flight and resettlement. The 'Personal Resources' box in figure 4.3 also includes fluency in the language of the receiving country. Testimony and common sense suggest the importance of language for adaptation (Canadian Task Force, 1988b).

Figure 4.3 posits that psychological resources exert both direct and indirect mental health effects. Simply put, this part of the model suggests that people who feel loved by their families and valued by their communities will experience better mental health than others who lack these reinforcements. The broken lines indicate a buffering effect: social support mitigates the psychological effect of bad experience. Personal resources have the same relationship to mental health as social. Selectively attending to present and future, rather than to the past, confers a mental health advantage.

The arrow linking personal resources and post-migration stress in figure 4.3 draws attention to a number of potentially important relationships. For example, language fluency may improve the chances of finding work. The arrow linking the two boxes is bidirectional, pointing out that it is equally plausible that employed people have a better chance of learning a new language than their jobless counterparts. A bidirectional arrow also links social resources to post-migration stress. Ethnic community contacts or private sponsors may help people find jobs. On the other hand, although employment and a steady income offer no guarantee of marital bliss, they almost certainly help.

Studies in mental health always include control variables like age and gender when analysing results. The reason is that long experience has demonstrated a strong association between these factors and mental health. Virtually every community study finds that women have higher rates of depressive feelings and of depressive disorder than men (Weissman and Klerman, 1977; Weissman, 1987), and that younger people are more prone to depression than their elders (Klerman et al., 1985; Eisenberg, 1984; Hirschfeld and Cross, 1982; Leaf et al., 1984). Failure to control for these factors can produce spurious inter-group differences. For example, finding an exceptionally high rate of distress among an immigrant group might constitute a spurious finding if, on the whole, they were younger than a comparison sample of indigens. Using age and sex as controls does not mean that research has answered all the important questions about how these variables jeopardize mental health. We still do not know whether male-female biological differences protect one sex while they place another at risk, whether societies that deny opportunity to one gender while conferring advantage on the other are to blame, or whether some interaction between biological predisposition and social disadvantage is the most likely explanation. Rather than using control variables mechanistically, this study includes qualitative data to help clarify how sex and age interact with other adaptive processes to affect mental health.

Selection bias mars many studies of the mental health of immigrants. If immigrants in resettlement countries have poor mental health, can one safely attribute their pathology to the stresses of resettlement, or are unhappy, disorder-prone people more likely than the well-adjusted to leave home? To a great extent, the Refugee Resettlement Project overcomes this methodological problem. The Southeast Asians did not choose to leave: they were forced from their homes, sometimes by government policy, sometimes by intolerable circumstance. Furthermore, they were exceptionally healthy. Only hardy, resourceful people could have planned a successful escape, then survived the rigours of flight. As if that selection process were not enough, the refugees who managed to reach a country of first asylum then had to convince immigration officials of their good potential. Canada's immigration officers chose the people they considered most promising – the healthiest, the best educated, the best workers, the people with the greatest social charm. A history of mental instability was an almost certain guarantee of rejection.

Any study spanning ten years is subject to attrition bias, the possibility that people with certain characteristics are more likely to drop out than others. In 1981, the Refugee Resettlement Project contacted and interviewed 1,348 people. Only 2 per cent of all those contacted refused an interview. Two years later, there were 1,169 reinterviews, a success rate of 87 per cent. In 1991, 647 of the original 1,348 people completed an·interview. This total, about 49 per cent of the original sample, included 40 people who had been interviewed in 1981, but not in 1983.

The loss of about half the original sample is disappointing. It is, however, important to view the loss in context. The RRP study retained twice as many respondents as other studies (Lewis, Fraser, and Pecora, 1988; Burwell, Hill, and Van Wicklin, 1986) that have attempted to follow highly mobile Southeast Asian refugees over a period of years. More importantly, exhaustive analyses suggest relatively little attrition bias. Age, gender, and education did not affect the chances of reinterview. There was a slight mental health trend: the least mentally healthy people in 1983 were the most likely to agree to a 1991 reinterview. The finding has one important implication: since psychiatric disorders tend to be persistent conditions, 1991 data may overestimate the amount of refugee psychopathology (Edwards, 1994).

Measures of Mental Health

Mental illness has been called a myth. One reason is that no one has succeeded in defining it.

Ostensive definitions of part of the spectrum of mental disorder are fairly easy. The filthy panhandler sitting on a heating grate in the heart of downtown listening to voices no one else can hear and the man standing next to him screaming, 'My knife is an instrument to redeem you from sin!' are madmen – people whom every known society would recognize as abnormal. It seems that all cultures consider apparently senseless, unpredictable, and potentially dangerous behaviour to be sickness. Their languages contain words that define the behaviours as illness, and they have culturally sanctioned ways of trying to control, if not to cure, madmen and madwomen (Beiser et al., 1973; Beiser et al., 1972; Murphy, 1976). Some societies consider the derangements these people suffer to be illnesses of the spirit or punishment for wrongdoing. The industrialized world calls them mental disorders: the panhandler with his voices would probably be called schizophrenic; the excited, grandiose, and threatening man might be in the throes of an attack of mania. Nguyen Bich, the handsome carpenter from Vietnam, smothered his common-law wife with a pillow while hallucinating that a woman dressed in white urged him to kill. Because Bich seemed so normal, both before and after the murder, his lawyer did not enter a plea of temporary insanity.

Hearing voices, seeing visions, and feeling that one has been singled out by some higher power are experiences so far out of the ordinary that most people recognize them as signs of sickness. Other, far less unusual disturbances are also called mental disorder. When Li Wuchin, the one-time factory owner from Saigon, tried to kill himself, he was neither grandiose nor hallucinating. He was understandably bitter and discouraged about being a janitor with no prospect of ever regaining the wealth and position he once enjoyed. He was ashamed that his wife had to work as a seamstress to help support their family, and he was shocked that his children did not respect him as Chinese youngsters should respect their elders. A few months before attempting to take his own life, he began to reminisce about the old days, before the communists came to Saigon. During the early morning hours, when it became increasingly difficult to sleep, he thought about killing himself. Sometimes Wuchin became so desperate that all he could do was cry to himself. His appetite dropped off, he lost about twenty pounds, and he developed constipation. The psychiatrist who saw him after the suicide attempt had no difficulty assigning his patient a psychiatric diagnosis of major depressive disorder.

With rates ranging from 6 to 8 per cent in the general population (Robins et al., 1984; Myers et al., 1984), depression is one of the most common forms of mental disorder. Before using depression as a measure of Southeast Asian refugee adaptation, the researcher has to answer two questions. First, is there anything 'real' about the construct of mental disorder when applied to Western populations, let alone Asians? Second, if depression is a useful construct in the Western world, in which it was developed, is there any justification for using it cross-culturally?

The Reality of Depressive Disorder

Like schizophrenia or mania, depression appears in lists of mental disorders like the American Psychiatric Association's *Diagnostic and Statistical Manual* (DSM-IV) or the World Health Organization's *International Classification of Diseases* (ICD-10). Their appearance in such lists signifies official and explicit inclusion among the range of phenomena that people in the Western world call mental illness.

Unlike the out-of-the-ordinary symptoms of schizophrenia and mania, however, Li Wuchin's experiences are familiar and understandable. Hasn't everyone, at some time or another, felt discouraged, sad, lonely, or ashamed, had periods when he or she found it hard to sleep, and perhaps even lost weight when they were not trying to? If this is the case, what qualifies Wuchin to be called a case of mental disorder?

Explicitly or implicitly, most definitions of psychiatric disorder incorporate four criteria: intensity, patterning, impairment, and persistence.

Although anyone can empathize with the feelings of a Li Wuchin – everyone has felt sad and discouraged at times – most people will never experience the profundity of his sorrow at being transformed from a rich man to a menial labourer, or the intensity of his hopelessness in recognizing that he would never again enjoy a position of authority in his family, let alone in society at large.

Depressed feelings are not the only possible reaction to stress. A constellation of vague bodily symptoms, including appetite loss, indigestion, pressure headaches, back pain, insomnia, and generalized weakness and fatigue, constitutes another dimension of human misery. Many authorities consider this pattern of symptoms a reaction to stress expressed in bodily, rather than psychic, terms. For this reason, it has frequently been called 'somatization' (Beiser and Fleming, 1986).

And so it was with Li Wuchin. Wuchin suffered from more than psychic symptoms. He also had frequent stomach upsets, constipation, and headaches – symptoms from the domain of somatization. Both the psychic and somatic symptoms were so severe that their co-occurrence might have alerted a mental health professional that Wuchin had passed from understandable distress into possible life-threatening disorder. However, by the time mental health professionals became involved with Wuchin, it was almost too late.

Symptoms from the domain of depression, common in everyday life, usually occur together. Likewise for the symptoms of somatization. It is, however, uncommon for symptoms to cross domains. In other words, expressions of depression and expressions of somatization rarely co-occur (Beiser and Fleming, 1986).

The psychiatric disorders described in the American Psychiatric Association's DSM-IV or the World Health Organization's ICD-10 are patterns of symptoms many of which span domains like affective expression and somatic upset. The idea that these unique co-aggregations connote something serious is implicit in all diagnostic systems. Unlike people with a few depressive *or* somatic symptoms whose discomfort is likely to be transient, individuals suffering a pattern of distress spanning more than one domain of suffering likely face a prolonged and persistent burden.

Although everyone has known sadness, the despair associated with depressive disorder is quantitatively and qualitatively different. Symptoms of disorder are more intense than in quotidian sadness. Furthermore, they spill over from the internal to the external areas of life, eventually interfering with work, frustrating social relationships, and obstructing well-being. People experiencing transient unhappiness can usually take pleasure in domains of their life other than the one causing their distress. Wuchin's depression pervaded everything: he took no pleasure in his children's school and career accomplishments; his brooding silence began to drive friends away; and his employers were unhappy with his work performance. In comparison with mentally healthy individuals, clinically depressed people like Wuchin are more prone to experience occupational and social failure, and even premature death (Murphy et al., 1986).

Depressive disorders may become chronic: 20 per cent of people with a disorder never recover, or recover only after a very long time. Another 15 to 20 per cent experience only partial recovery. Twenty-five per cent of the people who do recover, usually after a period of weeks or months, relapse within one year (Angst, 1986; Bronisch et al., 1985; Ceroni, Nevi, and Pezzoli, 1984; Prien et al., 1984; Keller and Shapiro, 1981; Keller et al., 1984; Sargent et al., 1990). Intense symptoms, unique patternings, the tendency of these patterns to persist, and the risk that symptoms will pervade other areas of life are the hallmarks of disorder.

Does Depression Occur in the Same Form in All Cultures?

Cultural relativists feel that concepts like depression are Western and eth-nocentric. They argue that applying such concepts in non-Western set-tings violates indigenous assumptions about the nature, antecedents, and consequences of behaviour. They also argue that, because of cultural dif-ferences, people describe illness differently and possibly even experience different symptoms.

A few years ago, a colleague called to invite me to attend a meeting about culture and psychiatric diagnosis. He said, 'We really need you to come because we want to have a mixture of relativists and universalists.'

'Which am I?' I asked.

Accusation mixed with pity coloured the tone with which he answered, '*You* think that disorders are the same in every culture. You're a universal-ist.' If my colleague's description of me is correct, it reflects an inclina-tion that I think is grounded in research, not in ideology.

From its early days, cross-cultural investigation has appealed to psychia-trists fascinated by the possibility of discovering exotic illnesses in cultures different from their own. The literature is replete with descriptions of *windigo, koro, latah,* and other exotic conditions, each supposedly culture-specific. Even though my colleague perceived me as a universalist, I have made at least one contribution to the exotic syndrome literature with a description of *pobough lang* among the Serer tribe of Senegal (Beiser et al., 1974). *Pobough lang* is a compulsion to eat sand. People affected by this socially disapproved behaviour hide their shame from others. If one elaborates the syndrome with descriptions of how some persons crave sand from termite hills, while others go in the dead of night to gather it from spots around the village well, it can begin to sound more and more bizarre. However, at a basic level, the behaviour is not that much different from a craving for soap chips that has been described among the rural poor in the Southern United States. The craving for soap chips is, how-ever, regarded as an idiosyncrasy, a condition that does not require inter-vention. Possibly because it may be a symptom of iron deficiency anaemia and, as a consequence, a frequent harbinger of mortality in the African Sahel, *pobough lang* is more than a personal idiosyncrasy. It is a full-fledged illness. Culture did not create the symptom pattern: it created its defini-tion.

Culture also affects packaging. Serer *marabouts* (traditional healers) speak of another illness, *m'befedin,* consisting of seizures, which may or may not be preceded by an aura, during the course of which people often hurt themselves, bite their tongues, or urinate, and which are usually followed by amnesia (Beiser et al., 1973). With one exception, the description perfectly matches a Western disease concept, grand mal epilepsy. The exception is that a *marabout* will call an illness *m'befedin* only if, during the course of a seizure, the unfortunate victim produces a lot of saliva. Although most European and North American neurologists would probably not consider it an important criterion of grand mal epilepsy, foaming at the mouth is vitally important to the Serer, who consider *m'befedin* a contagious disease with saliva its medium of transmission. To protect others, victims of *m'befedin* go into life-long quarantine.

Human physiology limits the range of ways in which people can feel distressed. Fear, for example, is a universal human experience. When its source is recognized, the affect is called fear; when it is not recognized, the feeling state is called anxiety; and when the source is recognized, but the reaction out of proportion to the stimulus, the condition is called phobia. When people are fearful or anxious, their heart rates speed up, producing an experience of palpitations. Blood vessels on the body's surface constrict, producing coldness along with numbing and tingling in the fingers and toes. In contrast to the physiologic over-reactivity provoked by anxiety-provoking stimuli, experiences of profound loss or of learned helplessness almost invariably result in physiologic under-reactivity, giving rise to feelings of immobilization and apathy together with symptoms like constipation and lethargy.

Since the Cantonese, Mandarin, Vietnamese, Khmer, and Laotian languages have no word for depression connoting an illness, some authorities have concluded that Asians do not experience depression in the same way North Americans or Europeans do (Obeyesekere, 1985; Leff, 1973, 1977). It has been proposed that Asian experiences of distress are dominated by bodily symptoms, which are often highly elaborated. In its most simplistic terms, the proposition states: North Americans psychologize distress; Asians somatize it (Kleinman, 1980; Tseng, 1975; Yap, 1965).

Research refutes this concept. Southeast Asian languages are rich in idioms like 'Do you find your life is sad and boring?' or 'Do you feel remorseful?' that clearly fall within the spectrum of depressive experience, even if they do not connote illness (Kinzie et al., 1982). The way in which symptoms of depression co-aggregate in community samples of Southeast Asians is identical to their patterning among North Americans. Somatization symptoms also co-aggregate identically in both groups, and, furthermore, they form a dimension completely independent of depression (Beiser and Fleming, 1986). These population-based data suggest that somatization is not a substitute for depression but that each is a separate and independent way of expressing and experiencing distress.

Although studies carried out in clinical settings often conclude that mental illness wears a unique face in different cultures, community-based research reveals that similarities across cultures are more striking than differences (Beiser and Fleming, 1986; Beiser, Cargo, and Woodbury, 1994). The researcher's perspective is part of the problem. If one relies on what patients in a clinic volunteer as their problems, one runs the risk of hearing only what people feel it is appropriate to talk about in such settings, rather than about all the things that may be bothering them. Even if they are feeling distressed, many Asian patients consider it inappropriate to report symptoms of sadness or anxiety to doctors. Such feelings are reserved for a trusted family member, a member of the clergy, or a fortune-teller. They are not legitimate tender for a medical encounter. Investigators have confused a reluctance to divulge symptoms with a lack of vocabulary to describe them. When they feel it is appropriate or likely to be helpful, Asians will confide psychic symptoms of depression to a psychiatrist with equal or even greater intensity than their North American counterparts (Cheung, Lau, and Waldman, 1980; Kinzie and Manson, 1983; Kinzie, 1985).

Despite the popularity of the apophthegm, Asians do not substitute somatic symptoms for psychological symptoms of depression. When asked appropriately, Asians report depressive symptoms just as Westerners do. Furthermore, the symptoms reported by Southeast Asians and resident North Americans co-aggregate in precisely the same ways. Statistical analyses of Refugee Resettlement Project data demonstrate that the depressive construct described in the American Psychiatric Association's *Diagnostic and Statistical Manual* is equally valid for Southeast Asian refugees and long-time residents of Canada (Beiser, Cargo, and Woodbury, 1994).

The debate about whether people from different cultural groups experience or express distress differently is more than an intellectual curio. It can affect the chances of receiving appropriate care. In his 1725 *Treatise of the Spleen and Vapours*, Richard Blackmore articulated his vision that 'Spleen' – which could be equated with contemporary concepts of depression – seemed characteristic of English distress, while other nations, especially those nearer the sun (colonials), seemed more prone to lunacy and disturbed imagination. Aside from needlessly shackling a clinician's ability to diagnose a patient's distress, emphasizing differences rather than universals in human suffering can perpetuate the kinds of stereotypes that misled Blackmore. The claim that Asians choose to express distress in one set of terms, North Americans in another, risks reducing human suffering to an affectation. Even when dressed up in modern liberal-looking clothes, stereotypes don't help.

Other Measures of Mental Health

Besides depression, the Refugee Resettlement Project focused on alcohol abuse, post-traumatic stress disorder (PTSD), and well-being.

Alcohol Abuse

Unlike depression – a condition that is suffered internally – alcohol abuse bothers others as much as, or more than, the person with the symptoms. Maladaptive in itself, alcohol abuse often leads to impaired work and social performance as well as domestic and social violence. Alcohol abuse is a delight for methodologists. This is because clinicians find it easier than with practically any other form of disorder to agree on when the diagnosis is appropriate (Helzer et al., 1990). Alcohol abuse is a potentially interesting barometer of adaptive distress. In comparison with other ethnic groups, Asians tend to have low rates of the disorder. However, immigrants who resettle in North America are prone to take on the host country's bad drinking habits (Scribner and Dyer, 1989; Chen, Ng, and Wilkins, 1996).

Post-Traumatic Stress Disorder

Although Chan Min Ran's garbage-strewn apartment in East Vancouver is a long way from home, distance does not protect her from memory. She says that her mental problems that began in Cambodia have become worse in Canada. When she was trying to escape, she was so preoccupied with survival she had no time to think. After she arrived in Canada, she began to reflect about the weather, about how big Vancouver was compared to what she was used to, and about how difficult it was to learn English. She forced herself not to think about her husband, about a son who would have been twenty-eight today, and about a daughter who would have been twenty-six.

Min Ran does not sleep well; Thomas says that he often hears his mother crying at night. Music and loud noises distract her and give her a headache. During her early years in Vancouver, Min Ran found work as an interpreter; however, she never held a job for long because her nervousness and distractibility interfered with her performance. The family survives today on what Thomas and his older brother earn from working in a warehouse.

At least once every night, a dream about the soldiers who came to take her and her family away disturbs Min Ran's sleep. On the date that would have been her daughter's birthday, Min Ran hardly sleeps at all. For the next three to four weeks, thoughts about her baby, her lost husband, and the rest of her family override everything else. The terrors of escaping from Cambodia keep coming back to her. At night, she paces the floor and cries. Although Thomas tries to help, Min Ran seems distant and inconsolable. One night, during her last spell like this, Thomas woke to the sounds of his mother's weeping. She was fumbling furiously with the front-door lock. He says Min Ran didn't seem to know him, or to understand where she was. She started yelling that she had to get out while there was still time. Thomas worries that one of these days his mother will run out on the street in her pyjamas and get into trouble.

Min Ran is depressed. She also has post-traumatic stress disorder (PTSD), a psychophysiological response to intense, catastrophic stress (Solomon and Mikulincer, 1988; Dohrenwend and Dohrenwend, 1974; Levav, 1998).

It took a long time for PTSD to find its way into official psychiatric thought. In part, this was because theory stressed the causal supremacy of personal predisposition over circumstance. For example, the first official catalogue of psychiatric disorder issued by the American Psychiatric Association (APA), the DSM-1 (1952), listed nothing resembling PTSD. The closest approximation was a condition called combat stress disorder. Although the name suggests that exposure to warfare could cause disorders, the description of the condition made it clear that the stresses of combat could make psychiatric casualties only out of people who were already vulnerable as a result of physiological make-up or developmental trauma.

Theory was not the only factor that led psychiatry to ignore evidence that holocaust survivors (Eitinger, 1961; Krystal and Danieli, 1994; Krystal, 1968; Kuch and Cox, 1992), prisoners of war (Basoglu et al., 1994; Bauer et al., 1993; Burges-Watson, 1993; Eberly and Engdahl, 1991; Kluznik et al., 1986; Speed et al., 1989), and victims of natural disaster (Shore, Vollmer, and Tatum, 1989; Green et al., 1992; Madakasira and O'Brien, 1987; McFarlane, 1988; De Girolamo, 1992) suffered psychological after-effects, evidence that might have contributed to formulating a psychiatric category. The resistance was partly a product of reluctance to create a medical justification for compensation claims by survivors, former prisoners, and discharged veterans. By the time the APA issued its first revision of the catalogue of psychiatric illness, the DSM-II (1968), combat stress disorder had disappeared. Nothing else in that edition of the official nomenclature came close to suggesting that external stress could result in internal upset. The next edition, the DSM-III (1980), was revolutionary in many ways. PTSD's sudden appearance was one of those ways. Pressure from veterans' organizations made it impossible to ignore the scientific evidence of profound and widespread psychological disturbances among the young men and women who had served in the Vietnam War. Social pressure helped force a revision in psychiatric thinking that made PTSD official, potentially compensable, and worthy of professional attention.

Aside from its pragmatic significance, official recognition of PTSD has forced revision of theory. The description of the syndrome acknowledges that catastrophic stresses like war, rape, or earthquakes can cause disorder in almost everyone, not just the personally vulnerable.

Studies of Vietnamese veterans (Keane, 1998), civilians traumatized by non-combat life experiences (Shalev, Orr, and Pitman, 1993), survivors of motor-vehicle accidents (Blanchard, Hickling, and Taylor, 1991) and natural disasters (Shore, Tatum, and Vollmer, 1986; Shore, Vollmer, and Tatum, 1989; Giel, 1998), and Holocaust survivors and prisoners of war (Levav, 1998) have all provided evidence consistent with the idea that extreme adversity gives rise to psychopathological consequences, and that the consequences may outlive the stressor itself. Research showing a dose-response relationship – that is, the greater the exposure to the stressor, the greater the likelihood of subsequent PTSD (Keane, 1998; Levav, 1998; Mollica, Poole, and Tor, 1998) – supports the posited aetiological link between adversity and psychopathology. Goldberg and colleagues (1990) provide some of the most telling evidence: fifteen years after the end of the Vietnam War, veterans who had been in combat had a far higher risk of developing PTSD than their non-combat-exposed monozygotic twins.

Research also suggests the potential usefulness of developing a typology of adversity. The utility derives from the possibility that different stressors can lead to different outcomes: for example, human-initiated disasters may have even more adverse consequences than natural disasters such as earthquakes (Giel, in 1998).

Still firmly ensconced in the DSM-IV(1994), the symptoms of PTSD are described as resulting from two underlying psychological disturbances: intrusion and avoidance. Intrusion refers to the penetration of thoughts, feelings, and images into sleep as well as conscious thought. Avoidance refers to psychic numbing, behavioural inhibition, and social withdrawal (Horowitz, 1982). Manifestations of intrusion include disturbed sleep, nightmares, and compulsive recollections. Those resulting from avoidance include loss of the ability to become interested in people or pursuits that might have seemed important before exposure to trauma, problems with intimacy, and emotional coldness.

Well-Being

Life is about more than avoiding pain. According to the World Health Organization's admittedly lofty definition, health is more than the absence of illness; it implies a state of psychological, social, and spiritual well-being.

Many North Americans are questioning the assumption that their nations' economic prosperity, technological advances, widespread literacy, and improved health care have actually improved individual quality of life. To help answer the question, 'quality-of-life' research has become a growth industry.

Psychological well-being is one of the core constructs in quality-of-life research. Research confirms what theory asserts: well-being is not the opposite of distress. The Affect Balance Scale is one of the most widely used measures in quality-of-life investigations (Bradburn, 1969). Simplicity accounts, in part, for its appeal. The test contains five questions about positive feelings; for example, 'During the past few weeks have you felt pleased about accomplishing something?' Five questions about negative states balance the positive items and complete the ten-item scale. 'During the past few weeks have you been feeling so restless that you couldn't sit in a chair for long?' is an example of a negative item. Population research demonstrates that people who endorse one negative item tend to endorse all of them, and that people who endorse one positive item endorse all of them. This patterning makes it possible to form a positive and a negative affect scale. Scores on these two scales have no relationship to each other. In other words, someone high on positive affect may also have a high negative affect score, or a low negative affect score. Furthermore, the determinants of positive and negative affect seem to be different. Negative affect scores tend to be associated with poor health and socio-economic disadvantage; positive affect, with participation in groups (Bradburn, 1969; Beiser, 1974; Diener, 1984).

Based on the mistaken premise that linguistic and cultural barriers make serious study of well-being difficult, if not impossible, North American research has routinely neglected ethnocultural minority groups. Cross-cultural theory that has tended to emphasize uniqueness and difference (Kleinman, 1982; Marsella, 1979) has also contributed to this neglect.

It is hard to imagine that the search for well-being is anything less than universal. In a truly pluralistic society, everyone's well-being is equally significant. Guided by these principles, the Refugee Resettlement Project incorporated the five-item positive affect scale as one measure of adaptation. With one exception, the measure worked very well. Translators working on the questionnaire were hard put to find an equivalent for the idiom embodied in the question 'During the past few weeks have you been feeling on top of the world?' Their difficulty reminded me of a previous experience with this item. Years before, as a research fellow at Harvard, I had used the positive affect scale in a community survey in rural Nova Scotia. Responses to the item made no sense statistically and, furthermore, bore no relationship to the other positive affect questions. It wasn't difficult to figure out why. On being asked the question, one woman replied: 'What does that mean? Do you think we're closer to the North Pole than you folks down in the States?'

Although the experience of well-being transcends cultural boundaries, affective tropes that describe feelings don't always survive translation. Although 'top of the world' obviously meant something to the people in Chicago, where the Affect Balance Scale was developed, the idiom's meaning did not carry over to rural Canada or to Southeast Asia. After omitting the item from the Refugee Resettlement Project questionnaire, we ended up with a four-question, culturally appropriate, and statistically sound measure of well-being (Devins et al., 1997).

The Refugee Resettlement Project's Questionnaire and Measures

To study the adaptation and mental health of the 1,348 refugees who made up the Refugee Resettlement Project's study sample, we constructed a questionnaire containing items about personal history, family, employment, language skills, cultural values, consumer practices, knowledge about rights in Canada, sources of social support, and health. The health section of the questionnaire inquired about symptoms of depression, anxiety, and somatization using a series of items derived in part from survey instruments widely used in North America and Europe

(Radloff, 1977; Robins et al., 1985; Harding, de Arango, and Baltazar, 1980; Beiser, Benfari, Collomb, and Ravel, 1976), as well as culture-specific measures of distressed affect (Kinzie et al., 1982; Beiser and Fleming, 1986; Beiser, Cargo, and Woodbury, 1994). The survey also included the positive-affect measure from Bradburn's (1969) Affect Balance Scale (omitting the 'top of the world' item) and a series of questions to assess alcohol abuse as well as post-traumatic stress disorder.

Results regarding depression, alcohol abuse, and PTSD are presented as if they were psychiatric diagnoses. Psychiatrists did not make them. Computers did.

To make a diagnosis, a psychiatrist interviews a client at length, tries to collect information from family members or friends, observes the patient over a period of time, and sometimes orders confirmatory laboratory or psychological tests. No community survey could afford the psychiatric fees required to assess everyone in this depth. Even if expense were no consideration, no community would tolerate the intrusion required for such intensive assessment. Even if funds and community patience were unlimited, clinical assessments would not guarantee validity. No matter how skilled, an individual clinician's performance will vary on a day-to-day basis. Fatigue, distraction, and other human failings compromise clinical reliability. It isn't only psychiatric judgment that is subject to unreliability. In one experiment, radiologists who examined cases they had judged once before, sometimes came up with different assessments on the second attempt. Factors accounting for the inconsistencies included tiredness, recent experience, and seemingly minor changes in the way in which information was ordered (Dawes, Faust, and Meehl, 1989).

The structured questionnaires used in most community surveys together with the rigorous training received by lay interviewers help to assure a solid reliability. Although many clinicians feel this is a case of reliability achieved at the price of flexibility, it is much prized by research workers.

No matter how dedicated to objectivity, clinicians cannot escape biases instilled by training, ideology, and personal idiosyncrasy. These biases can influence clinical assessments in a number of ways. For example, psychiatrists are probably more interested in depression than in substance abuse: if they find evidence of the former, they are more likely to pursue its investigation with a patient than they are to inquire if the person also happens to be drinking a lot. Structured interviews, however, ensure comprehensiveness of coverage with each respondent. Interestingly, the most common discrepancy between structured and clinical interviews carried out with the same research subject is that the structured format produces more diagnoses of alcoholism (Robins, 1989). Decision rules for computerized diagnostic algorithms are always explicit. If research dictates revision of diagnostic rules, it is easier to reprogram a computer than a clinician.

Clinicians' idiosyncrasies are not the only explanation for unreliable diagnosis. The respondent may be the source of unreliability as well. Presented with the same question on two different days, a respondent may offer an inconsistent response because he or she does not fully understand the question's intent. Items which do not interest a respondent very much, or which use unfamiliar terms to describe a feeling state, are likely to elicit unreliable responses (Sudman and Bradburn, 1974; Robins, 1989). Questionnaires typically use a number of items to tap an underlying domain. If a subject fails to understand or to answer a particular item, all is not lost. At the cost of sounding a bit repetitive in the actual interview situation, multiple questions on the same topic help ensure that nothing will be missed.

Although many epidemiological studies use something resembling clinical diagnosis as the measure of disorder, this is always an approximation at best. Typically, a trained lay interviewer poses a number of questions thought to measure criteria for psychiatric disorders as well as other questions designed to ensure that a given symptom like fatigue is likely a result of psychiatric disturbance rather than of physical conditions like anaemia. In early investigations of this type, psychiatrists examining responses to a questionnaire decided whether or not the individual qualified for a psychiatric diagnosis (Leighton et al., 1963; Srole and Fischer, 1978).

Computers programmed to replicate human judgments have now replaced this labour-intensive and sometimes unreliable diagnostic process. Creating a computer routine to make diagnoses of depressive disorder, alcohol abuse, and PTSD is straightforward and relatively simple. It is easy to forget that more than forty years of conceptual struggle and methodological investigation went into creating the algorithms now so readily generated by computers.

Do the algorithms measure anything 'real' or do they merely identify people who happen to be feeling upset at the time and who, left on their own, would be cured by the passage of time? Wuchin and Bich were suffering intense symptoms that interfered with their lives. Months after their onset, the symptoms showed no signs of abating. Professional intervention could have helped prevent the disastrous actions that brought the two unfortunate men to public attention.

Min Ran also has symptoms that are intense, persistent, and impairing. It would be hard to convince her, her family, or anyone who has met her that her suffering is anything other than 'real.'

FIVE

How Much Disorder and Who Is at Risk?

This chapter explores a number of questions: How much mental disorder did refugees have and how did these figures compare with rates for resident Canadians? Who developed a disorder, who did not, and why the difference? Why did some people who developed disorders recover, while others did not?

How Much Depression?

Depression is one of the most common of the mental disorders: at any given moment, it compromises the day-to-day functioning of 5 to 8 per cent of the population (Robins et al., 1984 Myers et al., 1984). In 1981, 6.4 per cent of the refugees and 5.2 per cent of the age- and gender-matched Vancouver sample were depressed.

Who Is at Risk for Depression?

Most community surveys report higher rates of depression for women than for men (Nolen-Hoeksema, 1987; Weissman and Klerman, 1977; Weissman, 1987), and for youth than for the middle-aged and the elderly (Klerman et al., 1985). Given such ubiquitous findings, it would be unthinkable to omit these factors when trying to investigate the risk of developing a mental disorder. In both samples – refugee and resident Canadian – young adults had higher rates of depression than older respondents. Compared to people thirty-five and older, young Vancouverites were twice as likely to be depressed. In 1981, the risk of depression for young refugees was one and one-half times higher than for those thirty-five and over. A common epidemiological finding, this pattern has aroused intense speculation (Weissman, 1987). It cannot be explained away as methodological artifact, and other data, including suicide statistics, are consistent in portraying the young as highly distressed and vulnerable (Eisenberg, 1984; Hirschfeld and Cross, 1982).

Contrary to the results of practically every other epidemiological study, including the data from the Vancouver comparison sample, male refugees in 1981 had a higher risk for depression than females. The results were a surprise not only because they ran contrary to the epidemiological literature, but because, before they came to Canada, female refugees probably experienced even more trauma than men. Rape, for example, was a major problem during escape as well as later in the refugee camps. According to testimony reported in the 1980s:

> During the last five years, approximately 2,400 [Vietnamese] refugee women suffered rape by pirates and some 1,000 women were abducted, frequently being passed among several boats. Only 43% of women abducted since 1982 are known to have survived. Piracy attacks on female asylum-seekers were generally sustained, brutal and multiple. (UNHCR, 1988, p. 84)

Selection helps explain the female refugees' relatively good mental health. When they looked for people to fill their quotas, immigration officers tended to eliminate single women. Although the selection process was not the most humanitarian imaginable, the immigration personnel were doing the job they had been assigned – to find the best possible candidates for successful resettlement. Single women, especially traumatized single women, were not a priority.

During the first few years in the country, Southeast Asian refugee men and women had a different experience of Canada. Their respective situations helped to explain male-female differences in rates of mental disorder. At first, the burden of finding a job and providing for their families (both the family members they brought with them to Canada and those they left at home) fell disproportionately on the shoulders of the young Southeast Asian men. By comparison, women were more likely to stay at home, where the traditional roles of homemaker and cultural guardian protected them, at least temporarily (Westermeyer, 1986). During their early years in Canada, resettlement stresses, experienced with particular acuity by young men, probably overwhelmed the predispositional vulnerabilities and role disadvantages that account for women's mental health disadvantage, at least as reported in most studies (see Turner and Avison,

1989; Weissman, 1987; Weissman and Klerman, 1977; Nolen-Hoeksema, 1987). In contrast with single women, most of whom came to Canada as part of a family with whom they continued to live, many young men escaped Southeast Asia on their own. Leaving their families behind in Vietnam, Laos, or Cambodia did not free young, unattached men from obligation. Wives and children, parents, siblings, aunts, uncles, and cousins were counting on them to send money or medicine which they could sell to make their lives in Southeast Asia a little easier. Family left behind expected that, in time, they would be brought to Canada.

Sitting in his prison cell, Nguyen Bich, the young carpenter who smothered his common-law wife, recalled the early days in Canada: 'When I first got here, I was so lonely. I wrote home all the time. Then, I had to stop writing to my wife and to my parents. At first, I told them everything was all right, but then I was ashamed to tell them that I couldn't get enough money to bring them here. So I stopped writing.'

Changes in Mental Health Risk over Time

The longer the refugees stayed in Canada, the better their mental health became. Figure 5.1 documents the improvement: with each successive wave of interviews, the rate of depression declined. Although the over-all mental health trends were positive, the tendency to improve with time did not affect everyone equally. Pockets of people within the refugee population stayed depressed. Other groups who were initially healthy came under increased risk during the refugees' first decade in Canada.

During the earliest years of resettlement, the availability of traditional roles insulated women from mental health risk; cultural attitudes stressing respect for wisdom and authority provided psychological support for the elderly; and the presence of a large, like-ethnic community gave the Chinese refugees a mental health advantage over the non-Chinese. However, between 1981 and 1983, rates of disorder among Chinese and non-Chinese became equal, and, in subsequent years, the Chinese never regained their initial mental health advantage. Consistent with Refugee Resettlement Project (RRP) results, other studies of immigrant and refugee resettlement also document an initial mental health advantage for women (Hinton et al., 1997; Beiser et al., 1997). The female advantage often proves evanescent. Staying at home, looking after children, and guarding tradition may be initially protective, but it offers few opportunities for women to learn the language and customs of the larger society. Without these tools, women risk isolation not only from their neighbours

Figure 5.1   Rates of Depression, 1981–91

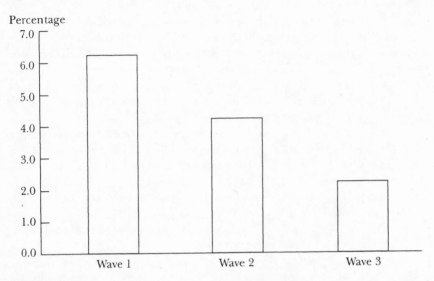

and larger community, but from their husbands and children, who learn about becoming 'mainstream' at work or at school (Garcia-Peltoniemi, 1991; Krupinski, 1967; Lasry and Schacter, 1975; Szapocznik and Kurtines, 1980). Refugee Resettlement Project data were consistent with these findings. By 1991, women and the elderly had lost their initial mental health advantage. Forced into a tough, competitive labour market and weighted down with family responsibilities, young men paid their resettlement dues early, and experienced high levels of distress. At first, the presence of family and the persistence of traditional roles may have insulated women and the elderly. These factors could not, however, protect them against the isolation that accrued with the passage of time.

If I Had a Job

'If I had a job,' Duong Quan confided, albeit loudly enough for her daughter to hear, 'they wouldn't treat me like this. Of course, they shouldn't be treating me like this anyway.' While our interpreter was translating to me what Quan was saying, the elderly woman darted a glance at the younger woman sitting on the sofa opposite us. Placidly rocking her baby, Hoa seemed oblivious to what her mother was saying. Perhaps she had a normally imperturbable nature. Perhaps she had heard the complaints so many times they no longer had an effect, even when voiced in the presence of a stranger.

The spring sunshine pouring into the windows of the small, neatly furnished house made the polished wooden floors gleam like mirrors. Dust particles flickered in the beams of light, obscuring the images on the muted TV. To outward appearance, it was a scene of perfect domestic tranquillity.

Mrs Duong Quan was, however, anything but tranquil. Earlier, when I had arrived to interview her daughter, one of the participants in the Refugee Resettlement Project, Quan had insisted that we have tea. Hoa's English had turned out to be good enough to make me regret the expense I had incurred in bringing along an interpreter. As the young woman and I proceeded with our interview, sounds of banging cupboard doors, clattering tea things, falling objects, exclamations of annoyance, and furious sweeping coming from the kitchen reminded us that, although Quan might be temporarily absent, she was not to be ignored. A few minutes of silence came as a surprise.

Quan re-entered the room wearing different clothes. In place of the red and white patterned sarong she had on when we first arrived, she was now dressed in a black silk blouse, with a mandarin collar that accentuated her sharp features and small glittery eyes, black pants with cuffs just below the knee, and flat-heeled black embroidered slippers. Quan now looked like a small elegant crow.

Hoa was a striking contrast to her mother. Her plump maternal figure was in perfect visual accord with her placid demeanour. Throughout our time together, Hoa alternated her attention between the infant sleeping restlessly on her lap and her four-year-old son tugging at her dress for attention. These distractions gave Quan the opportunity to redirect the spotlight from her daughter to herself.

Duong Quan nervously picked at her buttons, at her collar, and at the cuffs of her blouse as she began to repeat what was clearly an often-told tale. As she became increasingly secure in her recital, Quan's initial restlessness disappeared.

In 1955, Quan married the owner of a small tobacconist shop in Saigon. Working together, the young wife and her older spouse kept the business running, and eventually built up a local clientele to take the place of Mr Duong's former French customers. Although the work was hard and the hours long, Quan shouldered half the load, even after the couple's daughter, Hoa, was born. She worked in the evenings when her husband went to the cafes to gossip and drink coffee with his friends.

When I asked if she ever resented his behaviour, she seemed genuinely puzzled. What would she have to resent? That's what men in Vietnam did.

In 1964, Mr Duong was drafted to fight the Vietcong. A few months later, he was dead. Quan kept the shop going. She did very well. When Hoa married, Quan Duong hosted a wedding anyone could be proud of.

According to Quan, her son-in-law is nice enough. When it comes to bringing up children, however, both he and Hoa are lazy. For example, Quan points out, neither of them insists that the four-year-old learn Vietnamese; if he speaks to them in the English that he is learning from television, his parents often reply in English. Neither her daughter nor her son-in-law seems to understand her when she tries to stress to them that the boy and his new sister will never learn proper Vietnamese values unless they can speak the language. Quan leaves implicit the idea that nobody is better equipped to teach good behaviour than the childrens' grandmother – and she can't do it in English. It may already be too late for her little grandson. He is, in his grandmother's opinion, entirely too casual in the way he treats her. In Quan's opinion, her lazy son-in-law sets the boy a bad example. (The interpreter whispered to me later that the 'lazy' son-in-law holds down two jobs.) Duong Quan thinks the boy's father should be spending more time at home, an opinion that she can apparently hold even though it contradicts her equally strong feelings about her son-in-law's laziness.

Sometimes, Quan wonders if she did the right thing when she left her sisters, her friends, and her old way of life in Vietnam. However, she is plucky and determined not to let thoughts like that get the best of her. One of these days, she says, she will get a job and move out on her own. Then, they'll pay attention.

Other people in the RRP sample not only recovered from an initial experience of severe depression, but may have ended up psychologically fortified as a result of overcoming adversity.

Made Stronger by Circumstance

Le Quyen is intimidatingly efficient. Like many other people with the aura of being able to overcome anything, Quyen's veneer of inviolability conceals a core of personal vulnerability that she equates with weakness. The early years in Canada cracked Quyen's veneer.

In the fall of 1981, an immigration officer in Fir Lake, a northern British Columbia town, placed a long distance call to the Immigration Reception Centre in Vancouver. A would-be suicide, a young refugee woman, had appeared in the local hospital's emergency room. No one in the hospital spoke Vietnamese. When she saw staff trying to speak to her father, the young woman began to scream and cry hysterically. The immigration worker wanted to send his problem down to Vancouver.

After arriving by emergency air-lift, the young woman was taken directly to a mental health clinic. Throughout the assessment that followed, Quyen was tired and ashamed. She said that she had slit her wrist with a knife because there was nothing left to live for. Now that she had failed, the thin, petite refugee felt life would become even more difficult.

Le Quyen talked first to a psychiatrist, who wound up his interview by prescribing antidepressants. Afterwards, she spoke to a Vietnamese case worker. This woman's efforts and presence probably helped the young refugee more than the medications. The case worker found her new client a room in a residential hotel and some clothes to replace Quyen's soiled green sweatshirt and her too-large, red-checked slacks. When the worker left her alone on her first evening in Vancouver, Quyen was a little afraid; however, her new friend's telephone number tucked under her pillow made her feel better.

It is difficult to judge whether the worker's mothering response to her psychologically regressed client stemmed from professional know-how or from natural inclination. It doesn't really matter. Mothering was exactly what Quyen needed.

As a child, Quyen had been expected to be competent, hard-working, and self-reliant. When her galvanized exterior cracked, Quyen reverted to a nurture-hungry child. With a slightly sheepish smile stealing over her face, Quyen recalls the case worker's attentiveness, her patience during the long silences when her client found it hard to talk, and the hugs she offered when the pain of remembering made Quyen cry.

Quyen eventually began to talk. She began with stories about the Malaysian refugee camp where she had lived for more than a year. When they were trying to reassure Quyen that she was more capable than she gave herself credit for, the relief workers in the camp would say something like, 'You're small but you're tough.' That happened a lot. The handful of volunteers sponsored by international agencies could not keep up with the needs of the camp's forty thousand inhabitants. Their only hope lay in recruiting natural leaders among the refugees to help organize food distribution and to get medical care to people who needed it most. They picked Quyen. For some reason, people seemed to think she was strong and self-reliant. Quyen never understood how she could give that impression when, inside, she felt so frightened and so lonely.

Talking to the mental health worker about her family proved harder for Quyen because the memories made her so sad. Eventually, she did open up a bit. The eldest of eight children, she was a particularly good student – so good that her parents took the unusual step of encouraging her to pursue a medical degree. A successful manufacturer of jams and condiments, Quyen's father could afford to send a brilliant child to university. However, after Saigon fell to the Northern armies, money and position were no longer advantages. In the eyes of the new government, people like Quyen's father had ridden the backs of the poor to enjoy their privilege. To survive, the family sold off the treasures they had managed to hide from the North Vietnamese. Even so, the pattern of daily life became a monotonous struggle for food, occasionally punctuated by the terror of police interrogation. Quyen's father never returned from one of his interrogations. Instead, he was arrested and sent to a re-education camp. Several weeks later, the family learned that he had committed suicide. If the rest of them were to survive, they would have to escape.

One day, Quyen's aunt, her mother's younger sister, came to say good-bye. She, her husband, and their seven children had places on a fisherman's boat. Although Quyen's mother begged her sister to take her and her family with them, there was neither room on the boat for so many extra people nor enough money to buy places. In her mother's eyes, Quyen was not only the eldest, but the strongest and most ambitious of her children. She gave Quyen a gold brooch to bribe her way on board with her aunt's family.

It was hard for Quyen to leave her mother and the rest of her family, harder still since she had recently met a handsome young lawyer. Quyen's mother did not have to tell her daughter that she had an obligation to get her family out of Vietnam as soon as possible. By the time she left, Quyen had a secret fiancé and an additional promise to keep.

After spending a year in a refugee camp in Malaysia, Quyen came to Canada with her aunt and uncle's family. To gain Quyen's admission to the country, her aunt and uncle passed her off as their child. The family settled in Fir Lake, a mining town where no one else dressed like them or spoke their language. Like the other adults in the family, Quyen wanted to attend the government-sponsored English classes for refugees. However, her uncle had different plans. Since he was enrolled in the language program and his wife was working, it was only fitting that Quyen, their 'eldest daughter,' stay home to look after the younger children.

Quyen assumed the family would take turns: first, her uncle would complete the English-as-a-second-language program, then her aunt would enrol, and, after that, it would finally be Quyen's turn. Again, her uncle had different plans. To make use of her time in the evenings, when the family did not need her for babysitting, he found Quyen a job washing dishes in a restaurant. Going to language classes was out of the question. In her uncle's opinion, the only reason for learning English was to find work. Quyen already had a job – in fact, she had two – so there was no need to go to language classes.

Quyen didn't mind working hard. She didn't even mind being given the out-sized clothes no one else wanted. During the day, she was in the house with the children. In the evening, she washed dishes in the restaurant kitchen, and it really didn't matter what she wore. It did bother her that she never saw her wages, nor her share of the government allowance which the family received each month.

Asking her uncle for a share of the money turned out to be a mistake. In an outburst of anger, he screamed reproaches at her: Wasn't she properly housed and fed? Wasn't she secure with the family that had helped her get out of Vietnam? How could she ask for money when her adopted family had barely enough to get by each month?

Quyen might have hoped for support from her aunt, the closest substitute for a mother to whom she could turn. In retrospect, Quyen is able to recognize that her aunt was emotionally caught between a niece and a husband, each of whom, in a way, was right. Her aunt's only option was silence. Her small cousins were an even worse trial. Sensing their father's anger, the youngsters followed suit, turning on Quyen and doing whatever they could to make her feel she was an outsider.

Quyen next threatened to expose the truth about her identity to the authorities. She wanted to deal directly with the immigration officers so that she could claim her allowance independently of her uncle and his family. Quyen's uncle did not react as she expected. Instead of capitulating, or becoming even more hostile, he became frightened. He shared his fear with Quyen. If the government were to discover that the family had lied about Quyen, everyone could end up being deported.

The young woman realized her uncle was right. Acknowledging this fact meant there was no way out for her. Quyen wrote her mother a note apologizing for her failure to carry out her familial obligations. After leaving the note in her room, to be sent after her death, Quyen went to the kitchen, took out a knife, and slit her wrists. The wounds were not very deep. Before she could do herself too much harm, she passed out – probably more out of fear, pain, and exhaustion than from actual blood loss. When she woke up in the hospital emergency room where her family had rushed her, Quyen's only request was: 'Not go home.' Although she remembers saying it, Quyen is not sure whether she meant her uncle's house or Vietnam.

Who Recovers from Disorder and Who Does Not?

On reinterview in 1983, 19 per cent of the refugees suffering a depressive disorder in 1981 were still depressed. Some probably stayed depressed the entire time; others may have recovered, only to relapse one or more times during the intervening two years.

By comparison with the amount of effort expended on attempts to find the cause of depression, investigators have neglected the study of factors that might explain why some people recover without apparent after-effect from an episode of depression while, in other cases, the disorder tends to become chronic. The issue is important. Contrary to popular conception, many depressions are not evanescent. Each episode of illness increases the probability of recurrence and eventual chronicity (Angst, 1986; Bronisch et al., 1985).

Quyen may be one of the fortunate people who recover and remain healthy. When first interviewed in 1981, just days after her emergency air-lift to Vancouver, Quyen was clearly suffering a depressive disorder. On reinterview in 1983, she was well. During the two years between interviews, Quyen was able, at long last, to enrol in an English class. Her relationship with the case worker progressed to friendship, and finally to a point where she was calling the older woman 'my sister.' However, recovery came slowly. For the first year in Vancouver, Quyen felt chilled all the time, and it seemed to her that she caught colds more easily than other people. Although she cried less as time went by, and she began to regain the weight she had lost during her depressive illness, the young woman missed her mother and family. Talking to her new Canadian confidante usually helped when the loneliness became too hard to bear, or when she experienced the sudden abdominal attacks that her big sister told her Canadians called 'butterflies in the stomach.'

After she finished six months of government-sponsored English classes, Quyen found a day job at a delicatessen, and a night job as a waitress. Although her fourteen-to-sixteen-hour days were gruelling, having enough money to send back to Vietnam and to open a savings account that would eventually make it possible to sponsor her family to come to Canada made the effort seem worthwhile. Quyen even bought herself a television set, rationalizing this luxury as a way to help improve her English.

Quyen was a valuable employee. Not only did she work hard at the delicatessen, but she taught her employers how to make the delicious noodle and vegetable rolls wrapped in rice paper that people in Vietnam eat in the same way North Americans eat sandwiches. The Vietnamese 'salad rolls' quickly became one of the delicatessen's most popular items.

By 1983, Quyen had changed from a thin, mildly hypochondriacal, somewhat unkempt young refugee suffering from depression and panic attacks to a healthy, hard-working permanent resident of Canada helping, in a small way, to make her adopted country more cosmopolitan. Providing he or she can provide evidence of ability to provide financial support for ten years, a Canadian citizen or landed immigrant can apply to sponsor the application of a relative or fiancé for immigrant status. Quyen sent for her handsome lawyer late in 1983, and for her mother one year later.

Alcohol Abuse

During Nguyen Bich's trial, the prosecutor seemed to want to establish whether or not the defendant had been drinking the night he killed his common-law wife. For some reason, though, he dropped this line of questioning. Bich told me that he had been drinking.

According to popular belief, Asians don't drink. Although an obvious over-generalization, the belief has some basis in fact. According to most community surveys in North America, roughly 13.5 per cent of the adult population abuse alcohol at some point in their lives to the extent that they could be considered alcoholics (Robins et al., 1988). The comparative figure for Taiwan is about 7 per cent, and for Hong Kong, about 3 per cent (Helzer et al., 1990). People like Bich who violate the stereotype of the non-drinking, pacific Asian become the exception who prove the rule, the bad apples an immigration system should turn away if it were perfect. The fact is that Bich never touched alcohol when he was living in Vietnam. It was only after he came to Canada that he learned to crave the temporary relief drinking provided.

At the time of the first and second surveys of the Refugee Resettlement Project, only 1.5 per cent of the group were abusing alcohol. At the end of the refugees' first ten years in Canada, the rate remained exactly the same, 1.5 per cent.

In every society studied to date, men have been more likely than women to abuse alcohol (Helzer et al., 1990). The pattern was even more dramatic in the Southeast Asian refugee sample: there were no female alcohol abusers at any point during the ten-year study.

Men who drank were much more likely than non-abusers to be

depressed and anxious. Research reports (Helzer et al., 1990) suggest that the relationship between alcohol abuse and mental disorder is much weaker among North Americans than among the Southeast Asian refugees. Normative patterns may account for the differences. Social sanctions against drinking are much stronger in Southeast Asia than in North America. For young North American men, drinking is almost a rite of passage. In situations where drinking is rare, emotional distress may play a more powerful role in inducing alcoholism than under conditions in which the social situation and peer behaviour encourage it. Although such interpretations seem plausible, the very low rates of alcoholism among the RRP sample made it impossible to analyse the data in order to establish whether one pattern preceded the other. In other words, although it is possible that the Southeast Asian refugee men were drowning their unhappiness in alcohol, it is equally plausible that they were becoming depressed as a result of their drinking, or that adversity gave rise to both depression and alcoholism in men particularly susceptible to both.

Most of Canada's immigrants now come from Asia, and their rates of alcoholism, like those of the Southeast Asian refugees, are lower than the rates in the host society. Typically, however, after about ten years, new settlers take on the dominant society's bad habits, such as smoking and drinking (Beiser et al., 1997). Understanding whether the stress of resettlement or the seduction of wishing to emulate the host society or a combination of the two accounts for the assumption of unhealthy behaviours remains a research challenge with important public health implications. The fact that, in the RRP sample, men from rural areas of Southeast Asia were more likely than men from urban areas to be drinkers after they settled in Canada raises the interesting possibility that people experiencing the greatest amount of cultural dislocation may be the individuals most likely to pick up bad habits from their adopted society.

Post-Traumatic Stress Disorder

Even though the mental health professions were slow to acknowledge the proposition that trauma could affect individuals long after the experience, Western literature has, for hundreds of years, described people who suffered the psychological after-effects of combat, torture, and natural disasters. For example, Homer portrayed Ulysses returning from the wars psychologically scarred by his experiences (Figley, 1993; Shay, 1991). We predicted that many of the people in the RRP sample would be similarly scarred.

About 1 per cent of the general population suffers from PTSD (Davidson et al., 1991; Helzer, Robins, and McEvoy, 1987). In 1991, 7 per cent of the refugees in the RRP sample had symptoms of a magnitude sufficient to qualify for a diagnosis of PTSD (Gaind and Beiser, 1997). Chan Min Ran, sleepless and nervous in her chaotic apartment, is one of them. Min Ran's symptoms spill over: they interfere with her ability to get along with her children and with the outside world. The same is true for others with the disorder. Compared to other refugees in the RRP sample, the subjects with PTSD have more anxiety and depression, suffer higher rates of unemployment, are less likely to marry, go to the doctor more often, and are more likely to have to resort to welfare (Gaind and Beiser, 1997).

Research aimed at understanding PTSD has proliferated in recent years. Some investigators (Kinzie, 1986; Kinzie et al., 1986, 1989) have reported rates for Southeast Asian refugees as high as 50 per cent. Several factors probably explain the discrepancies between the extremely high rates reported by Kinzie and his colleagues, and the still high, but less dramatic, RRP findings. These factors include sample differences, time, and the dose-response relationship. Kinzie's sample consisted of Cambodian youth whose average age was seventeen; they, like Min Ran's son Thomas, would have been exposed to the stresses of war and of Pol Pot's regime when they were youngsters. Participants in the RRP study were older. Since traumatic stress is not only detrimental in itself but because it can interfere with critical phases of personality development (Garbarino and Kostelny, 1993; Goldson, 1993; Davidson and Smith, 1990), there is reason to predict that children exposed to war and violence might end up with higher rates of PTSD than similarly exposed adults. Time is the second factor. Research demonstrates that, the longer the time after exposure to stress, the greater the tendency for PTSD symptoms to fade (Solomon and Mikulincer, 1988). The RRP data on PTSD were collected after the refugees had been in Canada ten to twelve years, whereas the refugees in Kinzie and colleagues' study had been in the United States for approximately two and one-half years at the time they were studied. Dose and response is the third, and probably most important, part of the explanation. Kinzie and his colleagues based their PTSD estimates on studies of Cambodian refugees. If it were possible to quantify suffering, one could probably make a case that refugees from Cambodia, like Min Ran, suffered even more than refugees from the rest of Southeast Asia. The Refugee Resettlement Project sample contained very few survivors of Pol Pot's ferocity: the majority were from Vietnam and Laos.

To their great credit, organizations like Amnesty International and

Human Rights Watch have been sounding the alarm on vileness for many years. However, the problems often seemed remote, the horror diluted by distance. The arrival of refugees from Southeast Asia, Latin America, and the Middle East is bringing home to citizens of receiving countries such as Canada an increasing understanding of the prevalence of abuse, and of the amount of suffering it leaves in its wake.

SIX

The Stresses of Resettlement

Before coming to Canada, the exiles suffered oppression and loss in their home countries, fear and danger during flight, and the squalor and uncertainty of life in refugee camps. Figure 4.1 acknowledges that pre-migration stressors may have a lasting effect on refugee mental health. For a number of reasons, however, the Refugee Resettlement Project (RRP) interviews de-emphasized pre-migration experiences. First, we wanted to avoid scratching at psychic wounds that might be just beginning to heal in the air of newly acquired safety. Second, we were interested in producing results with practical or policy implications. Since receiving countries can do more to plan the reception of immigrants and refugees than to make up for what they experience before arriving, we focused our research on ways to improve hospitality rather than on documenting past adversities. Third, the comparatively few studies carried out prior to our own suggested that, in the early years of resettlement, post-migration stress affected mental health more profoundly than stresses occurring prior to the refugees' arrival in a new home (Westermeyer, Vang, and Neider, 1983b; Starr and Roberts, 1982).

The Past: Significant but Perhaps Evanescent

No matter what their individual histories, all the refugees in the RRP study shared one experience: on their way to Canada, they spent an average of twelve months incarcerated in refugee camps scattered throughout Southeast Asia (see fig. 3.1). Although none of the camps was pleasant, some were worse than others. During the years 1979 through 1981, the camps in Thailand were the worst in Southeast Asia, those in Hong Kong the best. The others – in the Philippines, Malaysia, and Indonesia – fell somewhere in between (Beiser, Turner, and Ganesan, 1989).

Most of the so-called Boat People escaped overland. Their destination was Thailand. The Thais soon became alarmed at the prospect of hundreds of thousands of people requiring shelter, sustenance, and supervision. In the hope of stemming the human tide, the Thai government began to make life as difficult as possible for the asylum seekers. One of their early acts was to press an abandoned jail called Sikhui back into service. As a refugee camp, Sikhui confined far more people than it had during its days as a prison. Refugees in the Thai camps quickly learned that complaints of being robbed or intimidated fell on deaf ears. A single woman was as likely to be raped by a guard as by another prisoner. Unlike refugees elsewhere, Thai camp inmates had no recourse to the world community. The national government did not permit agencies like UNHCR, UNICEF, the International Red Cross, Save the Children, or the World Council of Churches to work in the Thai camps as they did everywhere else.

During the late 1970s and early 1980s, Hong Kong was the only country to have 'open' camps. Under the open system, adults were permitted to leave the camps during the day in order to work in the crown colony's booming industries, and children could leave to attend school. The UN, together with international and local relief agencies, helped ensure that the refugees were reasonably well fed and clothed, as well as reasonably well protected. However, by the late 1980s, Hong Kong became an overly popular refugee destination, and camp conditions began to deteriorate. By the 1990s, camp conditions in Hong Kong were as bad as anywhere else.

The Malaysian, Indonesian, and Philippine camps were closed, overcrowded, and dangerous. Like the Thais, and unlike the people of Hong Kong (who initially profited from the influx of cheap and willing labour), the Malaysians, Indonesians, and Filipinos were hostile towards the Boat People. They feared that the stream of refugees would never end. Furthermore, they resented what they saw as a diversion of needed resources to the camp transients. However, the presence of international relief agencies helped ensure conditions superior to those prevailing in Thailand.

Although length of confinement in the camps did not predict postmigration adjustment, type of camp did. After resettling in Canada, the former inmates of the Thai camps had the highest levels of depression, Hong Kong the lowest, and internees from the other camps fell in between.

The demonstration of a 'dose-response' association enhances the credibility of theorized relationships between external events and mental health. For example, if there were a natural disaster an earthquake, one would expect the people closest to the epicentre to show the most psychic distress. Our refugee resettlement data showed that the worse the conditions in the camps in which they had been interned, the worse the refugees' mental health. However, this relationship prevailed only during the twelve-month period immediately following arrival. After that, the salience of camp internment apparently faded. By the end of the first year in Canada, the after-effects of refugee camp life on mental well-being disappeared (Beiser, Turner, and Ganesan, 1989).

Post-migration experiences, including unemployment and discrimination, had a more lasting impact.

Unemployment and Mental Health: The Early Years, 1981 and 1983

In answer to the question in our 1981 survey 'What worries you most at the present time?' one-third of the refugees responded: 'Jobs.'

Small wonder.

As do all but a privileged few, refugees have to work in order to make a living. Host countries are interested in putting refugees to work. High employment rates that suggest refugees are contributing their efforts and their taxes to the general good constitute evidence of success. Unemployment that eventually forces refugees onto the rosters of social assistance agencies challenges immigration and resettlement policies.

Work is important not only because it guarantees a pay cheque, but because its symbolic and social bonuses help maintain mental health. Work helps determine status, helps fill up and structure time, gives variety to life, and creates opportunities to make and meet friends (Warr, 1982). Unemployment is psychologically hazardous for everyone (Jahoda, 1982; Starr and Roberts, 1982; Dew, Bromet, and Schulberg, 1987; Kessler, Turner, and House, 1987a, 1987b; Bland et al., 1988). The effects of joblessness extend beyond the individual: unemployment can lead to increases in intrafamilial tensions, physical violence, separations, and divorce (Riegle, 1982; Clark and Clissold, 1982). It is therefore not surprising to learn that, in addition to condemning them to poverty, unemployment creates distress for refugees (Lin, 1986; Stein, 1986). Simply demonstrating that the links between unemployment and distress in the general population also hold true for refugees would amount to little more than an exercise in documenting the obvious. The Refugee Resettlement Project tried to go one step further. Rather than just studying *whether* unemployment was linked with depression in a refugee sample, we tried to investigate *why*.

Studies attempting to account for the relationship between joblessness and depression must deal with the question of sequencing: does losing a job lead to depression, or are depressed refugees less likely than the mentally healthy to find or keep jobs?

The RRP also investigated whether unemployment has the same meaning for refugees as for their hosts. Prior to coming to Canada and during the early years of resettlement, refugees undergo stress of a scale most people can hardly imagine. Does work have the same meaning for them as for people whose lives have never been shattered by war and horror? Do refugees feel it important to work because they hope to regain lost status, to find friends in the workplace, and to structure their time, or do worries about simple survival sweep aside all other considerations?

Because refugees typically experience high rates of unemployment during the early years of resettlement, investigating the effects of not working and the reasons underlying those effects are important. Of the refugees in the RRP sample, 68 per cent found jobs within the first year or two after they arrived in Canada; 22 per cent declared themselves unavailable; and 10 per cent reported that they had not been able to find work. The picture did not brighten over the ensuing two years. Many among the 22 per cent unavailable for work in 1981 – either because they were enrolled in government training programs or were at home with young children – shifted out of this category and were competing for jobs. By 1983, only 17 per cent classified themselves as homemakers, students, or too old to work. The 1983 unemployment rate climbed to a discouraging 18 per cent.

Although unemployment jeopardizes mental health, work does not guarantee psychological well-being. Underemployment – a situation in which, given a person's education or past jobs and experience, he or she is working at a lower-status job than might be expected – seems to create a mental health risk (Boman and Edwards, 1984; Vignes and Hall, 1979). Any hope refugees might have held about work as a route to regaining lost status had little chance of being fulfilled. About half the refugees who had jobs in 1981 felt that they were working at their appropriate ability level; the other half, that they were working below this level.

Table 6.1 describes the occupational background the refugees brought with them from Vietnam and compares this with the jobs they found during their first two years in Canada. The ten items listed as jobs in Vietnam

Table 6.1
Jobs Held in Vietnam and in Canada

Job In Vietnam	Percentage of Sample	Job In Canada	Percentage of Sample
Mechanic, electrician	11	Labourer	28
Owner, manager of business	10	Dishwasher	8
Seamstress, tailor	9	Carpenter	8
Teacher	7	Fruit picker	5
Labourer	4	Janitor	7
Secretarial worker	4	Seamstress, tailor	7
Jeweller	3	Mechanic	3
Fisherman	3	Other	34
Military service	3		
Cook, baker	3		
Other	43		
TOTAL	100	TOTAL	100

account for 57 per cent of the sample. The remaining 43 per cent of the refugees worked in so many different fields that listing their jobs would result in a dauntingly long table. Choice in Canada was nowhere near as great: seven categories covered the jobs that about two-thirds of the refugees were fortunate enough to find in the early years of resettlement.

Table 6.1 documents the refugees' occupational slide. During their early years in Canada, Vietnamese, Laotians, and Cambodians who owned and managed businesses at home or who were nurses, teachers, mechanics, and electricians became labourers, seamstresses, and dishwashers. The sociologists Bernard Blishen and Hugh McRoberts have developed a scale which assigns a prestige score to an exhaustive list of Canadian jobs (Blishen and McRoberts, 1976). According to this scale, university professors and physicians receive a score of 76; schoolteachers, about 70; owners and managers of small businesses, about 56; secretaries and typists, about 30; and labourers, dishwashers, and domestics, about 27. The scale helps to quantify the refugees' downward occupational drift. Refugees with less than eight years of formal education were holding Canadian jobs that were, on average, eight points lower in occupational prestige than the ones they had in Vietnam – about the distance between a construction foreman and a labourer. Better-educated refugees, who tended to have held higher-prestige jobs than the poorly educated in Vietnam, experienced an even greater drop in job status. The difference in prestige ranking between their jobs in the home country and in Canada, about thirteen points, was a statistically greater drop than the slide experienced by less-educated people. Thirteen points is roughly the prestige-rank difference between a teacher and a fruit-stand owner.

Employability

Most investigations into the reasons underlying refugee unemployment focus on how individual attributes like age, sex, education, and fluency in the language of the majority culture affect job opportunity. According to popular opinion, the young and the old have more trouble getting work than people in their middle years, and male sex, good education, and ability to speak the language of the host country all confer advantages in the job market (Canadian Task Force, 1988a).

According to RRP findings, younger refugees had an easier time finding jobs than older; Chinese had an occupational advantage over ethnic Vietnamese, Laotians, or Cambodians; and people who spoke English well were more likely to be employed than those with inferior language skills (Beiser, Johnson, and Turner, 1993). In 1981, shortly after the refugees first arrived, gender, level of education, and length of time in Canada did not affect employability. Two years later, however, men were more likely to be working than women, better-educated people enjoyed an occupational advantage over the less well educated, and the longer people had been in the country, the more likely they were to be working.

Expressed in terms of odds, a Chinese refugee was 1.5 times more likely to be working than a non-Chinese. Vancouver's Chinatown was a job resource, particularly for Chinese refugees and most particularly for poorly educated Chinese women who spoke little or no English. Unfortunately, employment in this economic enclave tended to be poorly paid and dead-end, offering no chance for advancement (Johnson, 1988).

In the Canadian population as a whole, youth between the ages of fifteen and twenty-four suffer higher rates of unemployment than older people. The job pattern in the Refugee Resettlement Project sample was the reverse: unemployment among refugees forty-five and older was twice as high as for people between the ages of fifteen and forty-four (see also Samuel, 1987). Why the difference? The refugees were willing to accept any kind of employment. For the jobs they were most likely to get – unskilled labour in factories or restaurants (Chan, 1987) – the stamina of youth probably acted as an advantage. In a job market with more opportunity, the experience of age might have counted for more. Many people have asserted that female and poorly educated refugees have a harder time finding jobs than males or the well educated. Our data suggest that this became true only after the refugees had been in Canada for a few years. One possible interpretation is that, in the early years, neither gender nor education bias affects selection for the menial jobs open to refugees. However, as the newcomers' aspirations increase, sex and education begin to make a difference in a male-dominated, education-valuing society (Chan, 1987; Samuel, 1987).

Studies examining the relationship between joblessness and depression must deal with the question of sequencing: does losing a job make people depressed, or are depressed refugees less likely than their psychologically healthy peers to find or keep jobs?

In some cases, sequencing could logically proceed in only one direction. For example, an individual's age and sex obviously predate employment and could not possibly be caused by it. By contrast, English fluency is a reciprocal variable, one of a class of factors in which direction is difficult to establish. Although command of English may determine employability, the reverse sequence is equally tenable: people who are working may be more likely to learn English than people who are not employed. Data presented in table 6.2 suggest that, in the early years of resettlement, the latter is the more likely sequence.

For the analyses in this table, we drew on the 1981 and 1983 interviews. At both interviews, we asked the refugees to rate their command of English on a three-point scale. A score of 1 meant they spoke no English; 2 meant a little English; and 3, a feeling of being in good command of the new language.

During the two years between interviews, the refugees' scores on this scale did not improve as much as one might have hoped. It was possible, nevertheless, to calculate an improvement index by subtracting the scores at wave one from the scores at wave two. To examine the association between employment and English fluency, we first excluded the 'not availables,' then divided the remainder of the sample into four different groups: UN-UN, meaning people who were not working in 1981 or in 1983; EM-EM, for people working at both times; UN-EM, for people unemployed in 1981 who had found jobs by 1983; and EM-UN, for people who were working in 1981 but who, by 1983, had lost their jobs. For each of these employment groups, table 6.2 lists the average change in English fluency, a positive score indicating improvement, a negative score indicating actual deterioration in language ability.

The consistently employed (EM-EM) and the people who succeeded in

Table 6.2
Employment and English Fluency

Employment Group	n	Mean Change	sd
1. UN-EM	79	0.241	0.068
2. UN-UN	65	−0.015	0.089
3. EM-EM	489	0.172	0.026
4. EM-UN	167	0.054	0.043

Note: Post-hoc comparisons using Student-Newman-Keuls procedure: EM-EM = UN-EM > UN-UN = EM-UN at $p < .05$

getting jobs (UN-EM) improved their command of English during the two years between interviews. People who lost their jobs (EM-UN) showed virtually no change in English ability, while the never employed (UN-UN) had a slight loss in fluency. In other words, learning English was more likely an effect, than a cause, of employment.

Refugees' answers to a question about English at work support this inference. In 1981, two-thirds of the respondents said they had to use English 'sometimes' or 'often' at work. By 1983, this proportion rose to 75 per cent. Apparently, by 1983, refugees who found work were advancing into positions requiring more English. Refugees (mainly Chinese) working for like-ethnic employers were an exception. They learned little, if any, English during their first few years in Canada (Johnson, 1988). If, as some authors have suggested (Stein, 1979; Johnson, 1988), learning the host country's language is key to occupational advancement, the short-term advantage of like-ethnic employment may have an important downside.

Canadian institutions were not very effective in helping refugees go to work. Most of the Southeast Asians found their first jobs either on their own or through informal networks of friends, families, or sponsors. Only a handful received help from Canada Manpower, the agency offering formal governmental assistance. Even though one might expect that as time went on, refugees would learn more about Canadian institutions, increased use of facilities did not follow increased knowledge. With the passage of the years, refugees used Canada Manpower less and less.

Job-training programs did not help as much as they should have. Of the people in a training program in 1981, 71 per cent were working in 1983. By comparison, only 56 per cent of the refugees who had not received training went on to find work by 1983 (chi square = 19.95, DF 2, $p < .001$). Since job training apparently improved employment prospects, it seems sad that relatively few people got into training programs. In 1981, only 12 per cent of all the refugees had been in a job program. By 1983, the percentage had increased only slightly, to 17 per cent.

Does Unemployment Cause Depression?

Are individuals the pawns or masters of their fate? Social science theorists tend to favour the first formulation. With respect to employment and mental health, a typical formulation would hold that poor economic conditions or discrimination in the job market – forces that might have made it difficult for the Southeast Asian refugees either to find jobs or to retain them – set in motion the process leading to elevated rates of depression. However, a reverse sequence is equally feasible. If they make a poor impression in a job interview, depressed people may be passed over in favour of another applicant. When depressed people do find a job, their psychological problems can interfere with their performance sufficiently to lead to dismissal. The issue of what causes what is more than theoretical. Unemployment is a problem not just for refugees and their families, but for the countries that admit them. Although Canada provides job training and employment counselling for refugees, solutions to the problem of joblessness remain elusive. If mental health were to prove a risk factor for unemployment, rather than vice versa, that particular sequencing might direct resettlement and employment agencies to pay more explicit attention to the mental health of their clients than they have in the past.

Refugee Resettlement Project data are provocative. The mental health of refugees who were laid off or fired declined. People who found jobs or who were re-employed improved. Although depressed people had no more trouble finding jobs than non-depressed, they experienced more difficulty holding onto them (Beiser, Johnson, and Turner, 1993).

Table 6.3, comparing levels of depression among four groups, illustrates these points. The first group, UN-UN, were unemployed in 1981 and again in 1983; at the opposite extreme, EM-EM were working at both times. The UN-EM were unemployed at time one but had found work by time two, while the EM-UN were people working at time one who had been fired or laid off by time two. If depression militated against finding a job, one would expect the UN-EM to have had lower depression scores at time one than the UN-UN. However, this was not the case: both groups had the same levels of depression in 1981, and the scores for both groups

Table 6.3
Employment Groups and 1981 Depression Scores

Group	n	Mean	sd
1. UN-EM	70	25.8	5.9
2. UN-UN	81	26.5	7.0
3. EM-EM	511	22.9	5.5
4. EM-UN	176	24.1	6.0

Note: Because of missing data, the numbers of subjects in tables 6.2 and 6.3 do not match. In a few cases, interviewers missed questions about depression; in others, they neglected to ask about English fluency.
Post-hoc comparisons using Student-Newman-Keuls procedure: UN-UN = UN-EM > EM-UN > EM-EM

unemployed at time one were higher than the EM-EM or EM-UN people, who were working. However, the EM-UN, the group who lost their jobs between 1981 and 1983, were more depressed than people in the EM-EM category, who managed to hold onto their jobs. In other words, although depressed people do not suffer a disadvantage in finding employment, they are more likely than the non-depressed to lose their jobs.

Vinh Thuy's story breathes life into the statistics in table 6.3. His diffidence, social awkwardness, and choppy speech suggest an inner tension to which Vinh readily admits. He does feel much better, however, than he did during his first year in Canada, when, going from job to job, he frustrated himself and everyone who tried to help him. The problem was that people were finding him jobs in construction or in gardening, and Vinh Thuy could not stand to be outdoors. In Vietnam, Vinh spent two years in a re-education camp, working in the fields. To amuse themselves, the camp guards played a game in which they would shoot at random at the inmates. Whoever killed the most prisoners was the winner. Vinh's agoraphobia, or fear of open spaces, is one of the legacies of his prison experience. After he finally told his story to a sensitive job counsellor, Mr Thuy was assigned a job sorting mail inside a post office. He is still working there.

Almost everyone, most of all the refugees themselves, wants to see newcomers succeed in their new home. If psychological disorder creates not only internal misery but the risk of losing a job, it becomes a problem of interest not only to psychiatrists but to anyone concerned about resettling refugees.

Underemployment and Mental Health

To be unemployed is to risk becoming depressed. However, work does not guarantee mental health. Underemployment, working at a level below what one might expect based on education or previous experience, is a potent stress for members of the majority culture.

Since underemployment seems the inevitable lot of most refugees, we were concerned about investigating its mental health effects in this population. In studies reported in more detail elsewhere (Beiser, Johnson, and Turner, 1993; Edwards, 1994), we constructed a scale measuring the fit between current job level and what would be expected based on educational background. A strong and statistically significant correlation between this scale and levels of depression among the Vancouverites demonstrated that working below one's level is a salient mental health stressor. The greater the gap between expected job level and actuality, the higher the level of depression. The findings did not hold true for the refugees. Although refugees may not have liked working below their level of skill, the discrepancy did not jeopardize their mental health.

Employment in 1991: Time Makes a Difference

The longer refugees stay in resettlement countries, the more likely they are to make a positive contribution to the economy (Stein, 1979; Caplan, Whitmore, and Choy, 1989). This trend held true for the Southeast Asian refugees in Canada. Figure 6.1 documents the good news.

Refugee unemployment rates dropped from 10 per cent in 1981 to 8 per cent in 1991, a rate lower than the national average. Although the refugees were not explicitly selected for their economic potential, as they would have been under Canada's immigrant selection program, their pattern of economic adaptation is very similar. According to Canadian economic analyses, it takes immigrants ten to twelve years to reach their full economic potential; when that happens, immigrants tend to outperform the indigenous population (deVoretz, 1995). These data should be reassuring not only to refugees discouraged by early frustrations but also to members of the host country. The rhetoric of intolerance notwithstanding, refugees do not come to countries like Canada intending to become parasites. The longer they stay, the more likely they are to contribute to the general economic good.

By 1991, the link between unemployment and depression was even

Figure 6.1   Labour Force Activities: The First Decade

Percentage

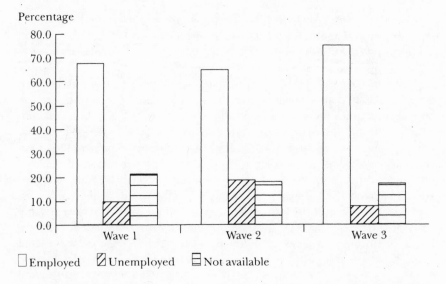

☐ Employed   ⧄ Unemployed   ⊟ Not available

stronger than it had been at earlier periods (Beiser, Hou, and Hyman, n.d.). Part of the reason may be that refugees who were not working after a decade in Canada were becoming part of a chronically unemployed, poor, and mentally unhealthy underclass. If this were the case, previous unemployment should have predicted future unemployment. However, according to RRP results, unemployment in 1981 and/or in 1983 was a very poor predictor of unemployment in 1991. Reference group comparison provides another possible explanation for the increasingly strong link between joblessness and poor mental health. According to this concept, the individual measures the adequacy of his or her achievements according to a norm provided by a reference group. For the refugees, particularly in the early years of resettlement, the most likely reference group was other refugees. The fact that, during the early years, everyone was struggling to find and keep jobs may have dulled the edge of disappointment for the unemployed. After ten years, however, most of the refugees were working. During the economic boom British Columbia was experiencing in 1991, former refugees who were not employed were deviant, not only in comparison with majority culture Canadians, but with respect to most of their fellow refugees as well.

Discrimination

In 1981, visible minorities accounted for 5 per cent of the population of Canada. By 1996, they had increased to 11 per cent.

National diversification can be a threat to inter-group harmony. In the past, immigrants and refugees in Canada have been frequent targets of ethnoculturally based discrimination (Avery, 1979; Thompson, 1996; Henry et al., 1995; Lieberson, 1982). However, in the 1960s – long before the Southeast Asian refugees arrived – Canadians had begun articulating the goal of a racism-free society. This vision was embedded, for example, in Canada's 1971 multiculturalism policy, as well as in more recent legislation such as the Canadian Charter of Rights and Freedoms of 1982, and the Multiculturalism Act of 1988. Although conceptual and methodological flaws limit its interpretability, a national survey (Palmer, 1997) suggests that contemporary Canadians portray themselves as a remarkably tolerant people. It would be comforting to think that, since the 1960s, goodwill, policy, and legislation have succeeded in wiping racism off the face of Canada. However, the evidence suggests that a meaner portrait still hangs in the Canadian attic. Racism in Canada is more elusive and subtle than it was heretofore. Rather than disappearing, racism has gone underground (Hamberger and Hewstone, 1997; Meertens and Pettigrew, 1997; Pettigrew and Meertens, 1995; Head, 1975; Henry et al., 1995).

The proposition that discrimination damages mental health seems so reasonable, and has been asserted so often, that it has become part of received wisdom (Canadian Task Force, 1988a; Lieberson, 1982; Portes, 1984). A search of the literature, however, reveals that rhetoric and admonition are much more common than research. This will not do. We need to know a good deal more about the extent to which immigrants and refugees who are members of visible minorities encounter discrimination, the methods they choose to handle it, and the mental health consequences both of exposure to this stressor and of coping strategies for dealing with it.

The 1991 RRP interviews contained a measure of perceived discrimination. Definitions of discrimination vary enormously. Ideology, politics, and experience shape definitions of discrimination and account for variations among them. However, research demands unambiguous, easily understood, and replicable measures. For the RRP study, we asked the following question: 'Some people have experienced discrimination, for example, being looked down upon, insults about one's race, being passed over for a promotion, because they belong to a particular racial group rather than because they lack English or other skills. *In Canada, have you been discriminated against because of your race?'*

One in four of the Southeast Asians answered 'yes.' Southeast Asian refugees taking part in a U.S. study (Roberts, 1988) reported higher rates of discrimination. Context may help explain the differences. Southeast Asian refugees are in the United States as a result of a bitter and humiliating period in that country's history. By contrast, Canada's response to the 'Boat People' crisis became a source of national pride, culminating in the 1986 United Nations award for humanitarianism.

As a group, the Southeast Asians in the RRP reported fewer experiences of discrimination than other groups, notably blacks and South Asians, sometimes have (Breton, 1978; Head, 1981; Wortley, 1996). Although there is no one-to-one link between discriminatory acts and the subjective perception of discrimination (Roberts, 1988), racism is more than subjective perception. In a study comparing black, Asian, and white perceptions of inequities in the criminal justice system, blacks were much more likely than the other two groups to report police discrimination against them. Perception accorded with objective reality: black men were twice as likely as Chinese or white males to be subjected to random police stops while driving a car, walking on the street, or idling in a shopping mall (Wortley, 1996).

We asked each of the refugees who reported at least one experience of discrimination where the experience had taken place, and what forms it had assumed. Most people reported that they had experienced subtle on-the-job discrimination.

Refugees with the strongest investment in their heritage culture were the most likely to report experiences with discrimination. Although this finding makes intuitive sense, another of the RRP findings seems initially counter-intuitive. The most highly acculturated refugees – respondents who had received some education in Canada and who used mainstream media the most – were the most likely to report discrimination. These results counter the claims by other researchers that participation in the host culture militates against feelings of discrimination (Aguirre, Seanz, and Hwang, 1989; Gordon, 1964). There are two likely explanations. First, the most highly educated refugees were probably the most likely to rise occupationally. By so doing, they may have become a threat to well-placed individuals and thereby elicited their animosity (Castles, Booth, and Wallace, 1984). It is, after all, easier to be tolerant of people who are different when they are invisible, than when they become competitors for jobs and positions. The second likely explanation is that English-speaking refugees who could read the majority culture's newspapers, watch its TV programs, and listen to its radio broadcasts were equipped to recognize the larger society's often subtle and elusive discriminatory messages.

Confronted with discrimination, the Southeast Asians in the RRP sample were more likely to cope with it through passive avoidance than through active confrontation (Beiser et al., n.d.). They were, in other words, more likely to choose what has been called emotion-focused coping, such as accepting unpleasant experience as a fact of life and not reacting, over problem-focused strategies, such as arguing or initiating formal complaints. Cultural conditioning probably helps account for the choice of passive over active coping. North American ideologies tend to value active coping and to devalue passive strategies for dealing with conflict. However, cultures that are more collectively oriented than North America's show a preference for resolving interpersonal conflicts with a view to mitigating tensions while preserving relationships (Gabrielidis et al., 1997; Kuo, 1995). Commentators have suggested that phenomenological reality is a product of the individual's inner state, on the one hand, and objective reality, on the other. Confronted with an uncomfortable phenomenological reality, Westerners often strive to change the objective reality. In very general terms, Asians are more likely to alter the inner state: 'Certain problems are held to be best handled by indirection and internal change' (Reynolds, 1976, cited in Aldwin, 1994, p. 111).

Situation is an equally important explanation for choosing passive coping. Many visible minority groups avoid active confrontation because they feel that the larger system does not welcome troublemakers (Feagin, 1991; Henry, 1978).

Along with a few other studies in the literature (Dion, Dion, and Pak, 1992; Moritsugu and Sue, 1983), the RRP has produced empirical evidence that discrimination has a damaging effect on mental health (Noh et al., n.d.). The results also demonstrate that emotion-focused coping mitigates the damage, while problem-focused coping has no effect. Ethnic identification played an interesting role in the mediation of distress. The more strongly identified an individual was with his or her heritage culture, the stronger the protective effect of emotion-focused coping.

The fact that minority groups feel themselves to be the objects of racially based discrimination is a problem for societies as well as for individuals. For countries like Canada in which national values dictate that no level of discrimination is tolerable, the fact that one-quarter of the Southeast Asians reported such experiences is morally discomforting. Perceptions of racially based discrimination also threaten social cohesion. Political scientists (e.g., Ignatieff, 1993) have pointed out that social cohesion in a civic society is possible only if the subcultural groups who make it up feel they are equally protected and have equal opportunity. If people who make up a nation do not feel equally safe within it, there is a danger of reversion to tribalism.

Since they were admitted as refugees, Canada had no right to expect the Southeast Asians to contribute to the economy. The moral and legal obligation flowed one way – from Canada to the people we agreed to protect. Nevertheless, within a decade the Southeast Asian refugees were contributing to Canada by working and paying taxes. Instead of feeling celebrated for their accomplishments, one-quarter of the refugees felt they had experienced discrimination; furthermore, the more they attempted to integrate by learning the language and participating in the wider society, the more strongly they felt the discrimination.

Moral imperative dictates the elimination of racially based discrimination. In addition, discrimination hurts its victims, militates against their ability to contribute to their adopted society, and threatens social peace. Perhaps it will never be possible to totally eradicate discrimination, but it has no place in a civilized society.

What about the Future?

Although other investigators have also found that post-migration stresses such as unemployment and discrimination affect mental health more profoundly than the traumas of uprooting, flight, and incarceration, the findings do not offer grounds for complacency. Every study of Vietnamese refugee resettlement, including our own, has focused on mental health during the early years of resettlement. Their tragic histories may yet return to haunt the memories and endanger the mental health of the survivors from Southeast Asia.

What is true about stresses from the past may prove equally true for more contemporary problems. For example, underemployment does not seem to affect refugee mental health during the first decade of resettlement. During my in-depth interviews, the refugees explained that hope for a better future for their children made up for the frustrations of knowing that personal fulfilment might never be possible. One cannot help wondering whether this rationalization will continue to satisfy people if opportunity continues to elude them over the years. As they become more 'Canadianized,' will their aspirations broaden, so that they once again match what they were when life was at its best?

Questions like these transcend the data in this book, and point up the limitations of short-term studies of refugee adaptation. Most analyses of migrant resettlement are one-time investigations, static snapshots from which researchers try to infer patterns of adaptation. By transposing three snapshots of the refugees, one taken shortly after arrival, the next two years afterwards, and the last after a decade in Canada, we have tried to move beyond the static, to create a moving picture documenting the efforts of people struggling to create lives in new places. Resettlement, however, is probably a lifelong process. Even our ten-year documentary is too short.

SEVEN

Social Support and Mental Health

Social support is difficult to categorize. Although figure 4.3 describes family and significant social groupings as social resources, it would be equally logical to call their absence the stress of loneliness.

Debates about categories are of no help to Nguyen Bich, the Vietnamese carpenter. Had he been able to bring his wife and children to Canada, he would never have met Anh My and ended up killing her. In theory, tragedies like Bich's should have been preventable. According to government guidelines, family unification is the cornerstone of immigration policy. Under the Immigration Act, any Canadian or permanent resident who is at least eighteen years of age can sponsor a spouse, fiancé, or dependent child to come to this country. The only caveat is that sponsors have to demonstrate that they can provide ten years of financial support for the persons they propose to bring to Canada. As Nguyen Bich quickly learned, putting aside enough cash to convince immigration authorities that he had the means to support his Vietnamese family for ten years was a severe test of resources and endurance. Conflicting definitions of family add to the refugees' problems. Although Canadian law is based on the assumption that 'family' means spouse and children, the Southeast Asian definition is wider. It includes parents, grandparents, and others consigned, in Western terms, to the more distant category of 'relatives.'

Social Support and Post-Traumatic Stress Disorder

According to the Refugee Resettlement Project (RRP) data, the availability of social support during the refugees' early years in Canada militated against the later occurrence or persistence of post-traumatic stress disorder (PTSD) (Gaind and Beiser, in unpub.). Support from others at critical phases of resettlement may either help protect against the emergence of later disorder, or facilitate recovery in cases in which a disorder has already occurred. Studies of children and adolescents exposed to war and violence are consistent with RRP findings; children with supportive social environments suffer fewer psychological consequences than their socially deprived counterparts (Losel and Bliesner, 1990; Chen, Kaspar, and Noh, 1997; Kaspar, Chen, and Noh, 1997). If disorder has already occurred, social support may help prevent chronicity.

Social Support and Other Forms of Psychopathology

Nguyen Bich, the twenty-seven-year-old carpenter who escaped from Vietnam, missed the wife and two young children he had left behind.

During the recession of 1982, the fish-processing plant where Bich was working laid off almost half its employees. One of the proverbial 'last to be hired, first to be fired,' Bich became an unemployment statistic. Too proud to go on welfare or on unemployment insurance, which, in his mind, were one and the same, Bich moved into a cheap, one-bedroom apartment that he shared with two other recently arrived Vietnamese. With a few tools he managed to buy, the former carpenter started to make and sell name-plates and bird-houses. All the money he made went into a common pool which Bich and his companions used to pay the rent and to buy food. Ashamed that he had no money to enclose with the letters he sent home, Bich stopped writing altogether.

When Bich heard that Ontario was recovering more quickly from the recession than British Columbia, he got on a bus for Toronto. Within a few weeks, he found a job. By putting together his pay as a night watchman with the money he was earning from his carpentry sideline, Bich felt he could soon start sending money home again. Just about then, he got a letter from his wife telling him she had divorced him and married someone else.

When a friend introduced him to Anh My, Bich was ready for some companionship. His friend told him that My had a hot temper and that she was flashy to the point of being vulgar. He cautioned Bich not to get serious. Despite the warnings, the overly shy Bich found Anh My's gregarious, breezy manner appealing. Looking back, he thinks it was she who decided they should live together, and he is certain that it was My's idea that they leave Toronto to go back to Vancouver. She was always complaining about the cold in Toronto. Even the fur coat he bought her with money he should have sent back to his former wife, his children, and his brothers in Vietnam didn't help.

Back in Vancouver, the couple moved into a furnished apartment near Chinatown. Bich found a job washing dishes on the night shift in a Chinese restaurant. Although he got less than the official minimum wage, he was afraid to complain because jobs were still scarce. When he first tried to suggest to Anh My that she look for work, she told him she needed time to settle in to her new surroundings. Two months later, when he raised the subject again, she screamed at him to mind his own business.

Bich was beginning to feel desperate about money. He never seemed to be able to save any. A man he met at church told him about a second-mortgage-partnership plan that would double Bich's money in a few months' time. After Bich gave the man four hundred dollars, he seemed to see less and less of his 'friend' at church. Soon, the man became so evasive that Bich began to worry that he would never see his investment again. He never did.

Even though he wasn't giving My any money for clothes, it seemed to Bich that his common-law wife kept cramming more and more flashy dresses into their small closet. Since he didn't want to start a fight, Bich never asked where My got the clothes or why she needed them. Because he worked practically every night, Bich rarely went out with his wife. When they did go out, he tried to avoid places where they might run into other Vietnamese. At the time, the young carpenter didn't analyse his reluctance to see his countrymen. He probably did not even think about the reasons until I asked him why during our first interview in his jail cell. All he could come up with then was that he felt uncomfortable because people seemed to be smirking.

A Vietnamese man who knew the couple slightly told me that, if Bich had left Anh My, everything would have turned out alright. Everyone who knew the pair wondered how Bich could allow himself to be fooled and to continue to let My lead him around by the nose.

By the time the couple had been in Vancouver for about a year, their relationship had seriously deteriorated. One day, Anh My discovered that Bich had been secretly sending some of his pay to his former wife in Vietnam. She yelled at him and called him names until he promised to start turning over his entire pay cheque to her. A few days later, My called a provincial social service agency to complain that Bich had been threatening to kill her. Anh My went to stay in a women's shelter for a few days while the police investigated the situation. Although My dropped her charges and went back to live with Bich, he felt hurt and humiliated. Bich became sad, lost interest in food, found it difficult to concentrate, and began to brood about what Anh My had said about him. Sometimes, when he woke up in the middle of the night, as he was now prone to do, he saw a shadow. My told him she had seen the same shadow. She thought it was her dead sister. After she told him that, the shadow became more distinct. It now looked more and more like a woman dressed in a long white dress. Whatever the shadow was, Bich was sure it meant evil.

The situation seemed more and more hopeless. One evening, Bich got so depressed that he went to a drugstore, bought as many sleeping pills as he could, came home, swallowed them, and lay down to die. When she came in later that night, My tried to wake him. She couldn't, so she called an ambulance. After a few days, the hospital released Bich with advice to get help from a local mental health clinic.

Bich soon discovered a new problem. Anh My began moaning in her sleep and calling out Caucasian men's names. Once he distinctly heard her say in English, 'Massage me Charley honey.' Asking My what was going on did not help. She told Bich he was imagining things, maybe even going crazy.

One Saturday night, Bich came home from the restaurant about 2:00 a.m. Anh My wasn't there. Bich couldn't sleep. Instead, he paced around the apartment smoking some of his wife's cigarettes. When she finally did get home, My was wearing one of her flashy new dresses and she had liquor on her breath. She wouldn't tell Bich where she had been. Instead, she laughed at him and told him he wasn't a man because he couldn't buy anything for her.

A film came down over Bich's eyes. He saw the woman in the long white dress. For the first time, she spoke to him. She said, 'Kill, kill.'

The next thing Bich remembers is lying on the bed next to Anh My. She had a pillow over her face and she wasn't breathing. Bich's hands were holding the edges of the pillow down. Bich swallowed all the pills he could find in the apartment. He wrote two letters, one to his former wife and one to the family who were caring for Anh My's two daughters in Vietnam. Before sealing the envelopes, he enclosed half his money in each. Then, he got into bed with My and fell asleep, expecting to die. Instead, he woke up in a hospital.

For whatever reason, Bich's lawyer did not mount a temporary insanity defence. Finding the young Vietnamese carpenter guilty of second degree murder, the judge sentenced him to a minimum of ten years in prison.

When I first visited Bich, he was in jail waiting to be transported to a medium security prison. The day before, he had tried to hang himself in his cell. Fortunately – at least for the justice system – Bich's shoelaces broke. Bich didn't feel fortunate at all. He was feeling miserable and wishing he had never come to Canada. As bad as life in Vietnam had been, it now seemed far preferable to what he had found in his new home. Although he was poor in Vietnam, Bich said he now realized life was better there because it was '… simple. I earned money and that was it.' Bich was worried about his prison sentence. It wasn't only the disgrace that worried him. He also felt it his responsibility to provide for the children in Vietnam – his own and My Anh's. How could a prisoner hope to do that?

He kept questioning how this terrible thing could have happened. In his own words:

> I ask myself whether I was a bad husband. I worked, I did everything my wife wanted me to do. I felt that a husband and wife should take care of one another and love one another. Sometimes, though, when I got back from work late, I would have no meal and I would have to wash my own clothes.

After my first visit with Bich, I spoke to one of the prison guards about him. Although I have no reason to believe that the guard was anything but a fair-minded man who felt as badly as I did about how things had turned out, we differed in where we found blame. I was inclined to think that the system of immigration and resettlement services had failed the young man our government had undertaken to protect. The guard, however, had some questions about his prisoner. He told me Bich was odd. For example, he always kept to himself and he never looked people in the eye. Through an interpreter, Bich told me he felt that people were angry with him because he had disappointed them. He also felt that they became impatient with his faltering English. Bich did not have to tell me that, in his culture, to look an authority figure in the eye would have been considered arrogant. Police guards in post-1975 Vietnam were not inclined to treat arrogance lightly.

The guard also told me that Bich kept copies of girly magazines in his bunk and that he had found razor slashes through some of the pictures, especially around the women's breasts and vaginas. When I asked Bich about this on a subsequent visit, he said that the magazines had already been in the cell when he arrived.

Passivity may not be the only quirk in Bich's nature. Perhaps, as the guard seems convinced, the young carpenter harbours some sexually sadistic traits. I could not, however, help thinking that early reunification with his wife and two children might have led his story to a different conclusion. As Bich knew only too well, the ten-year-support requirement translated into evidence of a steady job and money in the bank, two things he did not have.

Having already invested in Bich and others like him, it would seem a reasonable gamble for Canada to relax its guidelines for family reunification in order to allow young men, women, and children to be together during the period in their lives when they need togetherness most.

If Bich's psychiatric disorder could not have been prevented by a change in federal policy, were opportunities missed to mitigate its consequences? Given the chronic shortage of time in hospitals, together with the lack of staff equipped to help young refugees and immigrants from exotic cultures, Bich's perfunctory discharge comes as no surprise. Neither does his failure to follow the recommendation to go to a mental health clinic. Two-thirds of all Asian patients referred to mental health services from hospital emergency rooms never comply (Sue, 1983; Sue and Morishima, 1982). Appropriate referral and follow-through might have helped ensure that Bich received medication to help with his depression, and counselling would probably have helped him either separate from My Anh or learn how to live with her.

It is not altogether impossible that an astute diagnostician would have discovered that Anh My had mental health problems of her own. She did, after all, see even more vivid visions than Bich's. The story of their shared hallucination has some of the character of a classical 'folie à deux' in which a dominant personality (in this case, Anh My) influences the perceptions of a more passive partner. My's suggestion helped convert Bich's fleeting images into a formed hallucination of a woman in white. Anh My's temper tantrums, her irritability, and her periods of gregariousness, promiscuity, and heavy spending were all behaviours compatible with psychiatric syndromes like bipolar affective disorder or behavioural disturbances brought on by substance abuse. During one of our talks about Anh My, Bich suddenly remembered that, during the most tranquil period of their life together, when they were living in Toronto, My was seeing a doctor and taking pills for her nerves.

I last saw Bich two years after his trial and conviction. He was in a medium security institution designed for 180 prisoners but housing 230. Less depressed than he had been, he was still feeling guilty about Anh My and about his family in Vietnam. He hadn't been able to bring himself to tell his brothers or his former wife that he was in prison. His only visitors now were religious brothers from a nearby mission. 'My Vietnamese friends,' he said, 'have forgotten me.'

Bich was not wasting time in prison. He was learning English, attending school five hours per day in the hope of completing a high-school equivalence certificate, and making name-plates and wooden ornaments to sell. Above all, he was working with a lawyer on an appeal to have his crime changed from murder to manslaughter. If successful, he would be eligible for earlier parole. If not, it would be at least ten years before Bich could hope to leave prison. As I was leaving after our last visit, he said: 'They say that life begins at forty; if I don't get out for ten years, I'll be thirty-nine.'

Novels and drama usually locate the root of tragedy either in a hero's flaws or a society's malevolence. Reality rarely offers such unambiguous denouement. Since everyone has flaws and vulnerabilities, every immigrant and every refugee poses a risk of some kind for the host country. However, other than ensuring that countries like Canada eliminate people with known histories of crime and violence from their admission queues, individual screening can do little to prevent tragedies like Bich and My Anh's. Countries of asylum can try, however, to mitigate the loneliness faced by many refugees and which, in the case of one young and rather passive young man, exploded into a moment of rage and madness.

To be alone was to be in a situation of compounded jeopardy, a situation of obligation with no compensating support. Although its contemporary fragility makes the institution a bit suspect, marriage improves mental health for both men and women (Hirschfeld and Cross, 1982; Brown and Harris, 1978; Beiser, Turner, and Ganesan, 1989; Turner and Avison, 1989). Presumably, members of a couple support each other. Aside from the advantages of this primary relationship, a refugee household with a married couple is more likely than other types of households to contain extended family on both sides, the members of whom create a rich network of financial and social resources (Kibria, 1993).

Friends help. Sometimes they help make up for missing family. In the early years in a new country, immigrants and refugees typically look for friends and for social support among people from their own ethnic background (Canadian Task Force, 1988b). Theory and research suggest that the presence of a large like-ethnic community protects mental health. In a study of hospitalization for mental disorder, the psychiatrist H.B.M. Murphy found that admission rates among immigrant groups in Canada increased as the size of their ethnic representation in the community decreased (Murphy, 1973). Other research confirms these trends (Bland

and Orn, 1981; Starr and Roberts, 1982; Beiser, Turner, and Ganesan, 1989).

Based on his findings, Murphy formulated what he called 'critical mass' theory. The idea was that access to a critical mass of persons from a like-ethnic background protects mental health. The Vancouver of 1981 provided the conditions for a natural experiment with which to test critical mass theory. When the Boat People arrived in Vancouver, the city could boast a Chinese population of 150,000, one of the largest to be found in any North American city. There were virtually no Vietnamese, Laotians, or Cambodians. Critical mass theory would predict a mental health advantage for the Chinese over the non-Chinese refugees. According to RRP data, 3 per cent of the Chinese were suffering a diagnosable depression in 1981. The rate for non-Chinese was 12.1 per cent.

The chance that a Vietnamese like Nguyen Bich would develop a depressive disorder was four times greater than for a Chinese refugee male of similar age. Later studies have produced similar findings (Hinton et al., 1997).

The Chinese advantage did not last. By 1983, Chinese and non-Chinese rates were almost equal. This fact argues against inherent predisposition as an explanation for the 1981 findings. If genes were the explanation, the difference in rates should have persisted.

Experience is a more plausible reason. The Chinese were sojourners in Southeast Asia before they came to Canada. Their experiences as ethnic minorities in Vietnam, Laos, and Cambodia may have better prepared them than their Vietnamese, Laotian, and Cambodian counterparts for the marginal status of refugees.

Critical mass theory provides the most likely explanation of all. For the Chinese refugees, there was a ready-made like-ethnic community in place. For the others, there was no one. Explaining the advantage of a like-ethnic community is not straightforward. It seems plausible that a large Chinatown would offer employment opportunities to Chinese that might be denied to non-Chinese. For example, some research (Hirshman and Wong, 1984; Borjas, 1993) suggests that immigrants placed in a position of disadvantage by virtue of language deficiency can sometimes find work through social ties within the ethnic community. For the RRP group, however, the impact of the like-ethnic community on job prospects was minimal. Only a small number of marginally employable Chinese found work in Asian businesses that was not available to their non-Chinese counterparts (Johnson, 1988).

Economic benefit probably does not account for the like-ethnic community's protective effect on mental health. The inner life of the refugee offers a more likely explanation. In a strange country, it is comforting to have someone with whom to share memories of the sights, sounds, and smells of home. Friendships help overcome loneliness. Although the chemistry of friendship remains mysterious, having something as basic as a common ethnicity probably helps.

Aside from friendship, the like-ethnic community probably nurtures the inner life by protecting one's self-worth. Human beings learn who they are, and the value of their identities, from interacting with others (Cooley, 1902; Mead, 1934). Major life disruptions, such as becoming a refugee in a strange country, challenge basic assumptions about self-worth. North America offers little reassurance to immigrants and refugees from other places that their cultural histories make them worthwhile people. Ethnic enclaves like Vancouver's Chinatown offer a partial remedy for self-doubt. The language, institutions, and patterns of social interaction within the ethnic enclave provide a bridge between present and past, and a sense of historical continuity that helps preserve faith that the identity one began to form as a child has value, even in a radically new environment.

Powerful as it was in the short run, the like-ethnic community's effect on mental health provided relatively transient. By the time of the second RRP interview, two years after the initial survey, the Chinese mental health advantage had disappeared. In all likelihood, the intervening years gave the Laotians, Vietnamese, and Cambodians time to form like-ethnic communities of their own that erased the differential between them and the initially advantaged Chinese.

Although having a like-ethnic community in place helps new settlers, that happy circumstance may not be available. Someone always has to be the first to arrive.

Canada has host and sponsorship programs to welcome newcomers. Under the host programs, volunteers help orient new settlers to Canada, particularly to the country's system of schools, health care, transportation, and recreation. Sponsors are people who apply to bring immigrants and refugees to Canada and accept a legal obligation to support them. Canada's agreement to admit 40,000 refugees under private sponsorship and another 20,000 under government sponsorship created a natural experiment to test the proposition that 'levels of hospitality' (Aylesworth and Ossorio, 1983) affect resettlement: the more welcoming the host society, the better the mental health of new settlers.

Private sponsors were obliged to provide financial support for the person or family they sponsored for a period of one year, or until the person or family had achieved financial stability, whichever came first. Moved by the horrors of the Southeast Asian experience, most private sponsors did much more: they helped refugees find jobs, schools for their children, doctors, and dentists. Assuming that the level of welcome the privately sponsored group received would give them an advantage over those the government sponsored, whose point of contact was usually an over-worked civil servant, the RRP investigators predicted that privately sponsored refugees would enjoy better mental health than the govern-ment-sponsored. The prediction was wrong: there were no mental health differences between the two groups at any point in the study.

In retrospect, government and academics were more impressed with the virtues of private sponsorship than the refugees themselves. Most peo-ple predicted that the private sponsors' willingness to commit their time and personal resources to newcomers could be nothing but an advantage.

Housing was one example. When they arrived, government-sponsored refugees went to live in a motel for a few weeks, during which time they were expected to find more permanent housing. Since so few spoke English and since, in the overheated Vancouver economy of the early 1980s, vacancy rates were close to zero, it is a matter of some wonder that they succeeded. By contrast, many private sponsors took it upon them-selves to have a home waiting. One particularly wealthy group of spon-sors, who became frustrated with house-hunting, finally bought an entire apartment building. Now in control of the tenancy, they were soon able to house the family they had sponsored in the largest apartment in the building, which they equipped with TV, stereo, and a new car.

Nevertheless, in response to a survey, half of all privately sponsored Southeast Asian refugees and almost all the government-sponsored said that government sponsorship was preferable to private (Woon, 1987).

Intrusiveness was one of the downsides of private sponsorship. Feeling they were acting as good, concerned hosts, private sponsors called the ref-ugees at all hours and insisted on taking them to various activities. Some-times they forgot that refugee families, like all other families, need and value privacy.

Sponsors were sometimes insensitive to the refugees' needs. For exam-ple, they often found housing that the refugees could not afford once the sponsorship period terminated, or they looked for housing close to them rather than to the ethnic communities in which the refugees would have preferred to live.

Inequity also proved a source of discontent. Government-sponsored refugees all received the same treatment, whereas, in the words of one refugee, 'with private sponsorship, sometimes it depended on luck whether you met a nice group or not' (Woon, 1987, p. 141).

A subgroup of privately sponsored refugees in the RRP were, in fact, at greater risk for depression than the government-sponsored. These were refugees whose religions did not match their sponsors. Most of the sponsors were Christian or non-denominational; most of the refugees, either Christians, Buddhists, or members of one of the smaller Southeast Asian religious groups. Non-Christian refugees sponsored by Christian groups developed very high rates of depression.

Statistics summarize but cannot do justice to human stories like that of Tran Soon.

Soon's husband and three children brought the fifty-two-year-old woman to the emergency room of a general hospital. During the three to four months leading up to the hospital visit, Soon had practically stopped eating and sleeping, she cried most of the day, and the family suspected that she was hearing voices. Since she had always been religious, the family took no particular notice of the Buddhist family shrine she built in the living-room. However, when she started to burn scraps of paper, clothing, and bits of string at the shrine, the family became concerned that she might start a serious fire. They decided to bring her to a doctor.

During the first few days in hospital, the greying, thin little woman always dressed in black and always stayed very quiet. However, when her therapist brought in a Vietnamese interpreter, Soon started talking. After that, she rarely stopped talking. Although much of what she said was disjointed, themes that recurred throughout her rambles suggested some of the things that were troubling her.

Soon talked a great deal about her sponsors, a Christian church group to whom she obviously felt very grateful. The group had been very attentive. Shortly after the family arrived in Vancouver, one of the sponsors invited them to attend church with her on Sunday morning. Each Sunday after that, one of the sponsors would call with the same invitation. Later, the sponsors also started taking Soon and her family to church socials.

Like others from Southeast Asia, Soon and her family had difficulty understanding the concept of sponsorship. They could not grasp the idea that strangers would be willing to help them without wanting something in return. They hit on the idea that the sponsors probably wanted them to renounce Buddhism for Christianity. Feeling the weight of obligation, Soon and her family converted.

During her recovery in the hospital, Soon talked about what happened next. Her grandparents came to her in dreams, reproaching her for giving up her religion. Then she began to hear their voices during the daytime. She set up a shrine in her parents' memory, but then realized it was inappropriate for a Christian to act this way. When she thought of converting back to Buddhism, she heard Christ denouncing her for abandoning him.

Some fundamentalist groups used sponsorship as a coercive tool (Westermeyer, Vang, and Neider, 1983a). Having met and talked with some of Soon's sponsors, I don't think they meant to be coercive. They seemed genuinely surprised that Soon and her family had felt obliged to convert to Christianity.

The relative failure of Canada's large-scale experiment with private sponsorship by no means suggests that Canada or other countries should abandon host or sponsorship programs. First of all, there were successes that offset some of the difficulties. For example, the privately sponsored refugees were quicker than the government-sponsored to adopt constructive financial practices such as opening savings accounts and buying insurance, presumably because of their sponsors' tutelage (Johnson, 1988). Second, some sponsor relationships turned into long-term friendships, from which the refugees benefited (Woon, 1987; Westermeyer, Vang, and Neider, 1983b).

Sponsors and hosts could probably help newcomers best if they themselves had help. If new settlers experience their sponsors' interest as intrusiveness, and if they react in a way that conveys ingratitude, everyone ends up being frustrated. Sensitive guidance by the agencies that sponsor host and sponsorship programs would go a long way towards preventing misunderstandings and supporting newcomers so that they can reap the benefits of these potentially useful initiatives. Helpers often forget how vulnerable refugees are. The latter rightly perceive an imbalance of power between themselves and their hosts, even though they may overestimate the extent to which this differential can affect their status. Soon's story is a poignant illustration of how innocent intentions can be transformed into tragedy when those who try to help fail to recognize the power they exert over people who picture themselves as helpless.

EIGHT

Splitting Time to Handle Stress

Ideas about time and its passing are probably universal (Leach, 1961). However, factors like personal circumstance, culture, and psychological need affect the relative importance of past, present, and future, as well as the relationships among them. For example, preoccupation with the future and inattention to the past seem the 'natural' state of youth (Cottle, 1976). By middle age, contemplating the past is as important as forecasting the future.

Culture adds another gloss to the perception of time. White North Americans, who are the descendants of immigrants and pioneers, de-emphasize the past: at best, it is no longer useful; at worst, an impediment to the urge to 'get on with it' or to 'just do it.' By comparison, Asians venerate the past as a source of instruction, authority, and wisdom (Kluckhon and Strodtbeck, 1961; Fitzgerald, 1972).

Psychological need influences the perception of past, present, and future as powerfully as stages of the life cycle or the dictates of culture. Unfortunately, mental health ideas about time are too limited. Most mental health professionals tend to view perceptions that burst the bounds of past, present, and future as *ipso facto* evidence of pathology. Writers like Marcel Proust and James Joyce violated these boundaries for artistic ends. Although generations of readers have acknowledged the power of the resultant artistic revelations, there are mental health experts who still have reservations about the sanity of these authors. *Repression, amnesia,* and *fugue,* the words most readily invoked to describe inability or unwillingness to acknowledge one's past, all connote psychopathology. Blocking out the past *may* be a symptom, or precursor, of psychopathology.

However, under certain circumstances, it may be adaptive. It can help victims of brutality survive.

What Refugees Have to Say about Time

In December 1980, on my way back to Canada from a conference on human rights hosted by the Japanese, I stopped off in Bangkok, at that time one of Southeast Asia's most important refugee transit points. Since I was more or less in the neighbourhood, I wanted to take advantage of the opportunity to locate and interview refugees assigned to resettle in Vancouver. I thought that interviewing people while in camp, then following them after they arrived in Canada, would provide important insights about adjustment to change.

The mechanics were easy. The Canadian embassy arranged my entry to the three major transit camps, each surrounded by twelve-foot-high metal fences. One camp was located in downtown Bangkok; the other two, at the periphery of the city. Every week in each camp, a list on a centrally placed bulletin board announced the names of the lucky few selected for resettlement, the place they would be resettled, and the day they could expect to leave. Announcements over the camp loudspeakers requiring the people whose names I selected from the lists to report to camp headquarters soon became part of daily camp life.

Had I realized the anxiety this new routine would cause, I would never have initiated it. I did not understand how exquisitely attuned helpless people become to revisions in routine, how quick they are to interpret any change as bad news. The camp authorities, who might have been expected to know better, did not warn me. Perhaps they were no more aware than I how frightening a call to the camp office was. Desperate people always expect the worst.

Unfailingly cooperative, the refugees answered my questions about their lives, the adversities they had experienced, and their patterns of flight in as much detail as I required. Sometimes, at the conclusion of an interview, they offered me a basket or some other small handicraft as a gift.

Something struck me as odd. At the end of each interview, after thanking people for their cooperation, I always offered to return the favour by telling them anything they might wish to know about Canada. No one ever had any questions.

It proved an important observation, one that led to new insights about the psychological management of adversity.

Nong

The small ceiling fan in the cluttered camp office did little to move the soupy, mephitic air of the cluttered camp office, or to lower a temperature hovering around forty degrees centigrade. I idly wondered how Nong, the wiry, watchful, thirty-five-year-old man sitting in front of me, his black hair standing up in spiky defiance of the dampness, could stand to wear a long-sleeved flannel shirt and long green pants. Months later, when we met again in Canada, Nong told me he had been too worried to notice the heat. When the call to attend camp headquarters blasted from the loudspeaker, his first thought was that he and his family were not going to be permitted to leave the camp after all. Although the paper on the bulletin board clearly stated they were going to Canada the following day, Nong had learned not to trust promises.

He hadn't betrayed his apprehensiveness to me. Instead, with a never-changing, intense expression on his face, Nong had told me his story, his particular variation on the theme of suffering resulting from cruelty, repression, and fear that I had already heard from many refugees, and would hear from many more.

After covering all the material that interested me, I asked Nong my usual wind-up questions, 'Do you have anything you would like to ask me? Is there anything you've been wondering about Canada, or about Vancouver?' Like everyone else I had interviewed, Nong had no questions. Whether prompted by heat-induced impatience, exasperation at having the only gift I could offer turned down once again, or frustration at my continuing failure to explain this seemingly unnatural lack of curiosity, I became more aggressive than usual. I said, 'I find that hard to believe. You're scheduled to leave tomorrow afternoon. You and your family are going to live in a place you know nothing about. I come from that place. I don't understand why you don't take this opportunity to ask me some questions.'

In dramatic contradiction to North American stereotypes about Southeast Asian diffidence, Nong visibly bridled. Fortunately, our interpreter didn't censor Nong's reply, a reply I have never forgotten. 'You can ask that question,' he said, 'because you've never been a refugee. You don't understand how we think. *If* I get on that aeroplane tomorrow and *if* I see that we're really flying over an ocean, then I might allow myself to think we're going to Canada. When you live as we have for the past few years, never knowing what will happen, you live day by day. We do not think about the past. We cannot let ourselves think about the future.'

Toura

Toura taught me the same lesson.

A red cloth covered with a simple pattern of white swirls – it could have been someone's cast-off tablecloth – seemed to be the only thing she had to cover her slender body. The poverty and filth of the refugee camp in Thailand was an unworthy setting for the young woman's touching, fragile loveliness, a beauty of which she herself seemed incognizant. Was she really as innocent as she seemed, or had Pol Pot's killing fields taught her that a face kissed by moonbeams could be a liability?

During the few days I spent in the camp with Toura acting as my interpreter, I became convinced that the latter explanation was closer to the truth. She was, after all, not some innocent child of nature, but a sophisticated young woman from Phnom Phen, the product not only of a traditional culture that celebrated female beauty but of a French colonial system that left behind both Catholicism and the idolatries of food and fashion. Before Pol Pot's ascendance, Toura had been a medical student, taking courses taught both in Khmer and in French. After Pol Pot's soldiers executed her older brothers, the former medical student was sent to the forest to be re-educated, to be converted from an intellectual into a peasant. Toura's parents were sent to a different part of the forest, her younger sister to yet another. One day each year, the family was reunited.

On my last day of work in the camp, Toura was very excited. Her father had succeeded in locating an older brother who had migrated to California many years before. Now that they had a sponsor in the United States, the family would soon be leaving for Sacramento.

I told Toura how pleased I was for her. Then, feeling the need to say something more, I asked, 'What do you think you will do when you get to the United States?' She seemed not to understand. I elaborated my question: 'Do you think you might want to go back to medical school?' Until I asked my question, Toura's smile had been genuine. Now it dropped, to be quickly replaced by a tighter, controlled caricature. In the moment between smiling and putting on the mask of smiling, Toura's face communicated some of the incredulity, hurt, and fear my ignorant question provoked. Although polite and controlled, her response was not altogether forgiving. 'I'm not sure I'll still be alive tomorrow. How can you ask me about medical school?'

Both Nong and Toura call to mind the comments of Chaim E., victim of a terror that occurred thirty years earlier in time, and half a world away from Southeast Asia. Describing how he and his fellow inmates survived in the unthinkable environment of a Nazi death camp, Chaim E. said, 'You were not thinking for tomorrow because tomorrow's thoughts were bad. Today was already better than tomorrow' (quoted in Langer, 1991, p. 180).

Thomas Cottle, a psychologist who pioneered the study of the way people think about time, divided temporal perception into two components. 'Time relatedness,' the first dimension, refers to the cognitive linkages between past, present, and future. Under ordinary conditions, time-binding, in which past, present, and future are connected, forms the backdrop for thought (May, 1958; Loewald, 1972; Getsinger and Leon, 1979; Platt and Eisenman, 1968; Baskaukos, 1981). Nong, Toura, and Chaim E. were not living under ordinary conditions. To cope with adversity, they split the spheres of time apart.

Cottle also described 'time dominance,' the relative amount of focus placed on past, present, or future. Both the Southeast Asian and Jewish narratives suggest that abandoning past and future in order to focus on the present was a survival strategy.

Li Wuchin's story suggests that premature reintegration of past, present, and future, and refocusing on temporal spheres other than the present, can pose a threat to individual mental health.

Li Wuchin

One day, several months after I had returned from Bangkok to Vancouver, a community mental health agency called to tell me about Li Wuchin, the former Vietnamese industrialist and would-be suicide. Wuchin's attempt to cut the jugular vein in his neck was gruesome; though he did not succeed in killing himself, he had undoubtedly meant to.

Li Wuchin tried to kill himself with the old wooden-handled ice-pick he had found in the basement of the church in which he worked as a janitor. By that time, he and his family had been living in Vancouver for about one year. Hoping to establish as favourable rapport as possible before asking about his suicide attempt, my interpreter and I began the interview by focusing on his family's life in Vietnam and their escape to Thailand. A rich industrialist in pre-1975 Saigon, Wuchin automatically became a special object for the new regime's attention. Taking away his factories, his house, and his servants apparently was not enough. To deal with his potential threat to the regime, the authorities sent him to a re-education camp. A man who slept in the bed next to him was undergoing his third re-education. One morning, Wuchin woke to an incessant creaking sound. When he looked to the side of his bed, he saw his neighbour hanging by his neck from one of the ceiling rafters.

Wuchin did not incorporate much communist doctrine in camp. The main thing he learned was that escape was imperative. After his release, he banded his family together for a difficult overland trip through Laos. The Mekong River, separating Laos from Thailand, was the last barrier on their ten-day exodus. Wuchin chose a crossing point in the river heavily guarded by Thai soldiers, whose job was to drive refugees away from the border. To divert the guards' attention, Wuchin jumped into the Mekong, making as loud a splash as he could. While the sentries fired at him, the rest of the family crossed the river at a point now left unguarded. Miraculously, everyone survived.

At the time of Wuchin's suicide attempt, the Li family was living in a crowded but clean basement apartment whose rent consumed most of the salary the former industrialist now earned as a church janitor. Ms Li, who supplemented the family income by working as a seamstress, sat in on our interview. She agreed with her husband that the children were becoming Canadianized too quickly. Perhaps she was a little less concerned than he was. Their son's long hair bothered her, but not to the point of preoccupation, and she turned a blind eye to their daughter's dating – something she knew about, but that her husband only suspected.

A traditional East Asian man, Wuchin was concerned that his daughter was jeopardizing their family's face by going out without a chaperone. Dating a young man would be out of the question. Mr Li was upset about more than family face. He was worried about his own. In place of the authority he used to exert over workers and servants, he now took orders from others. Instead of the absolute obedience he could have expected from his family in Vietnam, he had to contend with his children's half-hidden disobedience, a situation that his wife's apparent complicity made even worse. As the months went by, Wuchin began to think more and more about his houses, his factories, and his servants in the old world. Soon his sleep became disturbed. Walking around the house in the early morning while his family still slept, he had more and more time for reminiscence. He lost his appetite, began to feel tired all the time, and was troubled by bouts of constipation. Although it was hard for him to admit, there were many times when he felt like crying.

The interpreter for my interviews with Mr Li was a wonderfully sensitive mental health worker from Hong Kong. Ordinarily, she was an excellent interpreter, waiting for, rather than prompting, my questions or the interviewee's responses, translating everything as idiomatically as possible, patiently repeating questionable phrases or nuances until we could be reasonably sure all three parties shared a common understanding. This time, the mental health professional in her became impatient with the interview's pace. She couldn't resist breaking in with a question of her own, which she later translated to me: 'Why, after all you've been through – all the suffering and the fear – did you do this? You're safe now, your family's together. Why would you try to kill yourself?'

Mr Li replied: 'I was thinking then about the past just as you are now. I still do. But when I consider the past, I don't think of myself in the re-education camp, or in the middle of the Mekong River. I think about life when it was at its best. Compared to that, I have nothing now, and I never will again.'

Handling Time: A Strategy for Survival

Like Nong, Toura, and Chaim E., Holocaust writers have described splitting off memories of suffering and of loss in order to survive and to glimpse the possibility of a personal future. With the restoration of normal, expectable conditions, memory is likely to reappear (Friedlander, 1979; Appelfeld, 1994).

Theory, Holocaust literature, and my interviews with Nong, Toura, Wuchin, and others converged to suggest that, under situations of extreme adversity, human beings resort to time-splitting, substituting what Thomas Cottle called 'atomistic' perception for the more usual mode in which past, present, and future are connected. Having split the three spheres of time apart, victims of overwhelming stress concentrate on the present, to the relative exclusion of past and future. For most, this proves an effective survival strategy. However, disappointed by present circumstance and with little reason to hope for a better future, Wuchin became increasingly seduced by hypnopompic reverie – shadowy images of better times that appeared while he was waking from sleep and his psychological defences were temporarily relaxed. Gradually, reverie shaded into nostalgic recollection and, from there, into despair.

Testing Concepts

The idea that, in order to survive extreme adversity, people split past, present, and future, and concentrate on the present seemed plausible. However, my small sample made generalizations impossible, while the method by which I had arrived at the formulation raised questions about validity. Although it seemed feasible that, like Nong, Wuchin, Toura, and

Chaim E., many other refugees try to cope with adversity by altering their time perspective, it was possible that these survivors were an exceptional group who employed a relatively idiosyncratic strategy. I was also concerned about the problem of the imperfect observer. Perhaps my own biases and preconceptions led me to focus on particular elements in these three encounters and to overlook others that might have led to a more useful formulation about how people cope with adversity.

Doubts like these call for cooler, more dispassionate investigative methods than collecting life histories. Although qualitative inquiry had helped me formulate what seemed an important insight, I felt that quantitative inquiry would help guard against an all too typical scenario in which compelling case material prompts someone with impressive credentials to formulate a theory and then to use his or her authority, together with the case material, to 'prove' the theory. Unfortunately, the behavioural sciences field is littered with this sort of tautology.

The Refugee Resettlement Project (RRP) provided the opportunity for relatively dispassionate examination of my theory linking time perspective and mental health. Testing theory with statistics requires the investigator to specify propositions or hypotheses. Seeing how well the results of a study conform to the hypotheses constitutes an important test of the usefulness of theory. I proposed the following hypotheses:

1. If time-splitting and avoidance of the past occur under conditions of adversity, refugees should show more future and present orientation and a greater tendency to split apart past, present, and future than people living under ordinary, more or less predictable circumstances.
2. The longer refugees live in a country of permanent asylum, the more likely they will be to begin reintegrating past, present, and future.
3. Time-binding brings a higher risk of depression than time-splitting, at least during the early years of resettlement.
4. Avoidance of the past militates against depression in the early years of resettlement.

Measuring Time Perspective

My measure of time perspective drew upon Thomas Cottle's studies of university students and young naval recruits (1967, 1969, 1976). I supplied the interviewers in our study with three sets of paper circles, one labelled 'past,' one 'present,' and one 'future.' Each set contained three circles, one small, one medium-sized, and one large. To measure the relative importance of past, present, and future – what Cottle called 'time

Figure 8.1   Patterns of Time Dominance (examples)

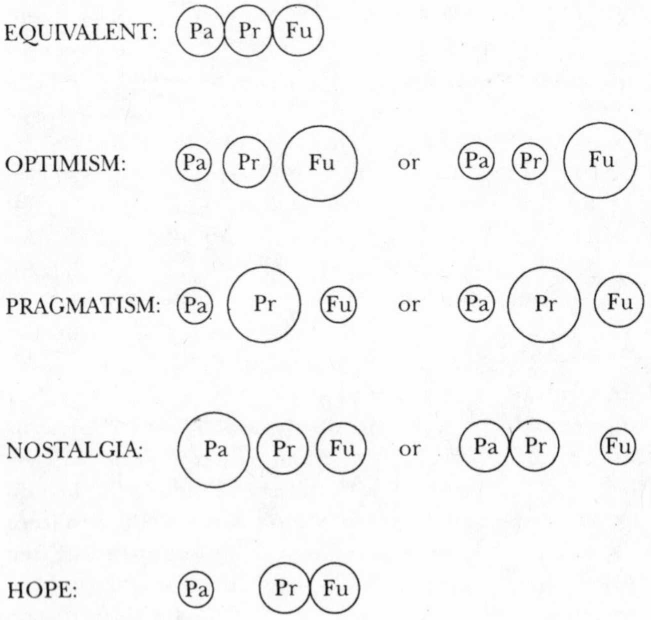

EQUIVALENT: (Pa Pr Fu)

OPTIMISM: (Pa) (Pr) (Fu)   or   (Pa) (Pr) (Fu)

PRAGMATISM: (Pa) (Pr) (Fu)   or   (Pa) (Pr) (Fu)

NOSTALGIA: (Pa (Pr)(Fu))   or   (Pa)(Pr) (Fu)

HOPE: (Pa)   (Pr)(Fu)

Pa = Past
Pr = Present
Fu = Future

dominance' – the interviewers asked the respondents to choose circles of different sizes: the larger the circle, the more important the perspective. Most of the choices fell into one of five different patterns, which we named as follows: *optimism*, in which the future is large relative to the other two domains; *hope*, in which future and present are equal, the past small; *pragmatism*, in which the present dominates; *equivalent*, in which all time zones are of equal size; and *nostalgia*, in which, as in Li Wuchin's case, the past seems to dominate present and future. Figure 8.1 illustrates these patterns.

The interviewers also asked study participants to show the relationships between past, present, and future by arranging the circles they had selected on a blank sheet of paper, in this way establishing their perceptions of 'time relatedness.' A simple scoring system assigned individual responses to one of three categories: *projection*, for patterns with a great

Figure 8.2   Time Relatedness Categories

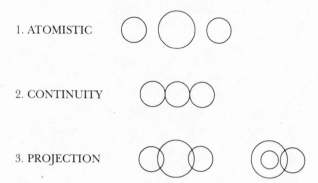

deal of overlap among past, present, and future; *atomistic*, for patterns of time-splitting; and *continuity*, for patterns falling between the two extremes. Figure 8.2 illustrates typical patterns for each category.

The 'circles test' has an appealing content validity: it seems to measure what it means to measure. Content validity, however, is no guarantee that a test means the same thing to research subjects as it does to investigators. Since other research workers suggest that sharing the assumptions underlying a test helps ensure validity (Dinges and Hollenbeck, 1978), we instructed the interviewers to explain the purpose of the test to each interviewee.

As a further check on validity, we asked a subsample of respondents why they chose a particular pattern of circles and arrangements. The answers suggested good understanding of the task. For example, many refugees chose a small circle to represent the past, setting it off to one corner of the page, or refused to choose a 'past' circle at all. A typical explanation was: 'I don't want to think about what's happened in the past and it's not connected to now. The important thing for me and my family is to build a good future.'

Hypothesis One: In Comparison with People Not Confronting Adversity, Refugees Are Less Focused on the Past and Demonstrate More Time-Splitting

Although neither gender nor level of education affected time perspective, age did. Older people like Li Wuchin, who had lost much and whose prospects of replacing their losses were slight, were more *nostalgic* and less *atomistic* than younger people (Beiser and Hyman, 1997).

Table 8.1a
Percentage of Refugees Choosing Different Patterns of
Time Relatedness in 1981, 1983, and 1991

	1981	1983	1991
Atomistic	76%	80%	38%
Other	24%	20%	62%

Table 8.1b
Percentage of Refugees Choosing Different Patterns of
Time Dominance in 1981, 1983, and 1991

	1981	1983	1991
Nostalgia	11%	12%	5%
Other	89%	88%	95%

Differences between refugee and Vancouverite time perspective in 1981 conformed to prediction. The refugees' time perspective was more *atomistic* than the Vancouverites'. Only 32 per cent of the Vancouver group described an *atomistic* perspective, compared to 81 per cent of the refugees who split past, present, and future apart.

Refugees and Vancouverites also endorsed different patterns of 'time dominance.' Whereas Vancouverite choices were fairly evenly split among all patterns of 'time dominance,' refugees tended to choose the future-oriented *optimism* and *hope* categories, and to avoid *nostalgia*, with its focus on the past (Beiser and Hyman, 1997).

Hypothesis Two: The Longer Refugees Live in Resettlement Countries,
the More Likely They Are to Reintegrate Past, Present, and Future
As table 8.1a demonstrates, refugee patterns of 'time relatedness' remained stable between 1981, the time of our first survey, and 1983, the time of the second. By 1991, the refugees were becoming less *atomistic*. In other words, they were now beginning to reintegrate time.

Ten years after their arrival in Canada, the refugees were allowing the past to touch the present and future. However, table 8.1b shows that they continued to place more emphasis on present and future than on the past. They were still avoiding *nostalgia*.

Hypothesis Three: Time-Binding Is Associated with Higher Risk for
Depression Than Temporal Atomism

Of the refugees holding an *atomistic* perspective in 1981, 6 per cent were
depressed. By comparison, the rate of depression among those with an
integrated view of time was 9 per cent. By 1983, the differences were even
more striking: people with an integrated perspective were twice as likely
to be depressed as those with an *atomistic* outlook. The differences were
statistically significant, even after taking factors like age, sex, ethnicity,
and employment into account in multivariate analyses. People who
dropped their *atomistic* stance in favour of time-binding between 1981
and 1983 paid a price in increased risk of depression. Conversely, the
mental health of refugees who shifted from time-binding to *atomism*
improved (Beiser and Hyman, 1997).

Associations between 'time relatedness' and depression are neither
inevitable nor immutable. The pattern of relationships never appeared in
the Vancouver sample and, by 1991, it had disappeared among the refugees. In other words, under normal circumstances, most people have an
integrated time perspective. Time-splitting helps people adapt to extraordinary circumstance. With the passage of time, it becomes increasingly
unlikely that temporal reintegration will jeopardize mental health.

If time-binding is a more natural state than *atomism*, what are the factors that promote it? According to RRP data, age, language ability, and
marital status are important. Youth and linguistic facility, factors associated with integration with the larger society, also promoted a change
from *atomism* to time-binding. People who married during the ten years
of the study were more likely to give up a pre-existing proclivity for *atomism* than others who stayed single. Marriage and children do, after all,
demand that people begin to make sense of where they have come from,
what they are doing, and what they can expect for themselves and their
families in the future.

A character in Joyce Marshall's (1996) short story 'The Rearing Horse'
says: '... for the living, things have to connect. At least, seem to.' No matter how effective time-splitting proves in the short run, temporal reintegration in the aftermath of catastrophe is probably inevitable. The
psychologist O.H. Mowrer (cited in May, 1958), for example, speaks of
time-binding as the natural state of being. Kirmayer (1992), Bartlett
(1932), Bruner (1990), and Neisser (1982) each refer to a natural tendency to 'weave experience into a seamless fabric' (Kirmayer, 1992) that
does not permit gaps in memory and events. Holocaust writings support

the concept of a natural push towards time-binding. Friedlander (1979), for example, writes: 'Memory must come, for memory is knowledge' (p. 17). Aaron Appelfeld recounts how, after liberation from the death camps, he and his fellow survivors suppressed memory, resorting to almost any distraction in order to do so. However, the recognition that the good was lost along with the intolerable created a psychological press for temporal reintegration. 'We knew that something warm and precious within us had been lost on the way to self-forgetfulness, something that we could not deny: parents, scenes from childhood, tribal whispers' (Appelfeld, 1994, p. 18).

Time-binding is a prerequisite for the important activity of 'imaginative reverie' (Kirmayer, 1992; Klinger, 1978), a cognitive state involving recollection of the past, together with contemplation of the present as prelude to what is yet to come. According to some investigators (Giambra, 1974), adults spend less time in reverie than children, probably because this form of thought is considered a waste of time for older people. Like maturation, circumstance may determine access to imaginative reverie. Danger and deprivation probably direct thought towards immediately practical goals, while escape from adversity, together with the appearance of new opportunity, liberate preconscious thought.

Hypothesis Four: Avoidance of the Past Militates against Depression
In 1981, in 1983, and again in 1991, *nostalgia* created a risk for depression. Over time, the refugees abandoned the time-splitting that initially conferred mental health benefit. By the end of their first decade in Canada, the refugees' 'time relatedness' patterns looked exactly like those in the majority culture's population. 'Time dominance' operated differently. In the early years of resettlement, only 12 per cent of refugees as compared with 23 per cent of Vancouverites chose *nostalgia* as their dominant cognitive mode. By 1991, only 5 per cent of the refugees were *nostalgic*. In other words, ten years after their arrival, they were avoiding the past even more strongly than when they first arrived. Probably for good reason.

Caught in the Past

Nong's and Toura's stories are compelling accounts of how refugees split off past and future in order to focus on the immediate present. His present and future boundaries more circumscribed than those of the youthful Nong and Toura, the dispossessed industrialist Li Wuchin retreated into nostalgic recollection, a path leading to depression. Elderly refugees like Wuchin, people with little stake in the present and few prospects for the future, are at high risk for nostalgia.

The elderly are not the only casualties of reminiscence. Tran Thu Lan, the youngest daughter of an elderly Vietnamese businessman, was pampered and spoiled as a child. Since he already had two sons to carry on his successful business, Lan's father was happy to let his pretty daughter have whatever she wanted. At the time her comfortable world of adoring parents and grandparents, indulgent older brothers, servants she could order around, private lessons, and party dresses fell apart, Lan was almost fourteen. She saw her parents for the last time when they bundled her and her two brothers onto a fishing boat with a hundred other people and pressed three things into her hands: her mother's ring, her grandmother's gold chain, and her father's gold watch. At first, Lan thought her parents were giving her keepsakes. Her mother explained that they were also giving her security. Gold could always be used for bribes. Even though everything else got lost at sea and in the refugee camp, Lan managed to arrive in Canada, five years after leaving her parents in Vietnam, with her valuables intact. Lan's two brothers found jobs as dishwashers. They rented a small two-bedroom apartment and enrolled in English-as-a-second-language classes. Busy schedules left the two young men with little time to worry about their apathetic younger sister, who seemed to want nothing more than to stay home, occasionally watch TV, look at the jewels she had brought from home, and brood about the parents she assumed had been killed. One night, Lan's brothers convinced the unhappy young woman to go with them to a party where she could meet other young Vietnamese. Even though there were people there from social classes she would have considered unworthy were she still in Vietnam, Lan enjoyed the party. Unfortunately, while Lan and her brothers were out, thieves broke into their basement suite and stole the jewels.

It seemed to Lan that the police were more intent on blaming her for not keeping the valuables in a bank safe-deposit box than in trying to help. She now understands how safe-deposit boxes work – but she no longer needs one. Since the robbery, Lan's brothers have become increasingly concerned about their young sister, who never leaves the house, and who seems to cry more and more about the past.

Keeping the Past out of Awareness

The idea that keeping memory out of awareness may protect mental health is not new. Sigmund Freud, the father of psychoanalysis, wrote about *Unterdrückung*, meaning 'pressing under,' a concept later elaborated by others as *suppression*, a psychological defence involving the temporary setting aside of painful percepts. Basing his conclusions on a study of successful people, the psychiatrist George Vaillant (1985) suggests that *suppression* is the most common and perhaps the most effective defence against internal conflict. Many psychiatrists draw a distinction between suppression and repression. They refer to 'suppression' as a more or less conscious act of inattention, and reserve the term 'repression' to mean motivated forgetting, a mechanism through which unwanted memories are forced into the unconscious (for further discussion of these terms, see Moore and Fine, 1990). The psychiatrist Lenore Terr (1994) suggests that an increase in symptoms invariably accompanies the return of painful, repressed memory. She goes even further to suggest that the presence of symptoms can help distinguish real memories from so-called false memory syndrome.

However popular, concepts like suppression and repression have limited usefulness. They are words that seem to explain, but really only describe. Although suppression and/or repression seem to describe how many of the Southeast Asian refugees were dealing with memory during their escape, their internment in refugee camps, and the initial phases of resettlement, the concepts do not explain *how* they were able to accomplish this feat. If forgetting is sometimes good, how do people consciously do it and sustain it, and why can't everyone do it?

Electro-physiological studies support clinicians' impressions that, by means of a poorly understood process, people reject aversive stimuli, in order to keep unwanted perceptions out of consciousness (Erdelyi, 1985, 1990; Luborsky and Crits-Christoph, 1989; Glucksman, Quinlan, and Leigh, 1985; Shevrin et al., 1992). In Shevrin's studies, for example, after studying interview transcripts and psychological test results obtained from people suffering pathological grief, clinicians identified key words and phrases that seemed to relate to each patient's underlying conflicts. While their electroencephalographic (EEG) responses were being monitored, the study subjects watched a tachistoscope that flashed conflict-related and neutral words, sometimes at subliminal exposure times of 1 millisecond, sometimes at supraliminal levels of 30 to 40 milliseconds. The EEG tracings demonstrated that, at subliminal levels, the brain recognized conflictual material, but at supraliminal levels, it did not. These results did not hold for the neutral words. In other words, the participants in this study appeared to 'know' unconsciously what they appeared not to know consciously.

According to Lenore Terr (1994), 'not telling' is one way to suppress thought. Experiences that people talk about are forgotten less easily than those never verbalized. Aaron Appelfeld, the Holocaust author, describes other 'marvellous instruments of oblivion' that, in the immediate aftermath of release from the concentration camps, helped him as well as other survivors to forget: 'sleep, bathing in the sea, and, above all, entertainment' (Appelfeld, 1994, p. 35). Appelfeld describes how, in the transit camps, former concentration camp inmates immediately began trading and bartering, in part to survive, in part to forget. He also describes spontaneously formed groups made up of people who, before the war, were actors and musicians and who now travelled from transit camp to transit camp to entertain. 'Feverish activity drew people into the depths of oblivion, and at night the entertainment troupes would come and finish the job' (Appelfeld, 1994, p. 33).

Reunification of past, present, and future does not occur without associated mental health risk. One reason may be that temporal reintegration, with the accompanying resurfacing of the past, may lead to *nostalgia*, a condition noxious to refugee mental health. Although psychoanalytic literature (Ellenberger, 1993; Young, 1995; Terr, 1994) tends to portray suppression of past traumas as a substrate for the emergence of psychopathology, autobiographical accounts and clinical studies suggest that individuals may suppress the past, not only as a manifestation of psychopathology, but as a way to cope with extreme adversity (Kirmayer, 1992; Friedlander, 1979; Appelfeld, 1994; Loewald, 1972). RRP data support the idea that suppression of the past can be an effective way of coping in the aftermath of catastrophe.

The principle that blocking out the past is not always pathological, but that it can be adaptive, is finding its way into the literature of therapy. For example, Spanier (1996) has described a program to prevent recurrences of depression. Teaching people to refocus on the present and future in preference to the past is integral to the technique. Study subjects treated with Spanier's program of short-term psychotherapy de-emphasizing the past were more likely to stay symptom-free than people receiving other forms of care.

If de-emphasis of the past is a useful therapeutic intervention in the general population, it seems reasonable that it might also help refugees whose circumstances discourage psychological investment in the present or the future. According to RRP data, groups at risk for *nostalgia* include the elderly, the unemployed, and people who speak little or no English. Counselling that emphasizes the present, paired with efforts to overcome the isolation imposed by joblessness and lack of language, could help.

No matter how effective as a short-term strategy, blocking out the past probably cannot go on forever. Although it may set in motion the maladaptive pattern of *nostalgia*, recovery of the past is a necessary part of knowledge, and a necessary component of the perception of self. Those who suppress eventually remember.

Reintegrating the Past

Ruth and Larry are survivors of the Holocaust of the Second World War. Fifty years after the event, they are patching its memories into the cloths of their lives.

Ruth

Ruth has been a close friend for forty years. She has an easy laugh, a slightly self-deprecating sense of humour, and a vivacity that still captivates. She came to Regina in 1952, an exotic gift to our Prairie city, where her captivating accent and *zaftig* good looks contributed to the maintenance of our high school's testosterone levels. She still looks and sounds wonderful. My friends and I knew that Ruth and her parents had come from Lithuania, and we knew, in a vague sort of way, that the family had survived the war in hiding. But Ruth talked about love affairs, politics, music, and poetry – never about the war.

Ruth now lives in Vancouver with her husband. She is director of continuing education programs for one of the universities. Her son and daughters, assorted in-laws, and grandchildren live nearby. Several years ago, during a visit to that fog-shrouded city, I happened to switch on the car radio. A talk-show host was interviewing Ruth about her Holocaust experiences, about her years in hiding with a Christian family, and about a sister who died in Auschwitz. When I called her, I said, 'Ruthie, I'm so surprised. All these years, and I never heard your stories. Now, you're telling the world. What happened?'

My old friend replied: 'There's something about getting to be fifty. You become more contemplative, and the memories start to come back.'

In 1995, Ruth went back to Lithuania with her husband and her daughters. I happened to be in Vancouver not long after their return. Ruth invited me to watch a video she had just edited from the dozens of reels of film tourists typically take when they go to an exotic place. But these films weren't about exotic places; they were from a place Ruth once knew as home.

We watched scenes of her visit to an undistinguished-looking brick building in her Lithuanian *shtetl*, the clinic where she had been born. The attendants there told her it was lucky she had come when she did. They would soon be replacing the delivery table they had been using for more than sixty years and where, without any doubt, Ruth's mother had delivered her. Pointing to a weathered, toothless old woman who was hugging her in one of the episodes on video, Ruth visibly *qvelled* (an almost untranslatable Yiddish word roughly meaning 'squirmed with pleasure'). This was the foster mother who had passed Ruth off as her own Catholic daughter during most of the war years.

The atmosphere darkened emotionally as the camera recorded the buildings and bare plots of land that had been the Jewish ghetto. Ruth's voice, usually characterized by a hint of laughter, turned to a near whisper as she said, 'And that's the building they were sitting in when they spotted us.'

During the early days of the war, when Jews were being used as slave labour for local projects, the adults were taken out to work during the day. The children, the elderly, and the infirm stayed behind in the ghetto. Since she was a big girl of six, Ruth's parents told her that it was her responsibility to look after her four-year-old sister while the adults were away. 'Looking after' meant being on the watch for any changes in routine. If anything unusual were to happen, Ruth and her sister were to run as fast as possible to their hiding place, a small, coffin-like space under the floorboards of one of the ghetto buildings. Under no circumstance were they to move until their parents came to get them.

One day, screaming and shouting broke out in the ghetto. As she had been instructed, Ruth ran to the hiding place with her sister. They stayed there for hours, the six-year-old trying to comfort her whimpering sister with reassurances that their mother would come to get them any minute. After a long while, her sister fell asleep, and it seemed to Ruth that the ghetto became very still.

When the four-year-old woke up again and began to cry that she wanted to go outside, pity overwhelmed her older sister's caution. No sooner had they stepped out the door when Ruth realized she had made a mistake. SS guards sitting in the building Ruth had pointed out to us in her film spotted them. They yelled at the children to stay where they were. The girls tried to run back to their hiding place, but were quickly captured.

That day's sweep through the little ghetto was part of the notorious *Kindertransport*, a program to remove all Jewish children to the Nazi death camps as quickly and efficiently as possible, an objective more easily accomplished when their parents were out of the way.

People who were useful for the moment were sometimes able to curry favours from the SS. A cousin of Ruth's mother was a surgeon whose skills the Nazis had called upon for their own care. He was the only Jew on hand to witness his little relatives being dragged onto the back of the last transport truck bound for Auschwitz. Sometime earlier, he had saved the life of a relative of the Nazi commandant who was overseeing the *Kindertransport*. Apparently the Jewish surgeon found the courage to say to the commandant something approximating 'You owe me one.' Years later, when Ruth was middle-aged, the elderly cousin told her that the commandant had replied, 'Take the older one.' It was the last time Ruth saw her little sister.

By now it was late, and we had drunk a lot of brandy. Although the video had stopped, Ruth, her husband, Cecil, and I sat in their darkened family room looking at test patterns on the screen. We stole an occasional, hopefully discrete glance at each other. Ruth broke the silence by picking up the story again. 'I know a lot about this from that old cousin. He lives in New York now. I went to see him recently ... because who knows? He's over ninety after all. He told me that he talked the commandant into letting my sister off the truck, too. But, by the time that happened, they'd already driven off. Morleshka [her pet name for me], I didn't want to hear that.'

The walls around our comfortable evening exploded. For a moment, we could all see the convoy of trucks at the edge of a little Lithuanian city, each one filled with children, the last one in line holding a frightened four-year-old crying for her mother.

For many years, Ruth simply didn't think about her life during the war. The postwar public mood probably reinforced the refugees' natural tendency to suppress the past. Soon after liberation, Holocaust survivors found themselves in what Lawrence Langer calls 'moral quarantine,' with the horror of their stories threatening both their credulity and the receptivity of potential listeners. Memory had to await a changed social context. The Eichman trial followed by the publication of books such as Hilberg's *The Destruction of the European Jews* (1967) helped open the floodgates of collective memory. Museums, movies, books, and documentaries now enshrine that memory.

Perhaps such collective acts of remembering made it possible for Ruth to begin resurrecting her own past. Still, the radio interview in which I heard Ruth talk about her first brush with recollection was a far cry from 'Morleshka, I didn't want to hear that.'

Her radio account seemed like a remote story, something akin to a Greek tragedy with principal characters who could do nothing to alter its inevitable unfolding. Public support and public utterance inevitably take on that quality. The old cousin's confession that more alacrity or greater persuasiveness on his part might have saved one more life changed the story from an epic to a personal event in which human frailty had played a possible role. If her cousin had been tried and found wanting, what about the six-year-old who had disobeyed her parents? Recapture of the past brings with it not only the memory of public tragedy, but the risk of disembedding presumed private shame.

Larry

Like Ruth, Larry is one of my oldest friends. He is also a child survivor of the Holocaust. Today, he is a highly regarded administrator in a U.S. hospital and medical school. Larry was born in Czernowicz, the Romanian city that was also my mother's birthplace and where she and my father first met. Although Larry and I often talked about going there, he to recapture memory, I to reconstruct a family history that began in a place I had never seen, we never thought it would be possible. For decades, the old country of our parents and grandparents was securely tucked away behind the Iron Curtain. However, in May 1996, one of my sons, a few friends, Larry, his wife, and I did go back.

Czernowicz is now Chernivtsi, no longer a part of Romania but of Ukraine. The trip was difficult but important. Despite the epidemic of amnesia that seems to have gripped Central Europe, we were able to find the mass grave where Larry's parents and brother were probably buried and to say Kaddish, the Hebrew prayer for the dead.

Despite forty years of friendship, I had never known much about how or, for that matter, what Larry had survived. I had always felt it better not to ask. There were no holds barred during the trip.

My son was amazed that Larry's confrontation with painful memory seemed to do so little to affect our friend's zest, his outpouring of information about everything we were seeing, his almost manic embrace of little pleasures like the taste of mamaligah (a traditional dish of corn mush), the sound of gypsy music in the restaurants, and the effects of the local vodka. In their different ways, Larry's skills in intellectual analysis and the vodka we numbed ourselves with each night helped maintain a tolerable distance between past and present.

Larry would also be the first to acknowledge that his wife, who has always been the source of his equanimity, didn't fail him on the trip.

After it was all over, Larry had this to say:

The trip made me realize how far I had come from those places and yet how close I remain to them. The trip also made me realize the paradox of human experience consists both in a need to remember and in the need to edit and to forget. If I did not remember all of the events we had traversed, life would be meaningless. If I did not forget selectively, life would be intolerable.

Coming to Terms with the Paradox

Ruth and Larry's odysseys into the past are not unusual. Liucija Baskaukos, a psychologist who worked with Lithuanian refugees, describes their 'impulse to restore the past' (1981). Flora Hogman (1985), another psychologist, asserts that, when severe disjunctures occur between past and present, '... detailed memories *must* be retrieved ... in order to recapture the lost world' (p. 396). She goes on to say that the retrieval of memory inevitably sets in motion a process of mourning, an experiencing of loss.

The retrieval of memory, mourning, and destructive nostalgia fit the experience of Li Wuchin, the dispossessed Vietnamese industrialist. However, although both Ruth and Larry were, and continue to be, disturbed by trips back in time, neither has become depressed or suicidal. Nor, one has to assume, do most others like them (otherwise someone would by now have noted an epidemic of suicide among survivors of their generation).

Many counsellors and therapists are convinced that people who have suffered trauma must confront their past, that uncovering painful memory is part of the process of recovery (Terr, 1994; Ellenberger, 1993; Bass and Davis, 1988; Herman, 1992). The United Nations International Children's Emergency Fund (UNICEF) has embraced this principle. With the help of non-governmental agencies working in refugee camps around the world, UNICEF is introducing a sweeping program of psychosocial care that begins with focusing refugees' attention on their past traumas. Recapture of traumatic memory is promoted as a necessary first step in coming to terms with horrible experience.

The theorists may be right. I hope that UNICEF's programs will help children who have been affected by severe trauma. However, Li Wuchin's experience makes me uneasy. His story underlines the need to consider context and timing before trying to force a confrontation with the past. When wounds are fresh, it may be too early.

What accounts for the difference between my two friends' relative equanimity in reintegrating past, present, and future, and in recovering and recounting suppressed memories, and Li Wuchin's inability to cope with his? The evidence suggests that success, financial security, temporal distance from the events, and, perhaps most of all, the security of friends and family promote constructive temporal reintegration.

In the final analysis, memory is not the same thing as *nostalgia*. Ruth's and Larry's stories suggest that, at the right time and under the right circumstances, it is possible to reassemble the shards of the past and, from them, create a mosaic of memory and present contentments, long-ignored pain, and hope for the future.

NINE

Profiles of Success

The painter Raoul Dufy draws attention to an object by leaving it out. In some of Dufy's canvases, the object – a sail on a boat, or a table – is a piece of blank canvas. Only the painted wall behind it and the objects placed on it give the table definition; only the backdrop of sky and water give the sail its substance. In his novel *The World According to Garp* (1978), John Irving details a family's comings and goings in the weeks following a bizarre accident. Lulled at first by mundane description, the reader slowly becomes uneasy, then chilled by the slow recognition that someone, a little boy, is missing. Revealing the child's death through his absence heightens the sense of tragedy.

Like painters and novelists, behavioural scientists sometimes define mental health by what it is not. Abnormal conditions like psychiatric disorder, unemployment, substance abuse, and public nuisance preoccupy behavioural science nosologists and phenomenologists. Whatever is left over is called normality.

Defining a phenomenon by its absence rather than its substance is an effective technique in art and literature. It does not work in science. Calling all refugees who do not develop health problems, who do not use welfare, and who manage to stay out of trouble well adjusted is inadequate because it conveys only the boundaries rather than the essence of good adaptation. The determinants of success are more than the absence of stresses that create failure: they are phenomena well worth studying in their own right.

The stories of refugees who were failing during their first years in Canada have much to teach. It is equally important, however, to understand the stories of refugees who dealt successfully with the early stresses of resettlement, who made the most of opportunity, and who, at the end of the first few years, seemed poised to become active, contributing citizens.

Refugees Who Were Succeeding

In *Anna Karenina*, Tolstoy writes that all happy families are alike: only unhappy families are interesting. Compared to the histories of the deviant and the troubled, the lives of the successful lack drama. Their ordinariness belies the enormity of the challenge Southeast Asian refugees faced during their early years in Canada, and how extraordinary it was that so many were able to rise to it.

Take the story of Quin Huang and his wife, Binh Ngo, who left Vietnam in 1978.

Mr Quin is a slight, gentle man. His bulbous forehead, made more prominent by premature baldness and thick glasses, gives him a look of grave intelligence. Looks like Mr Quin's, the kind which inspire confidence, are a great asset for professionals, at least for those professionals who, unlike Huang, are lucky enough to lead ordinary, expectable lives. Although he was a dentist in Vietnam, Mr Quin will probably never practise his profession again.

In order to qualify for a licence to practise in Vancouver, Huang would have to pass written examinations. Before he could hope to pass the examinations, he would have to take a refresher course at a Canadian dental school. The University of British Columbia told him they would accept him as an advanced student. Welcome as the news was, it did not solve the problem of providing for his family. Mr Quin and his wife both worked. However, paying the rent on their basement apartment, and buying food and clothes for themselves and their two little girls, left very little to send their respective fathers, mothers, brothers, sisters, aunts, and uncles still left in Vietnam. Without Huang's income – income the family would have to sacrifice if he went back to school – the family could not get by. There was also the language problem. Huang received three months of English-language training shortly after he arrived in Canada. His job in a produce market afforded little chance to add to the small vocabulary he acquired when he first came to Canada.

Although he is not the professional he hoped to be, Mr Quin says that does not really matter. He and his wife will continue working hard so that they can eventually bring the rest of their family to Canada and so that their two daughters will have a chance at the kind of success that now lies beyond their parents' grasp.

For now, Huang seems resigned. The promise of a future for his children offers enough psychological comfort to balance the recognition that his own years of training will probably never reward him with the status and the material well-being for which he might once have hoped. One cannot help wondering how long his stoicism will last.

Quin Huang's wife, Binh, speaks Vietnamese, French, and better English than her husband. Soon after the couple arrived in Canada, she began working in a fashionable part of the city where shops and restaurants use French and Italian names to try to enhance their cachet. Working behind the counter of a shop advertising itself as a 'boulangerie/ pâtisserie,' Binh charms her customers with her sunny manner. She also helps the more affected ones – Anglophones who like to chat with her in French – make believe they really are in France, or at least Montreal.

Binh recently convinced her employers that they could improve the shop's image by using fancy packaging for some of their products. When she showed the shop's owners some of her husband's artful wrappings, they hired him for the job. The couple bring in enough money to support their little Canadian family and to leave a little something to send back to their families in Vietnam. To Binh, it seems ironic that the government doesn't seem to mind the fact that they are sending Canadian earnings overseas. If it were easier to sponsor Binh's mother, her sister (a talented linguist), and her father-in-law (an exceptionally hard worker) to join them as immigrants, the money could all stay in Canada.

Or consider Suva. Like most Laotians, Suva has a five-syllable surname that most English speakers cannot pronounce. When he was in his early twenties, Suva, his mother and father, Suva's three teenage sisters, his nine-year-old brother, and his paternal grandparents fled their home. They were afraid the Pathet Lao would inflict the same reprisals the Communists in Cambodia and Vietnam were meting out to the middle class and to intellectuals they defined as the enemy. That was in 1978. Under the sponsorship of a group of families in Vancouver who had been moved by media reports about the Boat People, Suva and his family came to Canada in 1980.

The ensuing years were reasonably happy and productive. The family bought their own home, where, for awhile, they all lived together. One of the sisters went to work in a bank; the other two attended community colleges. After working for a few years, and serving a term as president of the Lao brotherhood, a community self-help and advocacy organization, Suva entered the University of British Columbia. In those days, shyly admitting his admiration for a physician who was one of his family's sponsors, Suva said he would like to pursue a career in the health field, either as a nurse or a physiotherapist. However, he later decided to take a degree in commerce. He now lives with his wife and two children in Toronto, where he runs a successful insurance company catering to the Laotian community.

By any standards, the people in these two families must be counted as successes. They are working or going to school, providing for themselves and for each other, educating their children, and learning one of their adopted country's languages. Some are involved with their own ethnic communities. They are in good health and, despite frustrations, seem reasonably content. Success is, however, uneven, and their integration limited. Although Suva and his sisters speak reasonably good English and are pursuing career paths similar to other Canadians in their age group, their father's English is limited, their mother's non-existent. Like Suva's parents, Binh and her husband spend their limited non-family time exclusively with members of their own ethnic group. Although Suva and his sisters have Canadian-born acquaintances, they feel the most comfortable when they are with other Laotian young people.

Even when there is goodwill, it seems difficult for newcomers and people born in Canada to become friends.

The Meaning of Integration

In keeping with its commitment to pluralism, formalized in the Multiculturalism Act of 1988, Canada has made integration the cornerstone of its resettlement policy. As is often the case, Canadians like to clarify their approach to issues through contrasts with the United States. In immigration and resettlement, the contrast is usually made between the U.S. pursuit of assimilation, 'a process of eliminating distinctive group characteristics' (Canadian Task Force, 1988a), and the Canadian ideal of integration, the 'process, clearly distinct from assimilation, by which groups and/or individuals become able to participate fully in the political, economic, social and cultural life of the country' (Canadian Task Force, 1988a).

Although the definition preferred by the Canadian Task Force assigns pride of place to political integration, the reality is that, for most newcomers, this form of participation in Canadian life comes late – if at all. Immigrants become politically active only after they are sure they can make a living and after they have learned enough English or French to make it possible for them to make deals in the various corridors of Canadian power.

Ideally, each newcomer to Canada develops his or her own unique pattern of integration, balancing past with present to create a synthesis of attitudes, skills, and vision of the future that is useful to the individual and that contributes to the common good. Integration involves options – deciding how much of the past to retain and how much of the present to incorporate into a new identity. Although the ideology of multiculturalism, with its emphasis on freedom of choice, should provide the optimum environment for immigrant resettlement, many newcomers experience pain as they go about the task of integrating into their new society. Lack of tools is one source of their pain. No matter what their situation, newcomers need to find work and to master the language of their adopted country. Without these minimal tools, successful integration will always remain elusive.

Learning English

Without language, one can never truly enter a culture.

No one has described the connection between language, emotion, and belonging more eloquently than Eva Hoffman. As a mature woman reliving the experiences of the thirteen-year-old Polish refugee she was when she came to Canada, Hoffman (1989) recalls that, although she seemed to be learning English words,

> ... the problem is that the signifier has become severed from the signified. The words I learn now don't stand for things in the same way they did in my native tongue. 'River' in Polish was a vital sound, energized with the essence of ... my river ... 'River' in English is cold – a word without an aura. It has no accumulated associations for me, and does not give off the haze of connotation. It does not evoke. (Hoffman, 1989, p. 106)

Because children seem to pick up words easily, their parents and teachers often assume their quick and easy mastery of a new language. According to the eloquent Ms Hoffman, mastery comes slowly and with attendant pain. Figure 9.1 shows that the refugees probably learned English more slowly and even more painfully than Ms Hoffman.

In 1981, very few people (16 per cent) spoke good English, and, by 1983, this proportion had increased to only 25 per cent. Data from 1991 are the most discouraging: ten to twelve years after they arrived in Canada, only one-third of all the refugees were fluent in English. In 1981, 16 per cent spoke no English; 10 per cent, in 1983; and 7 per cent, by

Figure 9.1   Learning English: The First Decade

Percentage

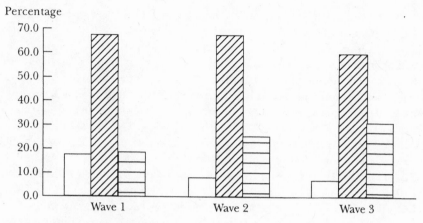

☐ None   ▨ Fair   ⊟ Well

the end of the study in 1991. There is a good chance that the hard-core 7 per cent will never acquire any of their host country's language.

In 1981, the correlation between the number of months refugees had been in Canada and their English proficiency was .21; by 1983, the relationship dropped to a statistically and substantively insignificant .07. These figures suggest an initial spurt in language acquisition in the early years of resettlement. Thereafter, the passage of time brought no guarantee of increased proficiency (see also Espenshade and Fu, 1977).

If time does not promote language mastery, what does? According to the Refugee Resettlement Project (RRP) data, being male, young, non-Chinese, unmarried, and well educated each conferred a critical advantage (Edwards, 1994).

Among elderly refugees, more than half spoke no English, even after ten years in Canada. A poorly educated person was six times more likely to speak no English than a well-educated refugee. The roles of youth and education in learning a new language are easy to understand; the first confers a physiologically based advantage in any learning that involves memory; the second, an advantage based on practice in honing intellectual skills. Resettlement policy also contributes to age-based disparities. Individuals deemed likely to enter the labour market are the most likely to be chosen to enter government-sponsored language-training programs. The result is that policy can promote the isolation of people already at risk of being cut off from society by virtue of their circumstances.

When the refugees first arrived in Canada, there were no Chinese/ non-Chinese differences in language ability. However, during the ensuing ten years, the non-Chinese were much more likely to learn English. Since single people and non-Chinese had less chance than their married or Chinese counterparts to be in the company of people fluent in their mother tongues, they probably had to speak more English on a day-to-day basis. Besides being the mother of invention, necessity may be the stimu- lus for practice.

The reasons underlying male/female differences in language proficiency merit more intense investigation. One reason stems from initial disadvantage. Fewer women than men spoke English when they arrived in Canada. During the ten years of the RRP study, women picked up English at the same rate as men. In order to catch up, they would, of course, have had to pick it up faster. Like the elderly, women did not have a good chance of attending English classes because many of them were judged unlikely to enter the labour market. Ironically, however, English classes had a larger impact on women's language learning than on men's. This was probably because, on the whole, men were better educated and had more chance of learning English at work. Although formal language training did help men, its effect was less than it might have been without the advantages conferred by previous training and opportunities for exposure in the workplace. English-language training made a bigger difference for women, who, compared to men, started at a lower level of proficiency, had less previous education, and were less likely to be employed in an English-speaking environment.

Although attending English classes and using the language at work were the most effective learning strategies, practising English with friends and hiring a private tutor also proved useful (see also Frideres, 1989).

Life is about seeking pleasure as well as avoiding pain. The two are not necessarily reciprocal; that is, freedom from anxiety and depression does not automatically guarantee a sense of well-being. Furthermore, removing factors that jeopardize mental health will not necessarily ensure contentment. For example, research results demonstrate the truth of the old adage that money can't buy happiness. Community studies have repeatedly shown that poverty creates a mental health risk for conditions such as depression. However, community studies fail to show any relationship between income and a sense of well-being. Happiness seems to be more dependent on meaningful involvement with other people than on money (Beiser, Feldman, and Egelhoff, 1972; Beiser and Leighton, 1976). RRP results are consistent with research about well-being in other populations. There is no relationship between levels of distress and English proficiency. However, language ability does predict well-being.

Successful Adaptation: From Construct to Measure

Binh, Huang, and Suva are exemplars of success. Their stories offer hints of what may have helped make them successful. However, these are only hints, not the type of 'hard' data one would want in order to make policy recommendations. Although it is difficult to define what hard data means, it seems self-evident that conclusions based on the observation of a large sample will be more convincing than those based on observing a few people. Results subject to the least possible amount of observer bias are easier to accept than those dependent on the particular perceptual apparatus of a particular individual. No matter how objective they believe themselves to be, observers can never completely free themselves of a tendency to notice data that fit with pet theories, and to fail to notice phenomena that do not.

It seemed a logical next step to take some of the ideas about success we had gleaned from studying individuals and test them out on the entire sample taking part in the Southeast Asian Refugee Resettlement Project. The first requirement for such a study was to create an objective measure of success.

The RRP measure of success combined three indices: employment, language fluency, and general health. We measured employment by answers to a simple question that Statistics Canada uses in its labour-force surveys: 'Are you working now?'; language fluency, by the answer to 'How well do you speak English?'; and general health, by the question 'Would you say your health is excellent, very good, fair or poor?' According to our definition, successful people were currently working or had a good reason for not being employed. Examples of the latter included students, the elderly, or housewives who were caring for children. To be classified as successful, people had to speak at least some English and to rate their health as good, very good, or excellent. People who did not fulfil these three criteria were rated unsuccessful.

This measure of success fulfils several research requirements. First, it is easy to understand. Second, it is easy to construct: other investigators would have no trouble replicating the measure. Third, it is straightforward. Others may well have different ideas about how to judge success, but there is no ambiguity about the RRP measure.

The category has an appealing face validity. Since success implies self-sufficiency, or taking steps that will lead to gainful work, employment seems a reasonable criterion of success. English proficiency is important because integration forms the cornerstone of Canada's immigration resettlement policy: the ability to speak one of the country's official languages is fundamental to successful integration. Employment and language facility are measures of the degree to which the refugees were conforming to the host country's expectations of them. The health question addresses internal feelings. Although deceptively simple, this 'general health' question is a surprisingly powerful predictor of mortality, regardless of actual physical health (Idler and Angel, 1990; Kaplan and Camacho, 1983).

In 1981, only 15 per cent of the refugees were successes according to the RRP's stringent standard. Time makes a great difference. By 1991, 86 per cent of the refugees were working, feeling healthy, and speaking English with moderate proficiency. Had we used a less demanding measure, success rates would have been higher. For example, a strictly economic measure might have equated success with working at a regular job. In 1991, 92 per cent of the refugees were working. Imposing the language and health criteria reduced the rates of success.

Other data suggest the validity of this measure of success. For example, the successful group were consistently happier than the unsuccessful. In 1981, the successful group's mean score of 7.1 (sd 2.0) on the well-being scale was higher than the unsuccessful group score of 6.5 (sd 2.1). The same pattern prevailed in 1983 (successful group = 6.5 [sd 1.7]; unsuccessful = 6.2 [sd 1.8]) and in 1991 (successful = 8.0 [sd 1.9]; unsuccessful = 7.4 [sd 2.1]). All differences are statistically significant at $p < .001$, meaning that the probability that such results could occur by chance alone is less than 1 in 1,000.

By 1983, 12 per cent of the refugees in the unsuccessful category had received some form of welfare support since their arrival in Canada. This was true for fewer than 1 per cent of the successfully adapting. In 1991, the differences were even more striking: at some time during their first ten to twelve years in Canada, 25 per cent of the unsuccessful refugees had been on welfare, compared with only 1 per cent of the success cases.

Success apparently spilled over into family relationships. By comparison with the successfully adapting, the non-successful complained more often that children were not listening to their parents, that they were responding to bad influences in Canada, and that they had too many distractions. Conversely, higher proportions of the successfully adapting felt that their relationships with spouses, children, and parents were better in Canada than they had been at home, and that their children were receiving higher quality education than would have been possible in Southeast Asia.

The way in which people handled time also distinguished the successfully adapting from the refugees who were experiencing difficulties. At time one there were no differences between the groups: about 13 per cent of both the successful and non-successful disclosed a *nostalgic* time perspective, one in which the past overwhelmed the present and the future. By time two, however, the proportion of successful adapters endorsing a *nostalgic* perspective shrank to 7 per cent, while among the non-successful it rose to 16 per cent. There were still differences between the successful and non-successful in 1991: 2 per cent of the former were *nostalgic* compared to 9 per cent of the latter. The successful were more likely than the non-successful to be *optimistic* or *hopeful*.

Does nostalgia make success less likely, or does present success make one less likely to reminisce about the past? Since the time perspectives of the two groups differed at times two and three, but not at time one, it seems likely that perspective is a consequence of the adaptive process, rather than a predictor. Compared with people who were struggling, the refugees successfully adjusting to life in Canada were more likely to abandon memories and past regrets in favour of the present and the future.

By way of summary: we defined success by employment, ability to speak English, and the subjective feeling of being in good health. People categorized as successful according to these criteria were happier than unsuccessful people, far less likely to have ever received welfare, more content with their family lives and with what was happening to their children in Canada, and less likely to dwell on the past.

Adapting to a new, unfamiliar culture was one of the greatest challenges the refugees faced during their first decade in Canada. The choices they made about balancing the familiar with the new affected their chances of achieving success.

Biculturalism and Successful Adaptation

Ethnic origin exerts a variable hold on individuals. For some, it defines their values, and the people they choose as spouses and as friends. For others, ethnocultural origin is best forgotten. Like everyone else, refugees differ in their degree of commitment to their culture of origin. For most, ethnic identification is not an 'all or none' issue. Instead, people retain elements of their past, simultaneously taking on elements of a larger culture in which they find themselves embedded (Sue and Sue, 1990; Phinney, 1990; Weinreich, 1989).

According to behavioural science theory, people who adopt a bicultural mode in the face of change – that is, one in which they retain their own cultural identity while incorporating elements of the new – are more likely to be successful than people who choose to assimilate completely to the new, or who retreat to the familiar while rejecting the new, or who reject both the old and the new (Berry, 1984; Beiser and Collomb, 1981). Consistent with such theory, Canada's national policy of integration promotes cultural retention together with participation in the larger society.

Given the amount of faith in the idea that integration constitutes the preferred mode for new settlers, the paucity of empirical research testing the proposition is surprising.

Integration demands a balancing of the competing tendencies to retain the values, practices, and skills an immigrant has when he or she comes to a new country versus the tendency to acculturate and adopt the norms and behaviours of the new society. The RRP investigated the supposed advantages of a bicultural orientation for the refugees in three spheres: language, adherence to the old, and accommodation to the new.

Language and Integration

The attitudes refugees held regarding their heritage languages and the languages of their adopted country provided enlightening information about the process of acculturation.

One of these attitudes was the importance attached to retaining mother tongues. During each of the three surveys, more than 90 per cent of all the refugees said they considered it either 'very important' or 'somewhat important' for children to be proficient in their mother tongue. There was no difference between the successful and unsuccessful groups. In other words, whether successful or not, the refugees were convinced of the importance of inter-generational passage of their heritage language.

However, there were interesting inter-group differences in willingness to make English part of intimate family life. During each of our surveys, we asked the respondents which languages they used at home – mother tongue exclusively, versus either English only or both mother tongue and

Table 9.1
Languages Refugees Spoke at Home in 1991

Context for Language Use	Language Spoken (Per Cent)		
	Mother Tongue	English	Both
With spouse:			
successful	93.3	1.8	7.0
non-successful	96.1	0.1	3.0
With children:			
successful	60.1	4.8	35.1
non-successful	72.8	2.8	24.4
With others:			
successful	32.3	2.4	65.3
non-successful	55.8	0.6	43.6

Note: Each of the differences between successful and non-
  successful groups is statistically significant.

English. Table 9.1 describes the answers to this question, broken down according to the person or people with whom interactions took place – spouses, children, and people other than spouses and children living in a household. Since only a portion of the refugees were married or had children, percentages are adjusted to take this factor into account. Likewise, not all households included people other than spouses and children. However, since virtually every refugee lived with at least one other person, responses to these questions provide an indication of the extent to which bilingualism became part of the home life of former refugees. The households of successfully adapting refugees were more likely to be bilingual than those inhabited by the less successful. The most intimate relationship, the relationship between spouses, remained the most intransigently unilingual.

Other RRP data show that the successfully adapting refugees were more likely than their non-successful counterparts to adopt Canadian customs. For example, observing children's birthdays is not a Southeast Asian practice. Children typically incorporate the host country's values more quickly than their parents. Celebrating birthdays is no exception. One adolescent from a traditional family told RRP staff a poignant story. Knowing that her family would do nothing to celebrate her sixteenth birthday, this young person bought herself a cake, which became the centrepiece of a fantasy party she conducted alone in her bedroom. Successful refugees showed more openness than the non-successful to incorporating new practices into their behavioural repertoires.

Adherence to the Old

According to a Chinese legend, popularized throughout Southeast Asia, there was once a great and highly cultured emperor who yearned to go to the moon. He directed his wizard to find a way. The wizard succeeded in building a rainbow bridge on which the emperor rode to the moon. Although the emperor would have liked to stay there forever, singing his poems to the moon fairies, and listening to theirs, he felt it his duty to go back to his people. So he went back to earth. After a time, feeling that he had once again earned a rest, the emperor called on the wizard to build the rainbow bridge again. Sadly, the wizard had to explain that there was no way back. The rainbow could only happen once. To help deal with his regret, the emperor proclaimed that every year, on the fifteenth night of the eighth lunar month, the anniversary of his trip, people would light candles and paper lanterns in honour of poetry and beauty. People still celebrate the mid-autumn festival.

Every culture has its own legends and customs. Even though they may leave home, people are understandably reluctant to give up beautiful things like the mid-autumn festival.

We constructed a scale to measure the importance the new settlers attached to traditional observances such as the ethnic new year, the mid-autumn festival, and an ancestor's death anniversary. Each scale proved psychometrically sound (internal reliabilities were 0.70 or higher). Average scores for both groups, successful and non-successful, fell in the positive range, suggesting a tendency to retain tradition. There were no intergroup differences in scores on this scale.

We also constructed two scales about health traditions. For the first scale, a measure of traditional beliefs about health, respondents were asked whether they (a) agreed strongly, (b) agreed somewhat, (c) were undecided, (d) disagreed somewhat, or (e) disagreed strongly with the following statements: (1) Acupuncture can cure rheumatism. (2) Huo (a bad wind) can make you sick. (3) All foods can be classified as either hot or cold. Strong disagreement received a score of minus 3, strong agreement plus 3, and the other responses received numerical scores between these two extremes. The resulting total scale scores could range from minus 9 to plus 9. The second scale measured health practices, what people did about health rather than what they said they believed. Using the same measure of intensity of agreement employed for the health belief scale, respondents reported whether or not they were likely to do the following: (1) avoid cold drinks if they had a cold; (2) avoid ice-cream if they had a fever; (3) avoid eating raw and cold food if they were not feeling well; and (4) avoid giving a child a bath if he or she had a high fever. For this scale, scores ranged from minus 12 to plus 12.

The successful and non-successful groups had virtually identical scores on both health beliefs and health practices in 1981, 1983, and again in 1991.

These results suggest that all the refugees were maintaining traditional beliefs and practices: the successfully adapting were as likely as the others to adhere to tradition.

Putting Old and New Together: A Key to Success

After only a few years in Canada, profiles of relative success were beginning to be etched. Compared to refugees who were experiencing adaptive difficulties, gainfully employed or otherwise productive people who were learning English and who felt healthy were also enjoying better mental health, and creating less social burden for Canada. Probably because they were doing well, people in the successful group were less nostalgic than the non-successful. When asked to compare life in Canada with their home country, the successful group reported that their family relationships were better, and that their children would probably receive a superior education.

Patterns of integration seemed to vindicate Canada's tortured commitment to multiculturalism. Successfully adapting refugees continued to value their heritage as much as those who were encountering difficulties. The difference was that successful people were more willing or able to incorporate the larger culture into their everyday lives.

The Respective Roles of Selection and Helping in Ensuring Success

Resettlement countries use two methods to try to ensure successful adaptation: selection and helping.

In theory, all refugees should experience equal opportunity of being selected for asylum. This never happens. Canada sets an annual quota of refugees – in recent years, somewhere in the neighbourhood of twenty thousand – to be selected from refugee camps in designated trouble spots such as Central America, the Middle East, or Southeast Asia. The selection process, loosely modelled on Canada's point system for determining immigrant eligibility, emphasizes attributes like good education, membership in a stable family unit, and the ability to speak English or French. In the opinion of resettlement authorities, these are the attributes most likely to predict successful adaptation.

After it opens its doors to refugees, no country, Canada included, provides sufficient welcome. Although the federal government provides job training and language instruction, these services target people deemed the most likely to enter the job market. In practice, this usually translates to mean young and middle-aged men. Women and the elderly tend to be left out.

If immigrants and refugees fail, as some do, the hard-line interpretation is that Canada is admitting either too many or the wrong kinds of people. By contrast, advocates for immigrants and refugees blame the system of resettlement services. If newcomers are not learning English or French, it is because either there are not enough classes or that the training offered is in some way inappropriate. If they fail to find jobs, it is because there are not enough job-training programs or because of discrimination in the marketplace.

Refugee Resettlement Project data make possible an investigation of the respective roles of selection and helping in ensuring successful adaptation.

Selecting for Success

Canada has adopted a hundred-point system for selecting immigrants. People who achieve a score of seventy normally qualify for admission. A profession that Canada needs, relatives already in the country, fluency in French or English, and formal education account for most of the points. Although the criteria for refugee selection are less formalized, the point system provides rough guidelines. According to RRP statistics, education is a good predictor of successful resettlement. Of refugees with more than a grade eight education, 33 per cent fell into the successfully adapting group in 1983, compared with only 17 per cent of people who had attended school for eight years or less (chi square = 34.7, DF 1, $p < .001$). People with twelve or more years of education were four times more likely to be successful than refugees with two years of schooling or less.

Theoretically, Canada selects refugees according to need and promise, turning a blind eye to factors like age, sex, and race. Sex and age prejudice can, however, creep into the implementation of any policy, even the most fair-minded. All things being equal, Canadian immigration authorities favoured younger refugees over the old, the married over the single, and single men over unaccompanied women or single mothers.

Statistics seem to support selection policy. Three to four years after they arrived in Canada, 31 per cent of all men fell into the success group compared with only 21 per cent of all women (chi square = 14.1, DF 1, $p <$ .001). Compared with women, men had an almost twofold advantage in getting and keeping jobs, learning English, and staying in good health.

Although the numbers are irrefutable, their interpretation is open to question. Do biology and pre-migration history predict adaptability, or does policy create a self-fulfilling prophecy?

Helping New Settlers Succeed

Selecting refugees on the basis of individual characteristics raises problems. Unlike immigrants, whose entry can and should be at least partly decided on the basis of the best interests of the receiving country, compassion supposedly dictates refugee admission. Ironically, selection criteria often bar people who need compassion the most. Lien, the young Vietnamese mother whose husband ran home to get something and missed the boat as a consequence, is an example. When I first met Lien, she was one of three thousand refugees living in San Yick Camp, an abandoned factory building on the outskirts of Hong Kong. Lien was depressed, worn out with worry about her husband back home, the four-year-old son who had escaped with her and his unborn sister or brother living in her bulging abdomen. Lien and her son were always hungry. Other refugees seemed to have goods or favours to trade for extra food. Lien had no goods to trade. When she first arrived at San Yick, she had refused to sleep with the guards. When I met her, she was in the seventh month of her pregnancy. Even if she might now be tempted, the guards were no longer interested.

Lien told me that, when she first came to the camp, she would sometimes be wakened by the touch of men's hands in the darkness. She got into the habit of sleeping during the day so that the four-year-old could keep watch. Lien might still be in San Yick if not for 'Women at Risk,' a program introduced by church groups and the Canadian Council of Refugees to sponsor unprotected single mothers.

Although physically safe in Canada, Lien is still at risk. She hears that her husband keeps trying to escape from Vietnam. So far, he has been caught and jailed seven times. Although he does not 'act crazy' as often as he did when he first lost his wife and child, he still has spells when he bangs his fist and his head against the wall, screams, and talks to himself. She knows that their separation is largely her fault. Still, she can't help feeling resentful sometimes; why didn't Thanh insist on staying on the boat so that he could protect her as any decent husband should? Is he crazy now because of a weak character that Lien should have recognized earlier? Thoughts like these run around constantly in her head; they make her feel sad and guilty. Although she knows it is unreasonable to be angry with Thanh, there are times when she can't help thinking: Where is he now, when the children and I need him? Lien needs emotional support, help with her youngsters, language training so that she can meet people, and a job.

Newcomers need assistance in order to integrate into Canadian life. Refugees have even more acute needs than other immigrants. On average, refugees are less well educated and less likely to have marketable job skills than other newcomers. For example, because of the point-system criteria, 75 per cent of all immigrants speak either English or French compared with only 10 per cent of all refugees (Canadian Task Force, 1988a).

Considering the urgency with which refugees need help, the apparent failure of employment programs is discouraging and provocative.

Reasons for failure are difficult to assess. Perhaps refugees are trained for the wrong things. For example, training programs concentrate on teaching occupational skills; they usually do not focus on how to act during a job interview. In addition, many programs do not seem to be geared to the job market. For example, Karenak, a thirty-year-old Laotian man, says he completed a six-month course as a bookkeeper:

> After I finished, I looked for a job. Every interview I went to, there were fifty or sixty people applying for the same position. That went on for months. One day, a friend told me he could get me on as an assistant gardener at the place where he was working. That job lasted until the boss laid us off for the winter. A friend I met there told me about a job killing and plucking chickens for another company. I'm still working there.

No matter how well trained refugees may be, the job market may not be prepared to absorb them. Labour market prejudice directed at visible minorities, documented in a number of Canadian parliamentary reports, including *Equality Now* (1984), the report of the Royal Commission on Equality in Employment (1984), and the report of the Parliamentary Committee on Equality Rights (1985), can thwart even the most motivated refugee.

Although Canada's Charter of Rights and Freedoms prohibits overt or covert discrimination, refugees from Southeast Asia probably get fewer breaks in the job market than native-born Canadians or immigrants from

Europe or the United States. They can't help being 'visible' or 'audible' minorities whose skin colour or accent compromises their chances of being hired for a job (Henry, 1978; Henry et al., 1995; Li, 1978).

Past advantages accruing from education and sex continue to affect the refugees' chances of acquiring important adaptive tools like language. Perpetuation of past advantage in a land of supposedly equal opportunity results, in part, from government policy. Although Canada places great stress on language and job training to promote successful integration, women and the elderly have less access to the programs than men and the young. Federal government programs providing full-time instruction in English or French together with living allowances, most of which target migrants destined for the labour market, effectively cut out refugee women and refugee seniors. Although a number of special programs aimed at women have been introduced, they suffer from erratic funding, lack of flexible scheduling, which often prevents mothers with young children from attending, and from a lack of emphasis on 'survival English,' as opposed to more esoteric aspects of the language (Boyd, 1977). The result is a double irony. House-bound women and seniors do not enjoy the opportunity to learn a new language through their work. Language fluency, which would make it possible for people isolated by circumstance to understand the radio or the television, to read newspapers, to communicate with their children and grandchildren, or to talk to their neighbours, is denied them. As a result of government oversight, the isolated can be made even more lonely (see also Samuel, 1987; Frideres, 1989).

Besides women, the elderly, and the poorly educated, Chinese refugees are less likely to acquire English than non-Chinese, and married people are less likely than unmarried. Although the Chinese refugees initially benefited from Vancouver's Chinatown, a source of employment for the marginally qualified, people who worked for like-ethnic employers acquired less English than people who found non-ethnically based jobs (Johnson, 1988).

These findings raise the spectre of social and ethnic ghetto. Research suggests that a like-ethnic community eases the process of resettlement, and that marriage confers a mental health advantage. Unless balanced by programs to integrate newcomers, these short-term structural advantages could promote the separation of ethnocultural communities rather than the piecing together of a new multicultural mosaic.

TEN

Please See Screaming

Fifteen years after the height of the 'Boat People' crisis, the wars in Bosnia were major front-page news, and the refugees of those wars, the major human interest stories. On 13 July 1995, Canada's national newspaper, the *Globe and Mail*, carried a front-page account about the fall of Srebenica to the Bosnian Serbs. The story described Serb soldiers herding Muslim women onto buses at gunpoint. The women were screaming because they had been separated from their husbands and sons, who were being kept behind. The women apparently knew what the rest of the world was to learn months later. The men and boys were to be executed. Like many newspapers, the *Globe* begins stories on the front page, then supplies a cross-reference to help the reader locate the remainder of the piece on a following page. Having finished the front-page text, the reader was instructed to 'Please see Screaming / page A10.'

The oxymoronic quality of 'please see screaming' captured some of the mood of North America in the mid-1990s. The 'Boat People' crisis had receded from consciousness, replaced by screams from El Salvador, Guatemala, Haiti, Somalia, Ethiopia, Bosnia, and Rwanda. With the list now appearing to be endless, and the possibility of doing anything meaningful to stop the cruelty increasingly hopeless, we retreat to the position of passive viewers, at a parade of worldwide horrors. This is what 'compassion fatigue' means. We no longer hear the screams; they have become peripheral cues, momentary alerts, that something is once again wrong, somewhere.

It is increasingly hard to imagine a world with no refugees. Canada's Department of Citizenship and Immigration doesn't waste time trying. Instead, it forecasts world 'hot-spots' most likely to produce a demand for refugee resettlement during a given period. Refugee quotas change from year to year. In 1997 the quota was set at about twenty thousand.

By international standards, Canada's refugee admission levels are generous. However, a growing public ambivalence not only threatens this generosity, but makes the strangers allowed to pass beyond the country's gates increasingly less welcome. At least four factors help account for Canada's overall swing from generosity to ambivalence: misinformation, lack of information, realistic concerns, and myth.

Misinformation

Guests who make life difficult for their hosts are not going to be welcome guests. The idea that immigrants depress local economies and rob the citizens of the host country of their jobs is a major check on hospitality. A sophisticated study covering five decades of immigration to the United States offers an important corrective. According to this study's results, immigration tends to result in increased earnings for the native born, particularly during periods of economic expansion (Kposowa, 1993). The most likely explanation is that immigrants and refugees take low-paying jobs or jobs rejected by indigens (Kposowa, 1993; Tienda, Jensen, and Bach, 1984; Heckman, 1992). Once they are working, immigrants consume high-cost goods and services produced, by and large, by the native born. The same study demonstrated future, as well as a contemporaneous, immigrant-inspired economic advantage. Immigration in the ten years prior to a decade of economic expansion had a significant and positive impact on the succeeding era. In other words, besides making a positive contribution during periods of economic expansion, immigration may help prepare economic regions to take advantage of future opportunity.

Canadian data are consistent. At worst, according to some analyses, Canadian immigration levels prevailing over the past decade have had no effect on unemployment levels or the economy in general. For example, the Economic Council of Canada (ECC) commissioned a series of studies looking for links between unemployment rates and either the level of population or its rate of growth. It found none. With respect to economic prosperity, the Council estimated that, on the basis of scale efficiencies alone, there would be a 0.3 per cent increase in per capita gross domestic product for every increase of one million people over current population levels. The Council estimated that the optimal population for Canada would be 100 million, a far cry from its current total of 30 million

(quoted in Coyne, 1995). According to one of Canada's leading economists, the typical immigrant family will, over a lifetime, pay forty to fifty
thousand dollars more into the public treasury than they consume in services (deVoretz, 1996). Thus, immigrants can be seen as an economic
windfall.

A larger population might well help Canada. However, the country's
citizens are not having enough babies to sustain the population at its
present levels, let alone allow for an increase. Since 1972, the national fer-
tility rate has been on the decline. It now stands at 1.7 babies born during
the lifetime of a family. This figure is well below the 2.3 births per family
that are needed simply to sustain current levels. Worse still, as the baby
boomers begin to enter their fifties, there is increasing concern about
how a small workforce of young people will be able to support the
boomers' health-care and social benefits. If there were no influx of young
immigrants, the 'dependency ratio' – the proportion of children and old
people to the working-age population – would rise from its current level
of 65 per cent to 85 per cent by 2045.

People worry about things other than the economy: for example,
peace and order. The briquets of fact and exaggeration about refugees
that the electronic and print media package for the public inflame too
much, inform too little.

For example, Asian youth gangs who spread crime, extortion, and
intimidation constitute a real problem in Canada's major urban centres.
The gangs also inspire engrossing reportage that probably exaggerates
the dimensions of the problem. In a 4 February 1991 broadcast on the
CTV national news network, reporter Dave Rinn said: 'Asian gangs have
escalated, turning the streets of Chinatown into a battleground for
supremacy. In the latest incident one man was killed and three others
were wounded, all Vietnamese refugees' (quoted in the National Media
Archive, 1993).

A major daily in one of Canada's most populous cities was among the
first of the popular media to capitalize on the public's fear of, and fasci-
nation with, Vietnamese gangs. In a series of articles appearing in the late
1980s, the paper described the gangs' demands for protection money
from small shopkeepers in Chinatown, their responsibility for a wave of
break-and-entry crimes at a level never before experienced in the inner
city, and the pitilessness with which they terrorized children in schools.

The reporter who had written the articles came to my office one day to
interview me about an entirely different topic. After the usual opening
exchanges, I told him that, before we began, I wanted to ask a few ques-

tions. His answers would help me decide if he was a responsible journalist and, therefore, somebody with whom I would be willing to cooperate. He was a fresh-faced young man, and he had cut himself shaving that morning. As he talked, his wobbling, oversized Adam's apple pulled at a shirt collar that was crying for attention from a laundry. His Vietnamese gang series was probably his first big success at his newspaper. Recognizing all these as signs of youth, ambition, and vulnerability, I felt a little guilty about challenging the veridicality of his reporting ... but not guilty enough to stop. After telling him that I had read his series on the youth gangs, I asked how many Southeast Asian youngsters were hard-core members of gangs. Apparently genuinely surprised by the question, he responded that he didn't know. 'The reason I'm asking,' I explained, 'is because your articles sound as if there might be hundreds, maybe even thousands, of Vietnamese kids marauding the downtown core. What's your ball-park estimate? Five thousand, five hundred, or fifty?' I already knew that the police department's best estimate was about fifty, and I assumed that my would-be interviewer had access to the same information. Nevertheless, once again, he said that he didn't know.·

After some extended verbal sparring, when it seemed clear that I would never get my answer, and that he might have to give up on his interview, the young reporter apparently decided drama might get us off the circular track that was tiring both of us. Referring to them by name, he asked me if I had heard about a particular gang. When I replied that I had, he told me that he knew how many members this gang had. He knew because, the week before, he had gone to a funeral of one its members who had been assassinated. The whole gang had showed up. 'How many came?' I asked. His response was, 'A lot.'

'Come on,' I said. 'How many is a lot?' Because he still resisted being pinned down, we repeated this exchange a few times. Finally, he broke and said: 'A whole carful.' I refused his interview.

Lack of Information about Refugees

The impact refugees and immigrants make on the institutions and economy of a host society is a realistic concern. Information about it should be part of continuing public debate about immigration policy. Unfortunately, public access to the information is limited and, too often, distorted.

In 1994, the Gallup organization of Canada allowed me to include four questions on one of their national surveys. The preface to the questions read as follows: 'Between 1979 and 1981, Canada admitted 60,000 Vietnamese "Boat People" as refugees. These questions are about what you think has happened since then.' The questions, all beginning with 'Please say whether you agree or disagree with the following,' were the following: (1) People who came to this country from Southeast Asia are as likely as any other Canadian to be working; (2) The refugees are using up more than their share of services like health care and social assistance; (3) Southeast Asian refugees are interested in giving something back to Canada; and (4) Accepting Southeast Asian refugees has cost Canadian taxpayers too much money.

Depending on the question, 10 to 12 per cent of all Canadians replied, 'Don't know.' Although the proportion of people admitting they knew so little about the refugees that they couldn't answer the questions may not seem terribly high, it must be remembered that the Southeast Asians arrived on a wave of national and international publicity about refugees never equalled before or since. If one in ten Canadians knows nothing about what happened to this well-publicized group, it seems reasonable to hypothesize an even greater level of ignorance about the less talked-about Tamils, El Salvadorans, Somalis, and Bosnians who have come to Canada since then.

Among those who did answer, the stereotype of the hard-working Asian may have prompted some of the majority – 52 per cent of respondents – to agree with the first proposition, that the former refugees were as likely to be working as other Canadians. In fact, the Southeast Asians were doing better than the general population. In 1991, the national unemployment rate was 10.3 per cent. The comparable figure for refugees was only 8 per cent. One in five of the remainder had started his or her own business. Some, like Quyen and her husband, were employing other Canadians. Others were teaching their former hosts new skills. Comparisons that take age and regional trends into account are more meaningful than gross figures. Regional trends are particularly important because, in 1991, Vancouver's economy was better than the rest of the country's. For people between twenty-five and forty-four, the age of most of the refugees, the national unemployment rate was 9.6 per cent, and, in Vancouver, 9.1 per cent. Measured against these exacting yardsticks, refugee unemployment was still a full percentage point lower than in the population as a whole.

Canadians may have been willing to concede that the Southeast Asian refugees were hard-working. Nevertheless, 39 per cent either agreed or strongly agreed that the refugees were using up more than their share of the country's health and social services. Some people probably forgot that the former refugees were now paying taxes to support the public programs they were supposedly overusing. In fact, since they had higher employment levels, the refugees were probably contributing more tax dollars per capita than people in the general population. Perhaps respondents to the Gallup poll thought that, even if they contributed a fair share of tax dollars, the refugees were excessive consumers of public services. According to the Refugee Resettlement Project (RRP) data, most refugees visited a doctor two to three times per year, just about the national average. The refugees were less likely to use social assistance than their majority culture counterparts.

One-quarter of the Gallup poll respondents disagreed with the statement 'Southeast Asian refugees are interested in giving something back to Canada.' During their first ten years in Canada, all the refugees became Canadian citizens, most at the earliest date of eligibility. In response to a question on our final survey asking them to list their most important sources of job satisfaction, the refugees assigned top ranking to good pay, steady work, and being useful to Canada.

Neither their unemployment figures nor their use of public services suggest that the refugees are a burden to the economy. Nevertheless, 43 per cent, slightly less than half of the Canadian public, feel that accepting the Southeast Asian refugees has, in the long run, cost the Canadian taxpayer too much money.

Although information like the Refugee Resettlement Project data should enter public debate, Canadians are not getting it. The media are a poor source. According to Vancouver's Fraser Institute, media analysis of issues relating to immigration is constantly shrinking. In 1989, for example, the Canadian Broadcasting System (CBC) devoted 21 per cent of its coverage of immigration issues to analyses of its social and economic effects. By 1992, this proportion had shrunk to 13 per cent. The Fraser Institute found that human interest stories are gradually replacing journalistic analysis. The problem is that human interest stories assign emotional manipulation as their first priority, with information often running a distant second. The effect on refugees is a double whammy. Not only is there a shortage of information about their adaptation, and practically no serious analysis of the opportunities and blocks created by public policy, the human interest coverage they do receive focuses much more on bad than on good news. The ratio of bad to good news coverage is about three to one (National Media Archive, 1993).

In the fall of 1994, to try to help correct excessively negative public per-

ceptions, I released the Gallup poll results together with Refugee Resettlement Project data. For a change, the media did pay attention to a good
news item. Usually tying the study results to a human interest story about
a successful individual or family, newspapers, radio stations, and TV chan-
nels devoted a week of coverage to my news. At about the middle of that
week, a TV crew came to my office. While they were setting up their lights
and cameras, the young, hypomanic host prowled my office in his Gucci
shoes, trying to decide whether the camera would like me better posed in
front of my books, seated at my computer, or standing with one of my cultural artifacts as a backdrop. After deciding on the books, he glanced at
the notes his researcher had given him about our interview. His eyebrows
shot up, a few creases crept across his flawless forehead, and he said: 'I
don't really understand why I'm covering this story. We're more interested in planes crashing than landing.' To be fair, it is important to recognize that 'the media' is not a monolith. Many who work in the industry –
if not yet enough – acknowledge a responsibility to inform, rather than to
inflame, public debate about immigration.

The Refugee as Mythological Construction

The term 'refugee' denotes someone who flees his or her home for protection, especially from war, violence, or persecution. In the three hundred years that have passed since the word was first applied to Huguenot
exiles from France, the term has evolved into a socio-political commentary on shelter from oppression. As signatories to the UN Convention,
more than one hundred of the world's nations have defined protection
de facto as not only a need but a fundamental human right.

Aside from its socio-political and legal meanings, the word *refugee* has a
unique evocative power. Although it is rarely articulated, there is a commonly shared psychosocial construction attached to the term: refugees
are survivors of oppression, plunged into poverty, purified by their suffer-
ings, and boundlessly grateful for safe haven.

Only the first part of the proposition is invariably true. Refugees are, by
definition, victims of adversity. The fact that they are not inevitably poor,
nor as pure or grateful as their hosts might wish, can be a source of
difficulty.

Refugees Are Not Always Poor and/or Pure

The date of 11 August 1986, is a watershed one in Canadian refugee history. On that morning, two lifeboats emerged from the fog off the coast

of Newfoundland. Designed to hold no more than 35 passengers, the boats were carrying 145 men, 4 women, and 6 children, all of them Tamils from Sri Lanka. After the sighting, the Tamils were whisked from the cold sea straight into a glare of publicity.

The Tamils' account of their flight from Sinhalese-dominated Sri Lanka, a miserable, month-long sea voyage on an Indian boat bound for Canada that ended with their being suddenly thrust into the Newfound-land fog in their overcrowded lifeboats evoked an outpouring of national sympathy. The sympathy did not last long. According to information gathered by a team of investigative reporters, the Tamils hadn't stepped, like Venus, naked and cold from the sea. They had paid a ring of professional smugglers approximately $3,500 per head, which had secured them sea passage from Hamburg to the coast of Canada. Rather than coming directly from Sri Lanka, where they might have justifiably claimed personal danger, they came from Germany, where they were already receiving asylum, albeit with no hope of being considered for permanent residence.

Anger with the Tamils fused with fears that Canada could not control its borders to set a full-blown 'moral panic' (Cohen, 1980) in motion. The Prime Minister recalled Parliament from its summer recess to consider this betrayal of Canada's goodness. During the ensuing debate in the House of Commons, orators vied with each other in expressions of outrage. The Leader of the Opposition even had the temerity to proclaim that the Tamils should have been turned back to sea. Parliament enacted legislation creating a complex and expensive reform of the refugee-determination process. Ostensibly, the purpose of the reform was to create machinery to carry out refugee policy more efficiently than in the past. However, the new legislation's subtext was obvious: Canada was going to get tough.

And it should. Canada's relatively open door has resulted in some abuse. Smuggling rings bring hundreds of people to Canada each year, instructing them that the phrase 'I claim refugee status' is their open sesame (Bauer, 1997).

Canada must be tough with the smugglers and other abusers of the system. At the same time, it must avoid displacing resentment from perpetrators of abuse to the people they exploit. International law defines a refugee as someone forced to leave home, or unable to go back to it, because of a well-founded fear of persecution. It does not require proof of poverty or willingness to stand in line in imaginary refugee queues. Anyone reaching Canada has the right to claim refugee status, and to have his or her case become the subject of a hearing. For years, people had been coming to Canada as individuals or in small family units, and quietly claiming asylum as refugees. Claimants able to convince immigration authorities that they satisfied the UN Convention criteria were allowed to stay. What the Tamils had done was neither illegal nor without precedent. However, they had come in a large group, they had lied to the authorities, and they were part of a cynical smuggling operation only too ready to take advantage of Canada's generosity. The public vented its anger on the Tamils, now relabelled queue-jumpers rather than victims – and wealthy queue-jumpers to boot.

The Tamils had defied the mythological construction of the refugee as submissive, pure, and poor. The resultant public antipathy was directed not only to them, but to subsequent asylum seekers. According to public opinion polls conducted at the time, disillusioned Canadians felt that no government response to the crisis could ever be too tough.

It seems unfair to condemn people for seizing an opportunity provided by national and international law. Whatever wealth the Tamils had did not confer immunity from persecution in Sri Lanka, nor would it assure them permanent asylum in Germany.

In fact, wealth and status sometimes invite oppression. Wealth does make it more possible to be a queue-jumper. However, people fearful for their own and their family's safety are unlikely to think about the niceties of waiting their turn. If they can find a way to get to the front of the line, they will. Most people would.

Canadians might have been expected to be disappointed with the Tamils for bending the truth as they had. Their anger was also understandable. However, the magnitude of the Canadian response seems totally out of keeping with the Tamils' offence. Overreaction is sometimes a signal of subconscious process. It is at least worth speculating that the Tamils incited so much reaction because they had betrayed the myth of the refugee as a survivor purified by suffering, and totally grateful to his or her helpers.

Additional Components of the Social/Mythological Construction of Refugee

Refugees who fail to live up to the receiving society's expectations of purity and poverty create problems for themselves and for others who come afterwards. Just as they cannot possibly know about such expectations and the consequences of their violation, new settlers are ignorant of other ideas about how they should behave. The fact that their hosts are themselves often hard-pressed to expressly articulate some of these ideas does not make life any easier.

Anthropological concepts concerning transition help illuminate unspoken expectations. According to anthropological observation, every society uses ritual to guide its members through the major life transitions of birth, marriage, and death. Less obviously, but no less importantly, most societies have rituals of integration, a set of expectations initiates must fulfil, and actions they must perform, as 'they' become 'us.' Sometimes, the process is set in motion by biological change. For example, puberty brings on profound biological changes and no less important changes in societal expectations, usually highlighted by rituals that stress communal responsibility. In other cases, the ticking of a social, rather than biological, clock determines the initiation of change. For example, the transition from dependent person to one expected to care for a family is usually set by social rather than biological standards. (Societies in which girls are expected to marry when they reach puberty are exceptions: here the two processes, biological and social, coincide.)

The integration of immigrants and refugees is a socially initiated ritual passage that seems to follow the three phases of transition described in anthropological theory: separation, limen, and aggregation (Turner, 1967).

The Tamils had violated the first rule of passage concerning separation: they hadn't waited for immigration officers to select them as worthy candidates. By contrast, the Southeast Asians had waited in refugee camps until some country deemed them a good risk. They had no choice but to obey the rule of selection. Unlike the Tamils, they were also poor and grateful. Because they fulfiled the initial requirements, the Southeast Asians passed from separation to limen quickly. 'Refugees' during the separation period, Canada quickly renamed them 'landed immigrants,' thereby signalling limenal transition.

The limen marks the passage between what people have been and what they will become. With past templates for thought and action now under constant challenge, and with the future only dimly visualized, the limen is an ambiguous state of being (Turner, 1967). For the Southeast Asians, the limenal period of landed immigrant status would last a minimum of three years, following which they would be eligible for citizenship, signifying the completion of their initiation.

Some expectations for limenal period initiates seem universal. All limenal passengers are supposed to be poor and to be content with their poverty, but to work hard in pursuit of full integration into the dominant society. Initiates are expected to respect authority. Many societal initiations involve a group, often determined by age, almost always by gender.

Participants in these age and gender 'classes' are expected to be companionable. Many societies regard initiates as unclean, requiring ritual purification before full membership is possible.

Limenal expectations created some problems for the Southeast Asians. Some expectations, such as the injunction to prove oneself through hard labour, were explicit, and the refugees responded. But other expectations, because they were harder to pin down, dimly perceived at best, and sometimes unconscious, created more difficulties. A retrospective examination of public demands that were sometimes conflicting, sometimes impossible, sheds light on these more obscure attitudes regarding newcomers in transition.

Some Impossible and Conflicting Demands

Some Southeast Asian refugees failed to live up to the expectation of comradeship. There were, after all, splits based on political and social factions, between North and South Vietnamese, between Vietnamese and Chinese. Trouble developing within the refugee community surprised and angered the larger society. The majority culture also criticized the refugees for creating and living within ethnocultural enclaves, for speaking their own languages among themselves, and for not interacting more with their Canadian hosts.

During the limenal period, initiates are supposed to submit absolutely to authority, to be reflective rather than active, and to be ready to receive new ideas and values, as wax receives a seal. The Southeast Asians could not always conform. Many had left family behind in refugee camps or in the home country. Upset about the world's apparent willingness to accept a political status quo in Southeast Asia, the refugees in diaspora formed organizations aimed at fomenting resistance to the communist takeovers in South Vietnam, Laos, and Cambodia. During the early 1980s, protest rallies marking the anniversary of the fall of Saigon were a source of embarrassment for Canada.

Neophytes undergoing ritual transition have nothing. They exist in what has been called 'sacred poverty.' Refugees are also expected to be poor, their poverty carrying over from the separation period into the limen. Nonetheless, they are also expected to work hard and to stay off welfare rolls. Work hard and expect little. Those who transgressed the rule by acquiring the means for conspicuous consumption, or through their children becoming over-achievers in school, invited social opprobrium.

Deeply rooted ideas about pollution also created problems for the new-comers. Since, at least the Middle Ages, and until the present day, the stranger has inspired fears of contagion. In a fascinating book, *Silent Trav-ellers: Germs, Genes, and the 'Immigrant Menace,'* Alan Kraut (1994) docu-ments the historical use of quarantine against travellers and migrants. Late in the nineteenth century and during the early years of the twenti-eth, peak years of migration to the United States, ritualized medical inspection of newcomers reached an acme of sorts on Ellis Island. Charged with identifying carriers of dangerous or 'loathsome' diseases, including insanity and idiocy, medical officers were set loose on thou-sands of would-be immigrants with a long list of conditions that could exclude entry.

Even though each Southeast Asian refugee received a medical exami-nation before being brought to Canada, the country's health-care institu-tions braced themselves for what they expected to be an overwhelming demand for their services. The demand never materialized. Even though long-term studies have demonstrated that certain Southeast Asian refu-gee subpopulations may be at risk for hepatitis B (Hurie, Mast, and Davis, 1992) or chronic infection by intestinal parasites (Gyorkos et al., 1992), the level of risk hardly justified the trepidation that greeted the refugees' arrival.

Disproportionate fear suggests determinants that transcend rational public health concerns. Fear of pollution may be a metaphor for fear of assault on tradition. According to Mary Douglas (1966), the concept of pollution fulfils a function for established societies. It is 'a reaction to pro-tect cherished principles and categories from contradiction.' Douglas asserts that what is unclear is unclean, citing as example the Levitican prohibition against the equivocal crustacean. Turner (1967) states that limenal personae may be feared because they can pollute those who have never been inoculated against them. Avery (1979) has documented the fear of ideological pollution that foreigners can sometimes arouse.

Because the idea that refugees can pollute their hosts can become a self-fulfilling prophecy, it is not only repugnant but potentially dangerous. Modern-day practices of quarantine analogous to the Ellis Island experi-ence can jeopardize health. During the winter of 1993–4, Dutch research-ers studied the health of refugees who, while waiting to be officially processed, were housed in an off-shore cruise ship. By the time health inspections took place, tuberculosis had spread not only among the refu-gees themselves, but among the staff. High initial rates of disease weren't to blame. Inadequate housing, poor ventilation, and a prolonged screening process caused the spread of the disease from a few carriers to the point where it became a mini-epidemic (van Loenhout-Rooyackers, 1994).

Tuberculosis, cholera, tetanus, and typhoid fever are common killers in refugee camps. The particular micro-organism associated with each of these diseases is never the sole cause of an epidemic. The sweep of an infectious illness through a refugee camp is almost always preceded by malnutrition and poor hygienic conditions that batter down host immune defences, thereby making it possible for micro-organisms to win the day (Arthur et al., 1992; Malfait et al., 1993). Despair is a more elusive, but perhaps no less powerful, pathogen than poor living conditions. A study of twenty-five thousand displaced Kurds in northwest Iran revealed that already high rates of respiratory illnesses, diarrhea, and typhoid fever increased just at the time they were forced to go home (Babille et al., 1994).

The concept of limenal pollution implies that the traveller is the problem. The source of pollution is genetic predisposition, exotic cultural practices, or unfortunate pre-migration experiences. History suggests a different construction. Despite their long lists of disqualifying conditions, the Ellis Island doctors never, at any period, rejected more than 3 per cent of all would-be immigrants (Kraut, 1994). However, the Jews who had fled Middle and Eastern Europe's pogroms and the southern Italians trying to escape the poverty of the Mediterranean basin who made it through Ellis Island subsequently suffered more illness and higher death rates than the American-born. The new settlers hadn't brought their diseases with them: they developed them in the United States. Exploitation in the workplace, poverty, overcrowding, unsanitary living conditions, inadequate access to medical services, anxiety, and disillusionment (half the Italian immigrants ultimately went back to Europe) were the most likely culprits (Kraut, 1994).

Things haven't changed. In the late 1990s, tuberculosis re-emerged as a major public health concern. Although they make up only 15 per cent of Canada's population, immigrants account for almost 60 per cent of all new cases of tuberculosis every year (Health Canada, 1995). The United States faces a similar situation. Foreign-born residents of the United States are four times more likely than native-born Americans to develop tuberculosis (McKenna, McCray, and Onorato, 1995). Newcomers, however, do not have active cases of tuberculosis when they arrive: rigorous screening rules this out. Many were probably exposed to tuberculosis prior to immigrating. During the process of resettlement, previously dormant infection becomes reactivated. Since immigrants in Canada are less likely to end up in the kinds of sweatshops that bred illness among their turn-of-the-century predecessors in the United States, and are less likely to be poor or to live in substandard housing, there may be other explanatory factors operating to explain high rates of tuberculosis among present-day new settlers. Anxiety and disillusionment are possible culprits. Since the immune system is exquisitely responsive to the state of emotional well-being, the idea that emotional distress may contribute to vulnerability to illness does not seem far-fetched.

When things go wrong, there is a tendency to look for scapegoats. Immigrants and refugees are convenient candidates. On 30 October 1995, the Parti-Québécois (PQ)–dominated government of the Province of Quebec held a referendum designed to give the PQ a mandate to declare sovereignty from Canada. The referendum was defeated by a vote of about 1 per cent. Conceding defeat on that night, the Prime Minister of Quebec, Mr Jacques Parizeau, assured a cheering crowd that there would be another referendum soon. Unlike this time, when 'money and the ethnic vote' had derailed the chance to separate from Canada, the sovereigntists would win the next round. Later that night, Mr Bernard Landry, the Minister of Immigration and Cultural Communities, checked into his hotel. When he heard the desk clerk's Hispanic name, he unleashed a diatribe about the immigrant vote. He frightened the clerk so badly that she called hotel security. Earlier in the campaign, Mr Lucien Bouchard, leader of the Bloc Québécois, Canada's official opposition party, which had been elected on a platform of separating Quebec from Confederation, tarnished his 'St Lucien' halo a bit by proclaiming that white Québécoises were not having enough babies. The clear implication was that 'the others' were having too many children. Musing on these events, a Vietnamese journalist sympathetic to the sovereigntist cause nevertheless had to conclude that 'minorities are acceptable as long as they don't get in the way of ... the majority' (Tu, 1995). The theme that the unclean can threaten existing power structures also threads its way throughout the proclamations of these three leaders, each of whom betrays in his statements the premium attached to a *pure laine* (pure wool) citizenry.

Good intention and reasonable speculation prompted initial concern for the Southeast Asian refugees' mental health. The concern can also be seen as a contemporary re-enactment of fears of pollution. Because the refugees had suffered so much before they came to Canada, the mental health and social services sectors braced themselves for what they expected would prove an enormous demand for services.

When the demand never materialized, new concerns arose about whether refugees were 'under-utilizing' services, or whether they were resorting to 'traditional' or 'unconventional' therapies. The truth, as Refugee Resettlement Project data show, is that, as a group, the Southeast Asians had remarkably good mental health. Reminiscent of the Ellis Island experience many years before, the newcomers did not bring illnesses with them. More than 50 per cent of immigrants who develop tuberculosis do so within the first five years after coming to Canada (Health Canada, 1995). The median latency period may be as short as one year for refugees (Jay Keystone, personal communication). The coincidence of maximal risk for developing tuberculosis and maximal mental health risk bears investigation.

Refugee Adaptation: Factors That Help and Forces That Impede

To those who might ask, How well do refugees adapt? the RRP study offers only a partial answer. One of the study's limitations is that it describes refugee resettlement in an industrialized country, and most refugees never reach such countries. Only 17 per cent of the world's refugees are in Western Europe, the United States, Canada, and Australia (Clinton-Davis and Fassil, 1992). The majority of the displaced live in the world's poorest countries, where they receive little attention, whether from research or in the form of services (Muecke, 1992).

The RRP data are an important commentary, however, on the question How did the refugees do in Canada? and, by extension, How might they be expected to do in similar, advantaged, industrialized countries? On the whole, they did fine. But their adaptation took time. For example, although everyone would like to see newcomers working within the first year of resettlement, both the Canadian and U.S. experiences suggest this is too optimistic an expectation. Unemployment rates stay high for the first few years, but they do eventually go down. The longer the refugees stayed in Canada, the more self-sufficient they became, a pattern that has also been observed in the United States (Caplan, Whitmore, and Choy, 1989; Fass, 1986; Strand, 1989). Simply knowing that, despite initial difficulties, the long-term prospects are comparatively bright might help refugees and their hosts alike.

Reassurance about future prospects can be no excuse, however, for a policy of complacency. Instead, it is important to understand the factors promoting and impeding employability, in particular, and adaptation, in general.

Recognition of credentials is one impediment about which refugees frequently complain. Prospective employers understandably want some assurance of training, either in the form of a certificate or a personal reference. Like anyone trying to find a job for the first time, refugees face a classic catch-22 situation. Having never worked outside their homelands, they have no references attesting to their 'Canadian experience.' This throws them back on the need for certification of previous training. The problem is that many refugees lack such certificates. It is hard to hold onto important documents during flight or during internment in refugee camps. Refugees who manage to hold onto their certificates often find that the papers don't do much good. It is hard to convince prospective employers that foreign training and experience equip someone for a job in Canada.

Quebec was probably the first province to acknowledge recertification difficulties. The province also recognized that by not allowing people to practise acquired skills, receiving societies were squandering human capital. Accordingly, the Division Scolaire et Professionelle of the Ministère des Communautés Culturelles et de l'Immigration created an orientation program for newcomers, as part of which it determines the North American equivalence of diplomas and arranges for special training needed to qualify for relicensure. Quebec has developed a model that should be emulated elsewhere.

According to Refugee Resettlement Project data, job training enhanced employment prospects. Nevertheless, only about one in eight refugees received it. Although some studies (Pedraza-Bailey, 1985) have suggested that state-supported professional retraining programs help refugees, the effect is far from overwhelming (Haines, 1988).

Employment-training programs need to analyse the reasons for their relative lack of impact on refugee communities. Self-scrutiny will probably point to the need for cross-cultural orientation for employment counsellors. Although Vinh Thuy's employment counsellor was sufficiently astute to eventually recognize that sending him to work at outdoor jobs ended in failure, it took three tries before she recommended an appropriate inside job. Had she known more about what life was like in Southeast Asian prison camps, the reason underlying Vinh's unsuccessful placements might have occurred to her sooner. To her credit, she was evidently supportive enough to encourage Vinh to keep coming back for help. Other refugees applying for job assistance find less encouragement, too often interpreting a counsellor's brusque manner, or what seems to them an overly casual acknowledgment of some skill they have worked hard to achieve, as a personal rejection (Canadian Task Force, 1988a).

Mental health and employment have a reciprocal relationship. Emotional disorder makes it difficult to hold onto a job, and unemployment creates a risk for depression. Preventing what seems to be a self-sustaining cycle of poor health and occupational impairment will call for the interdigitation of mental health and employment services.

The least well educated were the least likely to find work, and the least likely to understand English (see also Haines, 1987). Working and learning English are reciprocal processes. Although English does not confer much advantage in finding a job in the early years of resettlement – probably because most of the refugees initially work in menial positions – command of the language does promote occupational advance over the long term. People who learned English also enjoyed life more, probably because command of the language gave them access to the larger community's neighbourhoods, and to TV, movies, newspapers, and radio. Proficiency in English may have helped parents preserve their relationships with their Canadianized children and to prevent intergenerational clashes.

The fact that two-thirds of the refugees spoke little or no English after a decade of living in Canada is cause for concern. Language programs and regular contact with Canadians in the majority culture were the most effective learning vehicles. Ironically, women benefited from English classes even more than men, but were less likely to attend them. Since they were also more likely to be home with young children or, if they worked, to be employed in ethnic enclave industries that did not require English, women had less chance than men to use English in their everyday lives.

Family and community protect mental health. Nguyen Bich's story calls into question the logic of admitting someone as a refugee and then imposing economic constraints that block family reunification, most particularly in the earliest years of resettlement. The quantitative RRP data show that, even though most stories are probably less dramatic than Bich's, refugee mental health benefits from the presence of family. Relaxing the criteria for family reunification would be a humanitarian act that would support mental health. Early family reunification probably has tangible economic benefit, as well. According to other studies, the household is the basic economic unit for refugees, benefiting every member of the unit because it facilitates a blending of income from multiple sources such as the market, informal economy, and social assistance programs.

The opportunity to blend incomes at early, critical stages of resettlement facilitates the transition to self-sufficiency (Gold, 1992; Caplan, Whitmore, and Choy, 1989). Recent Canadian-based data show that individual immigrants from Europe economically outperform Asian immigrants. However, when the household becomes the unit of analysis, the picture reverses: Asian households outperform their European counterparts (David Ley, personal communication).

During their early years in Canada, the Chinese benefited from the presence of a large like-ethnic community in Vancouver. It provided a modest advantage in employment prospects for the Chinese over their non-Chinese counterparts (Johnson, 1988). More importantly, it created opportunities for social interaction that helped provide a carry-over between the culture the refugees had left behind and what must have seemed to them a very strange new society. In some ways, the ethnic community acted like a cocoon, providing protection for newcomers and a relatively soft landing. The existence of like-ethnic communities, and, in all probability, government support of them, stimulates the emergence of self-help or mutual assistance agencies that are advantageous, particularly during the early years of resettlement (Abhay, 1992).

What happens when there are no pre-existing like-ethnic communities? After all, someone always has to be the first to come, just as the ethnic Vietnamese, Laotians, and Cambodians were when they arrived in Vancouver in 1981. There is great potential benefit to be derived from sponsorship and hosting programs. However, a wish to help does not guarantee that the help will be sensitive or informed. To prevent tragedies such as Soon's religious conversion through a misguided attempt to please her sponsors, potential helpers will have to be helped. At a minimum, orientation and follow-up consultation programs should be made available to all potential hosts and sponsors.

Ethnic enclaves have disadvantages as well as advantages. Within five years after arrival, the initial advantage of a like-ethnic community had disappeared. What may have conferred initial advantage may have soured over the years, an idea captured in the concept of ethnic entrapment. Ethnic entrapment suggests that, although ethnic affinity and kinship help land newly arrived immigrants jobs in minority-owned establishments, these family and community bonds can trap newcomers like Quyen in economically exploitative relationships (Li, 1977). In the long run, immigrant employers may benefit more from the ethnic enclave economy than immigrant workers (Sanders and Nee, 1987). Another reason why the non-Chinese refugees eventually caught up with their Chinese counterparts was that the early years of resettlement provided an opportunity for a new ethnocultural infrastructure to become established that provided them the type of social support the Chinese had had all along.

Vietnamese and Laotians were more likely than Chinese to learn English and to make friends with non–Southeast Asian Canadians. Although Canadian multiculturalism policy emphasizes the importance of heritage culture retention, it pays equal attention to the advantages that accrue from participation in the larger society. In this respect, the non-Chinese cultivation of language skills and relationships that extend beyond ethnic boundaries may turn out to be tools for participation in Canadian society that will ultimately transform their mental health disadvantage into advantage vis-à-vis their Chinese counterparts. No research study can fail to call for more research, and this one is no exception. The changing functions of ethnic enclaves over time is a topic surely in need of investigation. Research can help point to ways in which the initial help provided by the like-ethnic groups can be supplemented by active programs of integration that will, over the long term, equip new settlers to participate in the larger society as well as in their indigenous communities (Hanson and Pratt, 1995).

Time changed many things for the refugees. Initially, women had a mental health advantage over men. Over time, this disappeared and the Southeast Asian women began to take on the pattern of mental health disadvantage that characterizes most women in most community surveys. The elderly, who were relatively protected at first, also became more vulnerable with the passage of time and, most probably, increasing isolation and erosion of stature. Resettlement is not a short-term or time-limited process. It probably affects people for most of their lives, and it affects them differently at different developmental stages.

Refugees and Immigrants

The report of a government-appointed commission to recommend changes to Canada's immigration laws (Immigration Legislative Review, 1997) suggests separating immigration and refugee legislation, rather than leaving them combined as they currently are. The commission based its recommendation on the observation that the general public is confused about the two concepts.

There are good reasons to support the commission's recommendation. First, as a receiving country, Canada should hold out different expectations for immigrants than it does for refugees. Immigrant human capital is expected to benefit the country. We should have no such expectations of refugees; if they do contribute, as most refugees have, that is a bonus rather than the fulfilment of a requirement. Another reason to separate the two classes of settlers is that they have different needs. Refugees are far less likely than immigrants to speak the host country's language when they arrive. Language training for refugees should be an important priority. There is also reason to believe that mental health needs will differ: refugees are, for example, at high risk for post-traumatic stress disorder (PTSD), but there is no reason that immigrants should have any higher rates of this disorder than the host country's population. Refugee mental health continues, however, to be a neglected topic. Finally, Canada admits refugees for entirely different reasons than it admits immigrants. We receive immigrants in the hope of benefit; we shelter refugees out of a sense of compassion.

Why Bother?

Generations of immigrants and refugees have thought of the United States as 'the place where, when you have to go there, they have to take you in.' Since its founding as a state, Israel provides the same sort of place, at least for all Jews. Canada and Australia have more recently joined the ranks of countries held up as examples of generosity in their treatment of the dispossessed.

Why should nations continue to provide asylum to the dispossessed? Refugee advocates maintain that, in admitting refugees, nations are not being generous, but merely complying with the terms of international treaties to which they are signatories. In other words, they are complying with international law. The argument is circular. Law usually codifies practice; leading refugee-receiving countries like Canada, the United States, Israel, Australia, and certain Western European countries shelter refugees, not because they are bound by law, but because the law these countries helped create reflects deeply rooted values and time-honoured practice.

According to UN estimates, there are 27 million refugees in the world. Repatriation is the officially preferred solution to this crisis of the dispossessed. To be repatriated is to be restored, to go home. The term has positive valence. Too often, the practice is anything but positive: it is an imposed, rather than a chosen, solution. Permanent settlement in so-called countries of first asylum is another potential solution. However, the fact that the poorest countries in the world currently provide initial asylum to almost 80 per cent of the world's refugees makes this an unlikely solution. For the foreseeable future, the demand for permanent asylum in the industrialized world will continue to be unrelenting.

By providing sanctuary to persons who, according to domestic values, are the victims of oppression, countries of asylum pass judgment on violations of human rights in the countries from which refugees come. For example, chapter 3 described recent Canadian and U.S. decisions to provide asylum to people fleeing persecution on the basis of their sexual orientation, violation of their assumed right to bear children, and practices such as female genital mutilation. These decisions constitute a de facto expansion of the concept of persecution. Such important precedents undoubtedly affect the practices of all countries that provide asylum, but they are also a commentary on the standards of refugee-producing countries. The case for making such comments is neither simple nor straightforward. Cultures that attempt to impose their own standards and values on others can be, at the very least, arrogant. They can also be dangerous. However, the inevitability of the 'global village' throws into relief the need for a definition of universal human rights that transcends local boundaries. Refugee policy, poised at the intersection between domestic and international politics, provides important commentary on the debate about human rights.

Aside from the overwhelming need for asylum and the opportunity to affect international political discourse, privileged countries should go on admitting refugees because their kindness to strangers at the gate is an affirmation of humanitarianism.

Max Weber, the great philosopher-scientist, observed that ethical imperatives like humanitarianism are not inimical to, but are a necessary component of, national self-interest. Policies of pure self-interest too easily become brutal and opportunistic. Rabbi Gunther Plaut (1995) has offered a similar observation. Countries admit immigrants out of self-interest: they should admit refugees as a reminder that self-interest is not the only factor that should drive behaviour.

Weber did caution, however, that altruism divorced from self-interest can be naïve. Viewed as an investment in 'human capital,' good settlement practice is both ethical and a good investment. Human capital refers to human skills and abilities that bring rewards in the labour market (Becker, 1975). The higher a person's human capital, the better equipped he or she is for capital-generating work. As nations achieve higher levels of aggregate human capital, the more productive they become, and the more internationally competitive. Schooling and on-the-job training are human capital 'investments' (Lord and Falk, 1980; Kposowa, 1993). Although economists don't usually refer to it as such, individual health seems another worthwhile investment. After all, unemployment created a risk for depression among the Southeast Asians, but depression compromised their ability to hold onto a job. The RRP study's results suggest that, if handled correctly, humanitarianism need not cost very much.

When times are difficult, as they were during the first half of the 1990s, receiving societies become less generous about admitting newcomers, and less willing to treat them well after they have been admitted. However, even if the costs of compassion were higher than they are, and the problems of adjusting to each other even more difficult than they are, countries such as Canada cannot refuse to provide haven for some of the world's people who have nowhere else to go. However, a welcome mat at the door is not enough. After the door has been opened, it is the warmth of the welcome that will make all the difference.

References

Abella, I., and H. Troper. (1982). *None is too many: Canada and the Jews of Europe, 1933–1948*. Toronto: Lester & Orpen Dennys.

Abhay, K. (1992). Leadership and management: A comparative study of MAAs. *Refugee Participation Network*. 13: 9–11.

Adelman, H. (1982). *Canada and the Indochinese refugees*. Regina: Weigl Education Associates.

Aguirre, B.E., R. Seanz, and S. Hwang. (1989). Discrimination and the assimilation and ethnic competition perspectives. *Social Science Quarterly* 70: 594–606.

Aldwin, C.M. (1994). *Stress, coping and development*. New York: Guilford Press.

American Psychiatric Association. (1952). *Diagnostic and statistical manual of mental disorders*. 1st ed. Washington, DC.

– (1968). *Diagnostic and statistical manual of mental disorders*. 2nd ed. Washington, DC.

– (1980). *Diagnostic and statistical manual of mental disorders*. 3rd ed. Washington, DC.

– (1994). *Diagnostic and statistical manual of mental disorders*. 4th ed. Washington, DC.

Angst, J. (1986). The course of major depression, atypical bipolar disorder and bipolar disorder. In *New results in depression research*, ed. H. Hippius, G. Klerman, and N. Matussek, pp. 26–35. Berlin: Springer-Verlag.

Appelfeld, A. (1994). *Beyond despair: Three lectures and a conversation with Philip Roth*. New York: Fromm International.

Arthur, J.D., L. Bodhidatta, P. Echeverria, S. Phuphaisan, and S. Paul. (1992). Diarrheal disease in Cambodian children at a camp in Thailand. *American Journal of Epidemiology* 135: 541–51.

Avery, D. (1979). *'Dangerous foreigners': European immigrant workers and labour radicalism in Canada, 1896–1932.* Toronto: McClelland and Stewart.

Aylesworth, L.S., and P.G. Ossorio. (1983). Refugees: Cultural displacement and its effects. *Advances in Descriptive Psychology* 3: 45–93.

Aylesworth, L.S., P.G. Ossorio, and L.T. Osaki. (1977). Stress and mental health among Vietnamese in the United States: Preliminary findings of a mental health needs assessment among Vietnamese refugees in Colorado. Paper presented at the Health, Education and Welfare Conference on Mental Health Needs of Indochinese Refugees, Denver, CO.

Babbie, E.R. (1992). *The practice of social research.* 6th ed. Belmont, CA: Wadsworth.

Babille, M., P. De Colombani, R. Guerra, N. Zagaria, and C. Zanetti. (1994). Post-emergency epidemiological surveillance in Iraqi-Kurdish refugee camps in Iran. *Disasters* 18: 58–75.

Bartlett, F.C. (1932). *Remembering.* Cambridge: Cambridge University Press.

Baskaukos, L. (1981). The Lithuanian refugee experience and grief. *International Migration Review* 15: 276–91.

Basoglu, M., M. Parker, E. Ozmen, I. Marks, C. Incesu, D. Sahin, and N. Sarimurat. (1994). Psychological effects of torture: A comparison of tortured with nontortured political activists in Turkey. *American Journal of Psychiatry* 151: 76–81.

Bass, E., and L. Davis. (1988). *The courage to heal: A guide for women survivors of child sexual abuse.* New York: Harper Perennial.

Bauer, M., S. Priebe, B. Haring, and K. Adamczak. (1993). Long-term sequelae of political imprisonment in East Germany. *Journal of Nervous and Mental Disease* 181: 257–62.

Bauer, W. (1997). Refugees, victims, or killers. The new slave trade? *International Journal* (Autumn): 677–94.

Baxter, D. (1997). Immigration to Canada: Youth tonic for an aging population. Urban Futures Institute, Vancouver.

Becker, G.S. (1975). *Human capital: A theoretical and empirical analysis, with special reference to education.* New York: National Bureau of Economic Research.

Beiser, M. (1974). Components and correlates of mental well-being. *Journal of Health and Social Behavior* 15(4): 320–7.

– (1982). Migration in a developing country: Risk and opportunity. In *Uprooting and surviving,* ed. R.C. Nann, pp. 119–46. New York: Reidl.

– (1988). Influences of time, ethnicity, and attachment on depression in Southeast Asian refugees. *American Journal of Psychiatry* 145(1): 46–51.

– (1998). Extreme situations. In *Adversity, stress and psychopathology,* ed. B.P. Dohrenwend, pp. 9–12. New York: Oxford University Press.

Beiser, M., R.C. Benfari, H. Collomb, and J.L. Ravel. (1976). Measuring psychoneurotic behaviour in cross-cultural surveys. *Journal of Nervous and Mental Disease* 163: 10–23.

Beiser, M., W.A. Burr, H. Collomb, and J.L. Ravel. (1974). Pobough Lang in Senegal: Analysis of a deviant behavior in biological and cultural contexts. *Social Psychiatry* 9: 123–9.

Beiser, M., W.A. Burr, J.L. Ravel, and H. Collomb. (1973). Illness of the spirit among the Serer of Senegal. *American Journal of Psychiatry* 130: 881–6.

Beiser, M., M. Cargo, and M.A. Woodbury. (1994). A comparison of psychiatric disorder in different cultures: Depressive typologies in Southeast Asian refugees and resident Canadians. *International Journal of Methods in Psychiatric Research* 4: 157–72.

Beiser, M., and H. Collomb. (1981). Mastering change: Epidemiological and case studies in Senegal, West Africa. *American Journal of Psychiatry* 138: 455–9.

Beiser, M., H. Collomb, J.L. Ravel, and C.J. Nafziger. (1976). Systemic blood pressure studies among the Serer of Senegal. *Journal of Chronic Diseases* 29: 371–80.

Beiser, M., G. Devins, R. Dion, I. Hyman, and E. Lin. (1997). Immigration acculturation and health. Report to the Health Canada National Health Research and Development Program, Project no. 6606–6414–NPHS, Ottawa.

Beiser, M., J.J. Feldman, and C.J. Egelhoff. (1972). Assets and affects: A study of positive mental health. *Archives of General Psychiatry* 27: 545–9.

Beiser, M., and J.A. Fleming. (1986). Measuring psychiatric disorder among Southeast Asian refugees. *Psychological Medicine* 16: 627–39.

Beiser, M., F. Hou, and I. Hyman. (n.d.). A ten-year study of unemployment, language and mental health among Southeast Asian refugees. Typescript.

Beiser, M., and I. Hyman. (1997). Refugees' time perspective and mental health. *American Journal of Psychiatry* 154: 996–1002.

Beiser, M., P.J. Johnson, R.J. Turner. (1993). Unemployment, underemployment and depressive affect among Southeast Asian refugees. *Psychological Medicine* 23: 731–43.

Beiser, M., and A.H. Leighton. (1976). Personality assets and mental health. In *Explorations in social psychiatry*, ed. H. Kaplan, pp. 178–94. New York: Basic Books.

Beiser, M., S. Noh, V. Kaspar, F. Hou, and J. Rummens. (n.d.). Perceived racial discrimination among Asian refugees in Canada. Typescript.

Beiser, M., and J.L. Ravel, H. Collomb, and C. Egelhoff. (1972). Assessing psychiatric disorder among the Serer of Senegal. *Journal of Nervous and Mental Disease* 154: 141–51.

Beiser, M., R.J. Turner, and S. Ganesan. (1989). Catastrophic stress and factors affecting its consequences among Southeast Asian refugees. *Social Science and Medicine* 28: 183–95.

Bennaum, P., R. Bennaum, and P. Kelly. (1984). *The people from Indo-China.* Victoria, Australia: Hodja Educational Resources Cooperation.

Berry, J.W. (1984). Cultural relations in plural societies: Alternatives to segregation and their sociopsychological implications. In *Groups in contact,* ed. N. Miller and M. Brewer, pp. 11–27. New York: Academic Press.

Berry, J.W., and T. Blondel. (1970). Psychological adaptation of Vietnamese refugees in Canada. *Canadian Journal of Community Mental Health,* 1: 81.

Black, J.H., and A.S. Lakhani. (1997). Ethnoracial diversity in the House of Commons: An analysis of numerical representation in the 35th parliament. *Canadian Ethnic Studies* (November): 13–33.

Blackmore, R. (1725). *A treatise of the spleen and vapours.* London: J. Pemberton.

Blanchard, E.B., E.J. Hickling, and A.E. Taylor. (1991). The psychophysiology of motor vehicle accident related post-traumatic stress disorder. *Biofeedback and Self-Regulation* 16(4): 449–54.

Bland, R.C., and H. Orn. (1981). Schizophrenia: Sociocultural factors. *Canadian Journal of Psychiatry* 26: 186–8.

Bland, R.C., G. Stebelsky, H. Orn, and S.C. Newman. (1988). Psychiatric disorders and unemployment in Edmonton. *Acta Psychiatrica Scandinavica Supplementum* 77: 72–80.

Blishen, B.R., and H.A. McRoberts. (1976). A revised socioeconomic index for occupations in Canada. *Canadian Review of Sociology and Anthropology* 13: 71–9.

Boman, B., and M. Edwards. (1984). The Indochinese refugee: An overview. *Australian and New Zealand Journal of Psychiatry* 18: 40–52.

Borjas, G. (1993). The intergenerational mobility of immigrants. *Journal of Labour Economics* 11: 113–26.

Boyd, M. (1977). Migration policy, female dependency and family membership: Canada and Germany. In *Women and the Canadian welfare state,* ed. P. Evans and G. Wekerle, pp. 142–69. Toronto: University of Toronto Press.

Bradburn, N.M. (1969). *The structure of psychological well-being.* Chicago: Aldine.

Breton, R. (1978). The structure of relationships between ethnic collectivities. In *The Canadian ethnic mosaic,* ed. L. Driedeger, pp. 55–73. Toronto: McClelland and Stewart.

Bronisch, T., H. Wittchen, C. Krieg, H. Rupp, and D. von Zerssen. (1985). Depressive neurosis: A long-term prospective and retrospective follow-up study of former inpatients. *Acta Psychiatrica Scandinavica* 71: 237–48.

Brown, G.W., and T.P. Harris. (1978). *Social origins of depression: A study of psychiatric disorders in women.* London: Tavistock.

Bruner, J. (1990). *Acts of meaning.* Cambridge, MA: Harvard University Press.

Burges-Watson, I.P. (1993). Post-traumatic stress disorder in Australian prisoners of the Japanese: A clinical study. *Australian and New Zealand Journal of Psychiatry* 27: 20–9.

Burwell, R.J., P. Hill, and J.F. Van Wicklin. (1986). Religion and refugee resettlement in the United States: A research note. *Review of Religious Research* 27: 356–66.

Canada. Parliament. Committee on Equality Rights. (1985). *Equality for all.* Ottawa: Supply and Services Canada.

Canada. Parliament. Special Committee on the Participation of Visible Minorities in Canadian Society. (1984). *Equality now.* Ottawa.

Canada. Royal Commission on Equality in Employment. (1984). *Report of the Commission on Equality in Employment.* Ottawa: Supply and Services Canada.

Canadian Task Force on Mental Health Issues Affecting Immigrants and Refugees. (1988a). *After the door has been opened: Mental health issues affecting immigrants and refugees in Canada.* No. Ci96–38/1988E. Ottawa: Ministry of Supply and Services Canada.

– (1988b). *Review of the literature on migrant mental health.* Ottawa: Ministry of Supply and Services Canada.

Caplan, N., J.K. Whitmore, and M.H. Choy. (1989). *The boat people and achievement in America: A study of family life, hard work and cultural values.* Ann Arbor: University of Michigan Press.

Carpenter, L., and I.F. Brockington. (1980). A study of mental illness in Asians, West Indians, and Africans living in Manchester. *British Journal of Psychiatry* 137: 201–5.

Castles, S., H. Booth, and T. Wallace. (1984). *Here for good: Western Europe's new ethnic minorities.* London: Pluto Press.

Ceroni, G.B., C. Nevi, and A. Pezzoli. (1984). Chronicity in major depression. *Journal of Affective Disorders* 7: 123–32.

Chan, K.B. (1987). Unemployment, social support and coping: The psychosocial response of Indochinese refugees to economic marginality. In *Uprooting, loss and adaptation: The resettlement of Indochinese refugees in Canada,* ed. K.B. Chan and D.M. Indra, pp. 116–31. Ottawa: Canadian Public Health Association.

Chan, K.B., and D. Loveridge. (1987). Refugees in transit: Vietnamese in a refugee camp in Hong Kong. *International Migration Review* 21: 745–59.

Chen, J., E. Ng, and R. Wilkins. (1996). The health of Canada's immigrants in 1994–95. *Health Reports* 7(4): 33–45.

Chen, X., V. Kaspar, and S. Noh. (1997). Social support networks and psychological adjustment in childhood and adolescence: A cross-cultural study. Paper presented at the 55th Annual International Council of Psychologists Convention, Padua, Italy.

Cheung, F.M. (1982). Psychological symptoms among Chinese in urban Hong Kong. *Social Science and Medicine* 16: 1339–44.

Cheung, F.M., and M.F. Dobkin de Rios. (1982). Recent trends in the study of the mental health of Chinese immigrants to the United States. *Research in Race and Ethnic Relations* 3: 145–63.

Cheung, F.M., B.W. Lau, and E. Waldman. (1980). Somatization among Chinese depressives in general practice. *International Journal of Psychiatry in Medicine* 10: 361–74.

Chui, T.W.L., J. Curtis, and R.D. Lambert. (1991). Immigrant background and political participation: Examining generational patterns. *Canadian Journal of Sociology* 16(4): 375–97.

Citizenship and Immigration Canada. (1996). *Total immigrant population*. Profiles: Immigration Research Series. Ottawa: Ministry of Supply and Services Canada.

Clark, A.W., and M.P. Clissold. (1982). Correlates of adaptation among unemployed and employed young men. *Psychological Reports* 50: 887–93.

Clinton-Davis, L., and Y. Fassil. (1992). Health and social problems of refugees. *Social Science and Medicine* 35: 507–13.

Cochrane, R., F. Hashmi, and M. Stopes-Roe. (1977). Measuring psychological disturbance in Asian immigrants to Britain. *Social Science and Medicine* 11: 157–64.

Cochrane, R., and M. Stopes-Roe. (1981). Psychological symptom levels in Indian immigrants to England: A comparison with native English. *Psychological Medicine* 11: 319–27.

Cohen, S. (1980). *Folk devils and moral panics: The creation of mods and rockers*. Oxford: Martin Robertson Press.

Convention relating to the status of refugees. (1951). Vol. 2, Human rights: A compilation of international instruments. Section O(82) (1950).

Cooley, C.H. (1902). *Human nature and the social order*. Glencoe, IL: Free Press.

Cottle, T.J. (1967). The circles test: An investigation of perceptions of temporal relatedness and dominance. *Journal of Projective Techniques and Personality Assessment* 31: 58–71.

– (1969). The location of experience: A manifest time orientation. *Acta Psychologica* 28: 129–49.

– (1976). *Perceiving time: A psychological investigation of men and women*. New York: Wiley.

Coyne, A. (1995). The case for open immigration. *The Next City* (Winter): 34–66.

Davidson, J., and R. Smith. (1990). Traumatic experiences in psychiatric outpatients. *Journal of Traumatic Stress Studies* 3(3): 459–75.

Davidson, J.R.T., D. Hughes, D.G. Blazer, and L.K. George. (1991). Post-traumatic stress disorder in the community: An epidemiological study. *Psychological Medicine* 21: 713–21.

Dawes, R.M., D. Faust, and P.E. Meehl. (1989). Clinical versus actuarial judgement. *Science* 243: 1668–74.

Dean, G., D. Walsh, H. Downing, and E. Shelley. (1981). First admission of native-born and immigrants to psychiatric hospitals in south-east England 1976. *British Journal of Psychiatry* 139: 506–12.

De Girolamo, G. (1992). International perspectives on the treatment and prevention of post-traumatic stress. In *International handbook of traumatic stress syndromes*, ed. J. Wilson and B. Raphael, pp. 935–46. New York: Plenum Press.

Devins, G.M., M. Beiser, R. Dion, L.G. Pelletier, and R.G. Edwards. (1997). Cross-cultural measurement of psychological well-being: The psychometric equivalence of Cantonese, Vietnamese, and Laotian translations of the Affect Balance Scale. *American Journal of Public Health* 87(5): 794–9.

deVoretz, D. (1995). *Diminishing returns: The economics of immigration policy.* Toronto: University of Toronto Press.

– (1996). Immigration to Vancouver: Economic windfall or downfall? http://www.sfu.ca/rim

deVos, G., and H. Miner. (1959). Oasis and casbah – a study in acculturative stress. In *Culture and mental health*, ed. M.K. Opler, pp. 333–50. New York: Macmillan.

Dew, M.A., E.J. Bromet, and H.C. Schulberg. (1987). A comparative analysis of two community stressors' long-term mental health effect. *American Journal of Community Psychology* 15: 167–84.

Diener, E. (1984). Subjective well-being. *Psychological Bulletin* 95: 542–75.

Dinges, N.G., and A.R. Hollenbeck. (1978). The effect of instructional set on the self-esteem of Navajo children. *Journal of Social Psychology* 104: 9–13.

Dion, K.L., K.K. Dion, and A.W.-P. Pak. (1992). Personality-based hardiness as a buffer for discrimination-related stress in members of Toronto's Chinese community. *Canadian Journal of Behavioural Science* 24: 517–36.

Dohrenwend, B.S., and B.P. Dohrenwend. (1974). *Stressful life events: Their nature and effects.* New York: John Wiley & Sons.

Douglas, M. (1966). *Purity and danger: An analysis of concepts of pollution and taboo.* London: Routledge & Kegan Paul.

Dyer, G. (1998). Immigration folly: How the 'new' francophones will save Canada. *Globe and Mail*, 28 March, p. D3.

Eberly, R.E., and B.E. Engdahl. (1991). Prevalence of somatic and psychiatric disorder among former prisoners of war. *Hospital and Community Psychiatry* 42: 807–13.

Economist. (1991). A survey of Canada: For want of glue. 29 June, p. 46.

Edwards, R.G. (1994). Southeast Asian refugees in Canada: Gender differences in adaptation and mental health. PhD diss. Wilfrid Laurier University. (*Dissertation Abstract International* 56: 11B).

Eisenberg, L. (1984). The epidemiology of suicide in adolescents. *Pediatric Annals* 13: 47–54.

Eisenstadt, S.M. (1954). Studies in reference group behavior. *Human Relations* 7: 191–216.

Eitinger, L. (1961). Pathology of the concentration camp syndrome. *Archives of General Psychiatry* 5: 371–9.

Ellenberger, H.F. (1993). The pathogenic secret and its therapeutics. In *Beyond the unconscious: Essays of Henri F. Ellenberger in the history of psychiatry*, ed. M. Micale, pp. 341–59. Princeton, NJ: Princeton University Press.

Erdelyi, L. (1985). The quantal nature of transmission and spontaneous potentials at the Torpedo electromotor junction. *Acta Physiologica Hungarica* 65: 81–93.

– (1990). Papaverine blocks the early outward currents in helix neurons. *Acta Physiologica Hungarica* 75[Suppl.]: 91–2.

Espenshade, T.J., and H. Fu. (1997). An analysis of English-language proficiency among U.S. immigrants. *American Sociological Review* 62: 288–305.

Fass, S. (1986). Innovations in the struggle for self-reliance. *International Migration Review* 20: 351–80.

Feagin, J.R. (1991). The continuing significance of race: Anti-black discrimination in public places. *American Sociological Review* 56: 101–16.

Figley, C.R. (1993). Foreword. In *International handbook of traumatic stress syndromes*, ed. J.P. Wilson and B. Raphael, pp. xvii-xx. New York: Plenum Press.

Fitzgerald, F. (1972). *Fire in the lake: The Vietnamese and the Americans in Vietnam.* Boston: Little, Brown.

Frideres, J.S. (1989). Visible minority groups and second language programs: Language adaptation. *International Journal of the Sociology of Language* 80: 83–98.

Friedlander, S. (1979). *When memory comes.* Toronto: McGraw-Hill.

Gabrielidis, C., C. Stephan, O. Ybarra, V.M. Dos Santos Pearson, and L. Villareal. (1997). Preferred styles of conflict resolution: Mexico and the United States. *Journal of Cross-Cultural Psychology* 28(6): 661–77.

Gaind, K.S., and M. Beiser. (1997). Post-traumatic stress disorder in Southeast Asian refugees after ten years in Canada. Typescript.

Garbarino, J., and K. Kostelny. (1993). Children's response to war: What do we know? In *The psychological effects of war and violence on children*, ed. L. Leavitt and N. Fox, pp. 23–39. Hillsdale, NJ: Lawrence Erlbaum.

Garcia-Peltoniemi, R.E. (1991). Epidemiological perspectives. In *Mental health services for refugees*, pp. 24–41. Bethesda, MD: National Institute of Mental Health.

Getsinger, S.H., and R. Leon. (1979). Impulsivity temporal perspective and post-hospital adjustment of neuropsychiatric patients. *Journal of Psychology* 103: 221–5.

Giambra, L.M. (1974). Daydreaming across the life span: Late adolescent to senior citizen. *International Journal of Aging and Human Development* 5: 115–40.

Giel, R. (1998). Natural and human-made disasters. In *Adversity, stress and psychopathology*, ed. B.P. Dohrenwend, pp. 66–76. New York: Oxford University Press.

Glucksman, M.L., D.M. Quinlan, and H. Leigh. (1985). Skin conductance changes and psychotherapeutic content in the treatment of a phobic patient. *British Journal of Medical Psychology* 58: 155–63.

Gold, S.J. (1992) *Refugee communities: A comparative field study*. Newbury Park, NJ: Sage.

Goldberg, J., W.R. True, S.A. Eisen, and W.G. Henderson. (1990). A twin study of the effects of the Vietnam war on post-traumatic stress disorder. *Journal of the American Medical Association* 263: 1227–32.

Goldfield, N., and N. Lee. (1982). Caring for Indochinese refugees. *American Family Physician* 26: 157–60.

Goldlust, J., and A.H. Richmond. (1974). A multivariate model of immigrant adaptation. *International Migration Review* 8(2): 193–225.

Goldson, E. (1993). War is not good for children. In *The psychological effects of war and violence on children*, ed. L. Leavitt and N. Fox, pp. 3–22. Hillsdale, NJ: Lawrence Erlbaum.

Gordon, M. (1964). *Assimilation in American life: The role of race, religion, and national origin*. New York: Oxford University Press.

Gore, S. (1978). The effect of social support in moderating the health consequences of unemployment. *Journal of Health and Social Behavior* 19: 157–65.

Green, B.L., J.D. Lindy, M.C. Grace, and A.C. Leonard. (1992). Chronic post-traumatic stress disorder and diagnostic co-morbidity in a disaster sample. *Journal of Nervous and Mental Disease* 180: 760–6.

Grinberg, L. (1984). A psychoanalytic study of migration: Its normal and pathological aspects. *Journal of the American Psychoanalytic Association* 32: 13–38.

Gyorkos, T.W., J.D. MacLean, P. Viens, C. Cheang, and E. Kokoskin-Nelson. (1992). Intestinal parasite infection in the Kampuchean refugee population six years after resettlement in Canada. *Journal of Infectious Diseases* 166: 413–17.

Haines, D.W. (1987). Patterns of Southeast Asian refugee employment. *Ethnic Groups* 7: 39–59.

– (1988). The pursuit of English and self-sufficiency. *Journal of Refugees Studies* 1: 195–213.

Halberstam, D. (1971). *Ho*. New York: Random House.

Halldin, J. (1985). Prevalence of mental disorder in an urban population in central Sweden in relation to social class, marital status and immigration. *Acta Psychiatrica Scandinavica* 71: 117–27.

Hamberger, J., and M. Hewstone. (1997). Inter-ethnic contacts as a predictor of blatant and subtle prejudice: Tests of a model in four West European nations. *British Journal of Social Psychology* 36: 173–90.

Handlin, O. (1951). *The uprooted: The epic story of the great migrations that made the American people.* Boston: Little, Brown.

Hanson, S., and G. Pratt. (1995). *Gender, work and space.* London and New York: Routledge.

Harding, T.W., M.V. de Arango, and J. Baltazar. (1980). Mental disorders in primary health care: A study of their frequency and diagnosis in four developing countries. *Psychological Medicine* 10: 231–41.

Head, W. (1975). The Black presence in the Canadian mosaic. Report submitted to the Ontario Human Rights Commission.

– (1981). *Adaptation of immigrants: Perceptions of ethnic and racial discrimination.* Toronto: York University Press.

Health Canada. (1995). *Tuberculosis in Canada: 1995 annual report.* Ottawa: Health Protection Branch, Health Canada.

Heckman, J.J. (1992). What has been learned about labor supply in the past twenty years? *AEA papers and proceedings: Lessons from empirical labor economics, 1972–1991.*

Helzer, J. E., G.J. Canino, H.G. Hwu, R.C. Bland, S. Newman, and E.K. Yeh. (1988). Alcoholism: A cross-national comparison of population surveys with the Diagnostic Interview Schedule. In *Alcoholism: Origins and outcome,* ed. R.M. Rose and J.E. Barrett, pp. 31–48. American Psychopathological Association Series. New York: Raven Press.

Helzer, J.E., G.J. Canino, E.K. Yeh, R.C. Bland, C.K. Lee, H.G. Hwu, and S. Newman. (1990). Alcoholism – North America and Asia: A comparison of population surveys with the Diagnostic Interview Schedule. *Archives of General Psychiatry* 47: 313–19.

Helzer, J. E., L.N. Robins, and L. McEvoy. (1987). Post-traumatic stress disorder in the general population: Findings of the Epidemiologic Catchment Area survey. *New England Journal of Medicine* 317: 1630–4.

Henry, F. (1978). *Dynamics of racism.* Ottawa: Secretary of State.

Henry, F., C. Tator, W. Mattis, and T. Rees. (1995). *The colour of democracy: Racism in Canadian society.* Toronto: Harcourt Brace.

Herman, J.L. (1992). *Trauma and recovery.* New York: Basic Books.

Hilberg, R. (1967). *The destruction of the European Jews.* Chicago: Quadrangle Books.

Hinton, L., Q. Tiet, C.G. Tran, and M. Chesney. (1997). Predictors of depression among refugees from Vietnam: A longitudinal study of new arrivals. *Journal of Nervous and Mental Disease* 185(1): 39–45.

Hirschfeld, R., and C.K. Cross. (1982). Epidemiology of affective disorders. *Archives of General Psychiatry* 39: 35–46.

Hirshman, C., and M.G. Wong. (1984). Socio-economic gains of Asian Americans, Blacks and Hispanics, 1960–1976. *American Journal of Sociology* 90(3): 584–607.

Hoffman, E. (1989). *Lost in translation: A life in a new language.* New York: Dutton.

Hogman, P. (1985). Role of memories in lives of World War II orphans. *Journal of the American Academy of Child Psychology* 2: 390–6.

Holmes, T.H., and M. Masuda. (1973). Life change and illness susceptibility. In *Separation and depression: Clinical and research aspects,* ed. J.P. Scott and E.C. Senay, pp. 161–86. Washington, DC: American Association for the Advancement of Science.

Horowitz, M.J. (1982). Psychological processes induced by illness, injury and loss. In *Handbook of clinical health psychology,* ed. T. Millon, C. Green, and R. Meagher, pp. 53–68. New York: Plenum.

– (1986). Stress-response syndromes: A review of post-traumatic and adjustment disorders. *Hospital and Community Psychiatry* 37: 241–9.

Hurie, M.B., E.E. Mast, and J.P. Davis. (1992). Horizontal transmission of hepatitis B virus infection to United States-born children of Hmong refugees. *Pediatrics* 89: 269–73.

Idler, E.L., and R.J. Angel. (1990). Self-rated health and mortality in the NHANES-I epidemiologic follow-up study. *American Journal of Public Health* 80: 446–52.

Ignatieff, M. (1993). *Blood and belonging: Journeys into the new nationalism.* Toronto: Viking Press.

Immigration act. (1976). In *Acts of the Parliament of Canada,* vol. 2, chap. 52.

Immigration Legislation Review. (1997). *Not just numbers: The future of immigration in Canada.* Ottawa: Minister of Supplies and Services.

Inkeles, A., and D.H. Smith. (1974). *Becoming modern: Individual change in six developing countries.* Cambridge: Harvard University Press.

Irving, J. (1978). *The world according to Garp.* New York: E.P. Dutton.

Jackson, I.V. (1991). The Convention relating to the status of refugees: A universal basis for protection. *International Journal of Refugee Law* 3(3): 403–13.

Jahoda, M.M. (1982). *Employment and unemployment: A social psychological analysis.* Cambridge: Cambridge University Press.

Johnson, P.J. (1988). The impact of ethnic communities on the employment of Southeast Asian refugees. *Amerasia* 14: 1–22.

Kallarackal, A.M., and M. Herbert. (1976). The happiness of Indian immigrant children. *New Society* 35: 422–4.

Kaplan, G.A., and T. Camacho. (1983). Perceived health and mortality: A nine-year follow-up of the human population laboratory cohort. *American Journal of Epidemiology* 117: 292–304.

Kaspar, V., X. Chen, and S. Noh. (1997). Provision of social relationships in child-hood and adolescence: Associations with perceived self-worth and loneliness. Presented at the biennial meeting of the Society for Research in Child Development, Washington, DC.

Keane, T.M. (1998). Psychological effects of military combat. In *Adversity, stress and psychopathology*, ed. B.P. Dohrenwend, pp. 52–65. New York: Oxford University Press.

Keilson, H. (1992). *Sequential traumatization in children.* Jerusalem: Magness Press.

Keller, M.B., G.L. Klerman, P.W. Lavori, W. Coryell, J. Endicott, and J. Taylor. (1984). Long-term outcome in major depression. *Journal of the American Medical Association* 252: 788–92.

Keller, M.B., and R.W. Shapiro. (1981). Major depressive disorder: Initial results from a one-year prospective naturalistic follow-up study. *Journal of Nervous and Mental Disease* 169: 761–8.

Kessler, R.C., J.S. House, and J.B. Turner. (1987). Unemployment and health in a community sample. *Journal of Health and Social Behavior* 28: 51–9.

Kessler, R.C., J.B. Turner, and J.S. House. (1987). Intervening processes in the relationship between unemployment and health. *Psychological Medicine* 17: 949–61.

Kibria, N. (1993). *Family tightrope: The changing lives of Vietnamese Americans.* Princeton, NJ: Princeton University Press.

Kinzie, J.D. (1985). Cultural aspects of psychiatric treatment with Indochinese refugees. *American Journal of Social Psychiatry* 5: 47–53.

– (1986). Severe post-traumatic stress syndrome among Cambodian refugees: Symptoms, clinical course, and treatment approaches. In *Disaster stress studies: New methods and findings*, ed. J.H. Shore, pp. 124–40. Washington, DC: American Psychiatric Press.

Kinzie, J.D., and S.M. Manson. (1983). Five years experience with Indochinese refugee psychiatric patients. *Journal of Operational Psychiatry* 14: 105–11.

Kinzie, J.D., S.M. Manson, D.T. Vinh, N.T. Tolan, B. Anh, and T.N. Pho. (1982). Development and validation of a Vietnamese-language depression rating scale. *American Journal of Psychiatry* 139: 1276–81.

Kinzie, J.D., W. Sack, R. Angell, G. Clarke, and R. Ben. (1989). A three-year follow-up of Cambodian young people traumatized as children. *Journal of the American Academy of Child and Adolescent Psychiatry* 28: 501–4.

Kinzie, J.D., W.H. Sack, R.H. Angell, and S.M. Manson. (1986). The psychiatric effects of massive trauma on Cambodian children: I. The children. *Journal of the American Academy of Child Psychiatry* 25: 370–6.

Kirmayer, L. (1992). Social construction of hypnosis. *International Journal of Clinical and Experimental Hypnosis* 11: 276–300.

Kleinman, A. (1980). *Patients and healers in the context of culture*. Berkeley: University of California Press.

– (1982). Neurasthenia and depression: A study of somatization and culture in China. *Culture, Medicine and Psychiatry* 6: 117–90.

Klerman, G.L., P.W. Lavori, J. Rice, T. Reich, J. Endicott, N.C. Andreasen, M.B. Keller, and R.M. Hirschfield. (1985). Birth-cohort trends in rates of major depressive disorder among relatives of patients with affective disorder. *Archives of General Psychiatry* 42: 689–93.

Klinger, E. (1978). Modes of normal conscious flow. In *The stream of consciousness*, ed. K.S. Pope and J.L. Singer, pp. 225–8. New York: Plenum.

Kluckhon, F.R., and F.L. Strodtbeck. (1961). *Variations in value orientation*. Evanston, IL: Peterson.

Kluznik, J.C., N. Speed, C. Van-Valkenburg, and R. Magraw. (1986). Forty-year follow-up of United States prisoners of war. *American Journal of Psychiatry* 143: 1443–6.

Kopvillem, P. (1989). An angry racial backlash: Increasing numbers of Canadians no longer share the vision of a multicultural society. *Maclean's*, 10 July, pp. 14–16.

Kposowa, A.J. (1993). The impact of immigration on native earnings in the United States, 1940 to 1980. *Applied Behavioral Science Review* 1: 1–25.

Kraut, A.M. (1994). *Silent travellers: Germs, genes, and the 'immigrant menace.'* New York: Basic Books.

Krupinski, J. (1967). Sociological aspects of mental ill-health in immigrants. *Social Science and Medicine* 1: 267–81.

Krystal, H. (1968). *Massive psychic trauma*. New York: International Universities Press.

Krystal, H., and Y. Danieli. (1994). Holocaust survivor studies in the context of PTSD. *PTSD Research Quarterly* 5(4): 1–5.

Kuch, K., and B.J. Cox. (1992). Symptoms of PTSD in 124 survivors of the Holocaust. *American Journal of Psychiatry* 149: 337–40.

Kuhn, T.S. (1970). *The structure of scientific revolutions*. Chicago: University of Chicago Press.

Kuo, W. (1976). Theories of migration and mental health: An empirical testing on Chinese-Americans. *Social Science and Medicine* 10: 297–306.

– (1995). Coping with racial discrimination: The case of Asian Americans. *Ethnic and Racial Studies* 18: 109–27.

Kymlicka, W. (1998). *Finding our way: Rethinking ethnocultural relations in Canada*. Toronto: Oxford University Press.

Langer, L. (1991). *Holocaust testimonies: The ruins of memory*. New Haven: Yale University Press.

Lasry, J. C., and E.B. Schacter. (1975). Jewish intermarriage in Montreal. *Jewish Social Studies* 37: 267–78.

Leach, E. (1961). *Rethinking anthropology*. London: Athlone Press.

Leaf, P.J., M.M. Livinston, G.L. Tischler, M.M. Weissman, C.E. Holzer, and J.K. Myers. (1985). Contact with health professionals for the treatment of psychiatric and emotional problems. *Medical Care* 23: 1322–37.

Leaf, P.J., M.M. Weissman, J.K. Myers, G.L. Tischler, and C.E. Holzer. (1984). Social factors related to psychiatric disorders: The Yale Epidemiologic Catchment Area Study. *Social Psychiatry* 19: 53–61.

Leff, J.P. (1973). Culture and the differentiation of emotional states. *British Journal of Psychiatry* 123: 299–306.

– (1977). Notions of the emotions. *Mental Health and Society* 4: 308–18.

Leighton, A.H., T. Lambo, C.C. Hughes, DC. Leighton, J.M. Murphy, and D. Macklin. (1963). *Psychiatric disorder among the Yoruba*. Ithaca, NY: Cornell University Press.

Levav, I. (1998). Individuals under conditions of maximum adversity: The holocaust. In *Adversity, stress and psychopathology*, ed. B.P. Dohrenwend, pp. 13–33. New York: Oxford University Press.

Lewis, R.E., M.W. Fraser, and P.J. Pecora. (1988). Religiosity among Indochinese refugees in Utah. *Journal for the Scientific Study of Religion* 27: 272–83.

Li, P.S. (1977). Occupational achievement and kinship assistance among Chinese immigrants in Chicago. *Sociological Quarterly* 18(4): 478–89.

– (1978). The stratification of ethnic immigrants: The case of Toronto. *Canadian Review of Sociology and Anthropology* 15(1): 31–40.

– (1992). Race and gender as bases of class fractions and their effects on earnings. *Revue Canadienne de Sociologie et d'Anthropologie / Canadian Review of Sociology and Anthropology* 29: 488–510.

Lieberson, S. (1982). Stereotypes: Their consequences for race and ethnic interaction. In *Social structure and behaviour: Essays in honor of William Hamilton Sewell*, ed. R.M. Hauser, D. Mechanic, A.O. Haller, and T.S. Hauser, pp. 47–68. New York: Academic Press.

Lin, K.M. (1986). Psychopathology and social disruption in refugees. In *Refugee mental health in resettlement countries*, ed. C.C. Williams and J. Westermeyer, pp. 61–73. Washington, DC: Hemisphere Publishing Corp.

Loesel, F., and T. Bliesener. (1990). Resilience in adolescence: A study on the generalizability of protective factors. In *Health hazards in adolescence*, ed. K. Hurrelman and F. Loesel, pp. 299–320. New York: Walter de Gruyter.

Loewald, H. (1972). *The experience of time: The psychoanalytic study of the child*. New York: Quadrangle Books.

Lord, G.F.I., and W.W. Falk. (1980). An exploratory analysis of individualist versus structuralist explanations of income. *Social Forces* 59: 376–91.

Luborsky, L., and P. Crits-Christoph. (1989). A relationship pattern measure: The core conflictual relationship theme. *Psychiatry* 52: 250–9.

Lysenko, V. (1947). *Men in sheepskin coats.* Toronto: Ryerson Press.

Macdonald, Sir John A. (1890). Editorial in *Empire* [Toronto], 2 October.

Madakasira, S., and K.F. O'Brien. (1987). Acute post-traumatic stress disorders in victims of a natural disaster. *Journal of Nervous and Mental Disease* 175: 286–90.

Malarek, V. (1987). *Heaven's gate: Canada's immigration fiasco.* Toronto: Macmillan.

Malfait, P., A. Moren, J.C. Dillon, A. Brodel, G. Begkoyian, M.G. Etchegorry, G. Malenga, and P. Hakewill. (1993). An outbreak of pellagra related to changes in dietary niacin among Mozambican refugees in Malawi. *International Journal of Epidemiology* 22: 504–11.

Marrus, M.R. (1985). *The unwanted: European refugees in the twentieth century.* New York: Oxford University Press.

Marsella, A. (1979). Depressive experience and disorder across cultures. In *Handbook of cross-cultural psychology,* Vol. 6, ed. H.C. Triandis and J. Draguns, pp. 237–89. Boston: Allyn and Bacon.

Marshall, J. (1996). *Blood and bone.* Toronto: Mosaic Press.

May, R. (1958). Contributions of existential psychotherapy. In *Existence: A new dimension in psychiatry and psychology,* ed. R. May, E. Angel, and H. Ellenberger, pp. 37–91. New York: Basic Books.

McFarlane, A.C. (1988). The phenomenology of post-traumatic stress disorders following a natural disaster. *Journal of Nervous and Mental Disease* 176: 22–9.

McKenna, M.T., E. McCray, and I. Onorato. (1995). The epidemiology of tuberculosis among foreign-born persons in the United States, 1986–1995. *New England Journal of Medicine* 332: 1071–6.

Mead, G.H. (1934). *Mind, self and society.* Chicago: University of Chicago Press.

Meerloo, A.M. (1946). *Aftermath of peace: Psychological essays.* New York: International Universities Press.

Meertens, R., and T.F. Pettigrew. (1997). Is subtle prejudice really prejudice? *Public Opinion Quarterly* 61: 54–71.

Mollica, R.F., C. Poole, and S. Tor. (1998). Symptoms, functioning and health problems in a massively traumatized population: The legacy of the Cambodian tragedy. In *Adversity, stress and psychopathology,* ed. B.P. Dohrenwend, pp. 34–51. New York: Oxford University Press.

Montero, D. (1979). *Vietnamese-Americans: Patterns of resettlement and socioeconomic adaptation in the United States.* Boulder, CO: Westview Press.

Moore, B.E., and B.D. Fine. (1990). *Psychoanalytic terms and concepts.* New York: American Psychoanalytic Association.

Moritsugu, J., and S. Sue. (1983). Minority status as a stressor. In *Preventive psychology: Theory, research, and practice,* ed. R.D. Felner, L.A. Jason, J.N. Moritsugu, and S.S. Farber, pp. 162–74. New York: Pergamon Press.

Morton, D., and J.L. Granatstein. (1996). *Victory 1945: Canadians from war to peace.* Toronto: HarperCollins.

Muecke, M.A. (1992). New paradigms for refugee health problems. *Social Science and Medicine* 35: 515–23.

Multiculturalism and Citizenship Canada. (1989). *Multiculturalism.* Ottawa: Ministry of Supply and Services Canada.

Munroe-Blum, H., M.H. Boyle, D.R. Offord, and N. Kates. (1989). Immigrant children: Psychiatric disorder, school performance and service utilization. *American Journal of Orthopsychiatry* 59: 510–19.

Murphy, H.B.M. (1955). *Flight and resettlement.* Paris: UNESCO.

– (1973). Migration and the major mental disorders: A reappraisal. In *Uprooting and after,* ed. C. Zwingmann and M. Pfister-Ammende, pp. 204–20. New York: Springer-Verlag.

– (1977). Migration, culture and mental health. *Psychological Medicine* 7 (4): 677–84.

Murphy, J.M. (1976). Psychiatric labeling in cross-cultural perspective. *Science* 191: 1019–28.

Murphy, J.M., DC. Olivier, A.M. Sobol, R.R. Munson, and A.H. Leighton. (1986). Depression and anxiety in a general population. *Psychological Medicine* 16: 117–26.

Myers, J.K., M.M. Weissman, G.L. Tischler, C.E. Helzer, P.I. Leaf, H. Orvaschel, J.C. Anthony, J.H. Boyd, J.K. Burke, M. Kramer, and R. Stolzman. (1984). Six-month prevalence of psychiatric disorders in three communities. *Archives of General Psychiatry* 41: 959–67.

National Media Archive. (1993). Immigration part I: The human interest story. *On Balance* 6: 1–8.

Neisser, U. (1982). *Memory observed: Remembering in natural contexts.* San Francisco: W.H. Freeman.

Noh, S., M. Beiser, J. Rummens, F. Hou, and V. Kaspar. (n.d.). Discrimination, coping and depression among Southeast Asian refugees in Canada. Typescript.

Nolen-Hoeksema, S. (1987). Sex differences in unipolar depression: Evidence and theory. *Psychological Bulletin* 101: 259–82.

Oberg, K. (1960). Cultural shock: Adjustment to new cultural environments. *Practical Anthropology* 7: 177–82.

Obeyesekere, G. (1985). Depression, Buddhism, and the work of culture in Sri Lanka. In *Culture and depression,* ed. A. Kleinman and B. Good, pp. 134–52. Berkeley: University of California Press.

Palmer, D.L. (1997). *Canadians' attitudes toward immigration: November and December 1996, and February 1997 surveys.* Ottawa: Strategic Policy, Planning and Research Branch, Citizenship and Immigration Canada.

Palmer, I. (1981). *Intergovernmental committee for migration.* Geneva: Intergovernmental Committee for Migration.

Parker, S., and R.J. Kleiner. (1966). *Mental illness in the urban Negro community.* New York: Free Press.

Pearlin, L., M.A. Lieberman, E.G. Menaghan, and O.T. Mullan. (1981). The stress process. *Journal of Health and Social Behavior* 22: 337–56.

Pedersen, S. (1949). Psychopathological reactions to extreme social displacements (refugee neuroses). *Psychoanalytic Review* 36: 344–54.

Pedraza-Bailey, S. (1985). *Political and economic migrants in America: Cubans and Mexicans.* Austin: University of Texas Press.

Pettigrew, T.F., and R.M. Meertens. (1995). Subtle and blatant prejudice in Western Europe. *European Journal of Social Psychology* 25: 57–75.

Phinney, J.S. (1990). Ethnic identity in adolescents and adults: Review of research. *Psychological Bulletin* 108: 499–514.

Platt, J.J., and R. Eisenman. (1968). Internal-external control of reinforcement: Time perspective, adjustment and anxiety. *Journal of General Psychology* 79: 121–8.

Plaut, W.G. (1995). *Asylum: A moral dilemma.* London: Praeger.

Porter, J. (1966). *The vertical mosaic: An analysis of social class and power in Canada.* Toronto: University of Toronto Press.

Portes, A. (1984). The rise of ethnicity: Determinants of ethnic perception among Cuban exiles in Miami. *American Sociological Review* 49: 383–97.

Pottier, R. (1982). Les Motivations des réfugiés indochinois – rapport de synthèse. In *Les Réfugiés originaires de l'Asie du Sud-Est,* ed. G. Condominas and R. Pottier, pp. 85–188. Paris: La Documentation française.

Prien, R.F., D.J. Kupfer, P.A. Mansky, J.G. Small, V.B. Tuason, C.B. Voss, and W.E. Johnston. (1984). Drug therapy in the prevention of recurrence in unipolar and bipolar affective disorders. *Archives of General Psychiatry* 41: 1096–104.

Protocol relating to the status of refugees. (1967). Vol. 2, Human rights: A compilation of international instruments. Section O(83) (1967).

Radloff, L. (1977). The CES-D Scale: A self-report depression scale for research in the general population. *Applied Psychology Measurement* 1: 388–401.

Regier, D.A., J.D.J. Burke, R.W. Manderscheid, and B.J. Burns. (1985). The chronically mentally ill in primary care. *Psychological Medicine* 15: 265–73.

Richmond, A.H., and J. Goldlust. (1977). Family and social integration of immigrants in Toronto. Ethnic Research Programme, York University, Toronto.

Riegle, D.W. (1982). The psychological and social effects of unemployment. *American Psychologist* 37: 1113–15.

Roberts, A. (1988). Racism sent and received: Americans and Vietnamese view one another. *Research in Race and Ethnic Relations* 5: 75–97.

Robins, L.N. (1989). Diagnostic grammar and assessment: Translating criteria into questions. In *The validity of psychiatric diagnosis*, ed. L.N. Robins and J.E. Barrett, pp. 263–78. New York: Raven Press.

Robins, L.N., J.E. Helzer, H. Orvaschel, J.C. Anthony, D.G. Blazer, A. Burnam, and J.D. Burke. (1985). The Diagnostic Interview Schedule. In *Epidemiologic field methods in psychiatry: The NIMH epidemiologic catchment area program*, ed. W.W. Eaton and L.G. Kessler, pp. 143–70. Orlando, FL: Academic Press.

Robins, L.N., J.E. Helzer, T.R. Przybeck, and D.A. Regier. (1988). Alcohol disorders in the community: A report from the epidemiologic catchment area. In *Alcoholism: Origins and outcome*, ed. R.M. Rose and J.E. Barrett, pp. 15–29. American Psychopathological Association Series. New York: Raven Press.

Robins, L.N., J.E. Helzer, and M.M. Weissman. (1984). Lifetime prevalence of specific psychiatric disorders in three sites. *Archives of General Psychiatry* 41: 949–58.

Robins, L.N., J.E. Helzer, M.M. Weissman, H. Orvaschel, E. Greenberg, J. Burke, and E.D. Regier. (1984). Lifetime prevalence of specific psychiatric disorders in three sites. *Archives of General Psychiatry* 41: 949–58.

Robins, L.N., and D.A. Regier. (1991). *Psychiatric disorders in America: The epidemiologic catchment area study*. New York: Free Press.

Roskies, E. (1978). Sex, culture and illness: An overview. *Social Science and Medicine* 12: 139–41.

Rumbaut, R.G. (1985). Mental health and the refugee experience: A comparative study of Southeast Asian refugees. In *Southeast Asian mental health: Treatment, prevention, services, training and research*, ed. T.C. Owan, pp. 433–86. Rockville, MD: National Institute of Mental Health.

– (1988). Portraits, patterns and predictors of the refugee adaptation process: A comparative study of Southeast Asian refugees. In *Refugees and immigrants: Cambodians, Laotians, and Vietnamese in America*, ed. D.W. Haines, pp. 138–90. Totowa, NJ: Rowman and Littlefield.

Rumbaut, R.G., and K. Ima. (1988). *The adaptation of Southeast Asian refugee youth: A comparative study*. Washington, DC: U.S. Office of Refugee Resettlement.

Salvendy, J.T. (1983). The mental health of immigrants: A reassessment of concepts. *Canada's Mental Health* 31: 9–12.

Samuel, T.J. (1987). Economic adaptation of Indochinese refugees in Canada. In *Uprooting, loss and adaptation: The resettlement of Indochinese refugees in Canada*, ed. K.B. Chan and D.M. Indras, pp. 65–75. Ottawa: Canadian Public Health Association.

Sanders, J.M., and V. Nee. (1987). Limits of ethnic solidarity in the enclave economy. *American Sociological Review* 52(6): 745–67.

Sargent, J.K., M.L. Bruce, L.P. Florio, and M.M. Weissman. (1990). Factors associated with one-year outcome of major depression in the community. *Archives of General Psychiatry* 47: 519–26.

Satzewich, V., and P.S. Li. (1987). Immigrant labour in Canada: The cost and benefit of ethnic origin in the job market. *Canadian Journal of Sociology* 12: 229–41.

Schurman, R.A., P.D. Kramer, and J.B. Mitchell. (1985). The hidden mental health network: Treatment of mental illness by nonpsychiatrist physicians. *Archives of General Psychiatry* 42: 89–94.

Scotch, N.A. (1963). Sociocultural factors in the epidemiology of Zulu hypertension. *American Journal of Public Health* 53: 1205–13.

Scribner, R., and J.H. Dyer. (1989). Acculturation and low birthweight among Latinos in the Hispanic HANES. *American Journal of Public Health* 79: 1263–7.

Shalev, A.Y., S.P. Orr, and R.K. Pitman. (1993). Psychophysiologic assessment of traumatic imagery in Israeli survivors of noncombat events. *American Journal of Psychiatry* 150(4): 620–6.

Shay, J. (1991). Learning about combat stress from Homer's Iliad. *Journal of Traumatic Stress* 4: 561–79.

Shepherd, J. (1987). Coping in America: Contextual variables in the adaptation of female refugees and immigrants. *Social Development Issues* 11: 72–86.

Shevrin, H., W.J. Williams, R.E. Marshall, R.K. Hertel, J.A. Bond, and L.A. Brakel. (1992). Even-related potential indicators of the dynamic unconscious. *Consciousness and Cognition: An International Journal* 1: 340–66.

Shore, J.H., E.L. Tatum, and W.M. Vollmer. (1986). Psychiatric reactions to disaster: The Mt. St. Helen experience. *American Journal of Psychiatry* 143: 590–5.

Shore, J.H., W.M. Vollmer, and E.L. Tatum. (1989). Community patterns of post-traumatic stress disorders. *Journal of Nervous and Mental Disease* 177: 681–5.

Solomon, Z., and M. Mikulincer. (1988). Psychological sequelae of war: A two-year follow-up study of Israeli combat stress reaction casualties. *Journal of Nervous and Mental Disease* 176: 264–9.

Spanier, C. (1996). Maintenance interpersonal psychotherapy for recurrent depression: Biologic and clinical correlates and future directions. Paper presented at the Eighty-sixth Annual Meeting of the American Psychopathological Association on Psychotherapy in the 1990's: Mechanism, Indications, Efficacy, and Survivability. New York.

Speed, N., B. Engdahl, J. Schwartz, and R. Eberly. (1989). Post-traumatic stress disorder as a consequence of the POW experience. *Journal of Nervous and Mental Disease* 177: 147–53.

Srole, L., and A.K. Fischer, eds. (1978). *Mental health in the metropolis: The midtown Manhattan study.* New York: New York University Press.

Starr, P.D., and A.E. Roberts. (1982). Community structure and Vietnamese refugee adaptation: The significance of context. *International Migration Review* 16: 595–618.

Statistics Canada. (1997). *The Daily*, www.statcan.ca, 4 November.

Stein, B. (1979). Occupational adjustment of refugees: The Vietnamese in the United States. *International Migration Review* 13: 25–45.

Stein, B.N. (1986). The experience of being a refugee: Insights from the research literature. In *Refugee mental health in resettlement countries*, ed. C. Williams and J. Westermeyer, pp. 5–23. Washington, DC: Hemisphere Publishing.

Stoffman, D. (1977). Making room for real refugees. *International Journal* (Autumn): 575–80.

Strand, P.J. (1989). Employment predictors among Indochinese refugees. *International Migration Review* 18: 50–64.

Sudman, S., and N.M. Bradburn. (1974). *Response effects in surveys*. Chicago: Aldine.

Sue, S. (1983). Ethnic minority issues in psychology: Re-examination. *American Psychologist* 38: 583–92.

Sue, S., and J.K. Morishima. (1982). *The mental health of Asian Americans: Contemporary issues in identifying and treating mental problems*. San Francisco: Jossey-Bass.

Sue, S.W., and D. Sue. (1990). *Counseling the culturally different: Theory and practice*. New York: Wiley.

Szapocznik, J., and W.M. Kurtines. (1980). Acculturation, biculturalism and adjustment among Cuban Americans. In *Recent advances in acculturation research: Theory, models, and some new findings*, ed. A. Padilla, pp. 139–57. Boulder, CO: Westview.

Tarling, N., ed. (1993a). *The Cambridge history of Southeast Asia*. Vol. 1, *From early times to c.1800*. Cambridge: Cambridge University Press.

– (1993b). *The Cambridge history of Southeast Asia*. Vol. 2, *The nineteenth and twentieth centuries*. Cambridge: Cambridge University Press.

Terr, L. (1994). *Unchained memories: True stories of traumatic memories, lost and found*. New York: Basic Books.

Thompson, V.L.S. (1996). Perceived experiences of racism as stressful life events. *Community Mentalh Health Journal* 32: 223–33.

Tienda, M., L. Jensen, and R.L. Bach.. (1984). Immigration, gender and the process of occupational change in the United States, 1970–80. *International Migration Review* 18: 1021–44.

Toronto Star. (1998). Pol Pot is dead. 16 April, p. 82.

Troper, H. (1984). The historical roots of current Canadian refugee policy. In *Refugee resettlement: Southeast Asians in transition*, ed. R.C. Nann, P.J. Johnson, and M. Beiser, pp. 189–98. Vancouver: Refugee Resettlement Project.

Tseng, W.S. (1975). The nature of somatic complaints among psychiatric patients: The Chinese case. *Comparative Psychiatry* 16: 237–45.

Tu, T.H. (1995). The PQ's narrow ethnic vision. *Globe and Mail*, 11 November, p. D-1

Turner, R.J. (1983). Direct, indirect and moderating effects of social support on psychological distress and associated conditions. In *Psychosocial stress: Trends in theory and research*, ed. H.B. Kaplan, pp. 105–55. New York: Academic Press.

Turner, R.J., and W.R. Avison. (1989). Gender and depression: Assessing exposure and vulnerability to life events in a chronically strained population. *Journal of Nervous and Mental Disease* 177: 443–55.

Turner, V. (1967). *The forest of symbols: Aspects of Ndembu ritual.* Ithaca, NY.: Cornell University Press.

Tyhurst, L. (1951). Displacement and migration: A study in social psychiatry. *American Journal of Psychiatry* 107: 561–8.

– (1977). Psychological first aid for refugees. *Mental Health and Society* 4: 319–43.

United Nations High Commission for Refugees (UNHCR). (1988). *Minutes.*

– (1995). *The state of the world's refugees.* New York: Oxford University Press.

Universal declaration of human rights. (1948). Vol. 1, Human rights: A compilation of international instruments. Section A(1) (1948).

Vaillant, G.E. (1985). An empirically derived hierarchy of adaptive mechanisms and its usefulness as a potential diagnostic axis. Paper presented at the World Psychiatric Association Regional Symposium: New Perspectives in Psychiatric Research. *Acta Psychiatrica Scandinavica* 71: 171–80.

van Loenhout-Rooyackers, J.H. (1994). [Risk of tuberculosis in the inadequate handling of refugees seeking asylum]. *Nederlands Tijdschrift voor Geneeskunde* 138: 2496–500.

Vega, W.A., B. Kolody, and G. Warheit. (1985). Psychoneuroses among Mexican Americans and other whites: Prevalence and caseness. *American Journal of Public Health* 75: 523–7.

Vignes, A.J., and R.C.W. Hall. (1979). Adjustment of a group of Vietnamese people to the United States. *American Journal of Psychiatry* 136: 442–4.

Warr, P. (1982). Psychological aspects of employment and unemployment. *Psychological Medicine* 12: 7–11.

Weinberg, A.A. (1961). *Migration and belonging: A study of mental health and personal adjustment in Israel.* The Hague: M. Nijhoff.

Weinreich, P. (1989). Conflicted identification: A commentary on identity structure analysis concepts. In *New identities in Europe*, ed. K. Liebkind, pp. 219–36. Aldershot: Gower.

Weissman, M.M. (1987). Advances in psychiatric epidemiology: Rates and risks for major depression. *American Journal of Public Health* 77: 445–51.

Weissman, M.M., and G.L. Klerman. (1977). Sex differences in the epidemiology of depression. *Archives of General Psychiatry* 34: 98–111.

Wells, K.B., A. Stewart, R.D. Hays, A. Burnam, W. Rogers, M. Daniels, S. Berry, S. Greenfield, and J. Ward. (1989). The functioning and well-being of depressed patients: Results from the Medical Outcomes Study. *Journal of the American Medical Association* 262: 914–19.

Westermeyer, J. (1986). Migration and psychopathology. In *Refugee mental health in resettlement countries*, ed. C.L. Williams and J. Westermeyer, pp. 39–59. Washington, DC: Hemisphere Publishing.

Westermeyer, J., T.F. Vang, and J. Neider. (1983a). Migration and mental health among Hmong refugees: Association of pre- and postmigration with self-rating scales. *Journal of Nervous and Mental Disease* 171: 86–91.

– (1983b). Refugees who do and do not seek psychiatric care: An analysis of premigratory and postmigratory characteristics. *Journal of Nervous and Mental Disease* 171: 92–6.

Woon, Y. (1987). The mode of refugee sponsorship and the socio-economic adaptation of Vietnamese in Victoria: A three-year perspective. In *Uprooting, loss and adaptation: The resettlement of Indochinese in Canada*, ed. K.B. Chan and D.M. Indra, pp. 132–46. Ottawa: Canadian Public Health Association.

Wortley, S. (1996). Justice for all? Race and perceptions of bias in the Ontario criminal justice system – a Toronto survey. *Canadian Journal of Criminology* (October): 439–67.

Yap, P.M. (1965). Phenomenology of affective disorders in Chinese and other cultures. In *Transcultural psychiatry*, ed. A.V.S. de Reuck and R. Porter, pp. 84–108. London: J. & A. Churchill.

Young, A. (1995). Reasons and causes for post-traumatic stress disorder. *Transcultural Psychiatric Research Review* 32: 287–98.

Zolberg, A., and L.L. Woon. (1997). Why Islam is like Spanish: Cultural incorporation in Europe and the United States. Paper delivered at the conference 'Inclusion and Exclusion: International Migrants and Refugees in Europe and North America,' New School for Social Research, New York, 6 June.

Index